IMAGES
of America

LANSING

On the cover: Please see page 35. (Courtesy of the Lansing Historical Museum.)

IMAGES
of America

LANSING

Laura Phillippi and Nolan Sunderman

ARCADIA
PUBLISHING

ISBN 978-0-7385-6192-9

Published by Arcadia Publishing
Charleston SC, Chicago IL, Portsmouth NH, San Francisco CA

Printed in the United States of America

Library of Congress Catalog Card Number: 2008928372

For all general information contact Arcadia Publishing at:
Telephone 843-853-2070
Fax 843-853-0044
E-mail sales@arcadiapublishing.com
For customer service and orders:
Toll-Free 1-888-313-2665

Visit us on the Internet at www.arcadiapublishing.com

This book is dedicated to the citizens of Lansing, who make the community a special place to live and work.

Contents

ACKNOWLEDGMENTS

In 1990, the Lansing Historical Society formed to save Lansing's Santa Fe Railroad depot. With this goal achieved, the group founded the Lansing Historical Museum and diligently collected historical photographs, documents, and artifacts to preserve Lansing's history. This book would not have been possible without the Lansing Historical Society's efforts.

I would like to thank Arcadia Publishing editor Ted Gerstle for giving us the opportunity to share our history with the world through this book project. His advice and support were invaluable throughout the process.

There are several people who ensured the success of this project. The Leavenworth Public Library reference desk staff pulled reel after reel of microfilm for the research component of this book. Mary Kay Menard from the Leavenworth Public Library graciously scanned our Kansas State Penitentiary slides. Sr. Kathleen Mary Connelly from the Sisters of Charity Archives in Leavenworth provided assistance with scanning the photographs in this book. The staff at the Kansas Historical Society Archives should be commended for their dedication to helping researchers like myself. Lifelong resident and local historian Gene Young provided historical background to the photographs in this book. The staff at the Lansing Correctional Facility and Lansing Unified School District 469 also assisted with this project.

I wish to thank the individuals whose donated photographs enhanced the story of the history of Lansing. There are a few special people who fostered my interest in history. For the past 40 years, my father, Samuel Phillippi, has taught social studies and for the past 20 or so years has taken me to museums and encouraged me to explore our past. Drs. Joyce Thierer, Christopher Lovett, and Karen Smith from Emporia State University influenced my decision to go into public history. Drs. David Goodlett and Robert Luehrs from Fort Hays State University greatly improved my writing and methodology.

Finally, I would like to thank my supervisor, Nolan Sunderman, for his support and the city of Lansing for giving me the opportunity to preserve and educate others about the unique history of Lansing, Kansas.

— Laura Phillippi

INTRODUCTION

Along the banks of the Missouri River are the grounds of the oldest penitentiary in the state of Kansas. For more than 140 years, the Gothic-inspired Kansas State Penitentiary (now known as the Lansing Correctional Facility) has stood as a beacon across the landscape. Throughout the years, the prison has seen many changes in the communities surrounding it. Delaware City vied unsuccessfully with Leavenworth, the first incorporated city in Kansas, to become the county seat of Leavenworth County. As a result, Delaware City's population moved away, and the settlement died. Many of the Delaware City residents moved to the town of Progress. William Taylor Lansing and his friend John Schmidt purchased 90 acres and plotted the land in 1878. The pair named the land the town of Lansing. Eventually Lansing and Progress combined into one town.

The small village of Lansing found a neighbor in the prison. The prison provided jobs, business, and project assistance to the community. The two entities have grown together throughout the years. The prison employs 700 staff members and 300 contract employees. In 2006, Lansing's population totaled 10,705. The city also has a strong military influence due to many veterans and current service personnel who live in the community. Current personnel serve at Fort Leavenworth, the oldest continuously running army fort west of the Mississippi River. Fort Leavenworth is also home to the Command and General Staff College where American and international military personnel attend classes to prepare for leadership roles in their respective militaries.

Lansing has a rich history, including "Lansing Man." Lansing Man refers to the collection of bones found on the Concannon farm by Michael Concannon, his father, his brother, and George White in February 1902. A Carbon-14 test indicated that the remains date back to between 2660 to 5020 BCE. In 1977, the Kansas State Historical Society placed the Lansing Man Archeological Site on the Kansas Register of Historic Places.

Another historic area is Mount Muncie Cemetery. Established in 1866, the cemetery is one of the oldest in Kansas. Over 28,300 people are buried here, including Gov. Thomas Carney, the second governor of Kansas; Fred Harvey, the Santa Fe Railroad entrepreneur; and U.S. Supreme Court justice David Josiah Brewer.

In 1959, Lansing became incorporated and since then has experienced rapid growth. With the increase of commuters between Kansas City and Fort Leavenworth, the two-lane U.S. Highway 73 could no longer handle the traffic. Several downtown Lansing buildings had to be torn down to make way for the addition of two lanes to the highway. In 2006, the city of Lansing embarked on a two-year Main Street System Enhancement project with the Kansas Department of Transportation. The project added more turn lanes and other features to improve safety on the highway. U.S. Highway 73/Kansas 7 is one of the busiest north–south highways in Kansas. Currently, more than 24,000 vehicles pass through Lansing daily, and the number of vehicles is projected to increase to 45,000 by 2024.

Lansing is living up to its motto, "the City with a Future." In 1960, 1,261 people called Lansing home. In 2006, the population had grown to 10,705. In 2007, *Money Magazine* recognized Lansing in its "Top 100 Best Places to Live." Lansing is a good place to raise a family and retire.

The purpose of this book is to capture the history of a small village's transformation into a prosperous community.

One

Founding

Lansing's founding father, William Lansing Taylor, served in the Civil War with the 7th Missouri Infantry and was captured by the Confederates. Taylor promised not to fight the South again in order to gain his freedom. In 1862, Taylor broke his promise and joined the Kansas Volunteer Cavalry under the name of James William Lansing. After the war, he became a hospital steward at the Kansas State Penitentiary and later opened a general mercantile, which included the post office and an apothecary business.

Choosing a location for a new town often depended upon the resources of the area. Leavenworth is located on the banks of the Missouri River and became the first incorporated city in the state of Kansas in 1854. During the 1800s, Leavenworth served as a gateway for many travelers heading to the West to start a new life. Traders exchanged commodities on the banks of the Missouri River, and entrepreneurs built lucrative factories such as the Great Western Manufacturing Company in Leavenworth. With the addition of Fort Leavenworth, an important military installation in the Great Plains, the rich agricultural land in the area, and the Kansas State Penitentiary, Taylor and his partner, John Schmidt, must have believed the area south of Leavenworth was an ideal location for a town to prosper.

Taylor and Schmidt purchased 90 acres of land, which was platted as Schmidt's Subdivision in 1878. On May 21, 1880, a surveyor completed the survey of the land and turned his map over to the Leavenworth County register of deeds. The town of Lansing grew slowly with the assistance of the Kansas State Penitentiary. Taylor remained an important figure in the community until his death on March 20, 1886. He is buried at Mount Muncie Cemetery in section 24, lot 178, grave 1. His descendants are still in the area. Taylor and Schmidt founded a small community that would grow into a prosperous city rapidly approaching a population of 11,000.

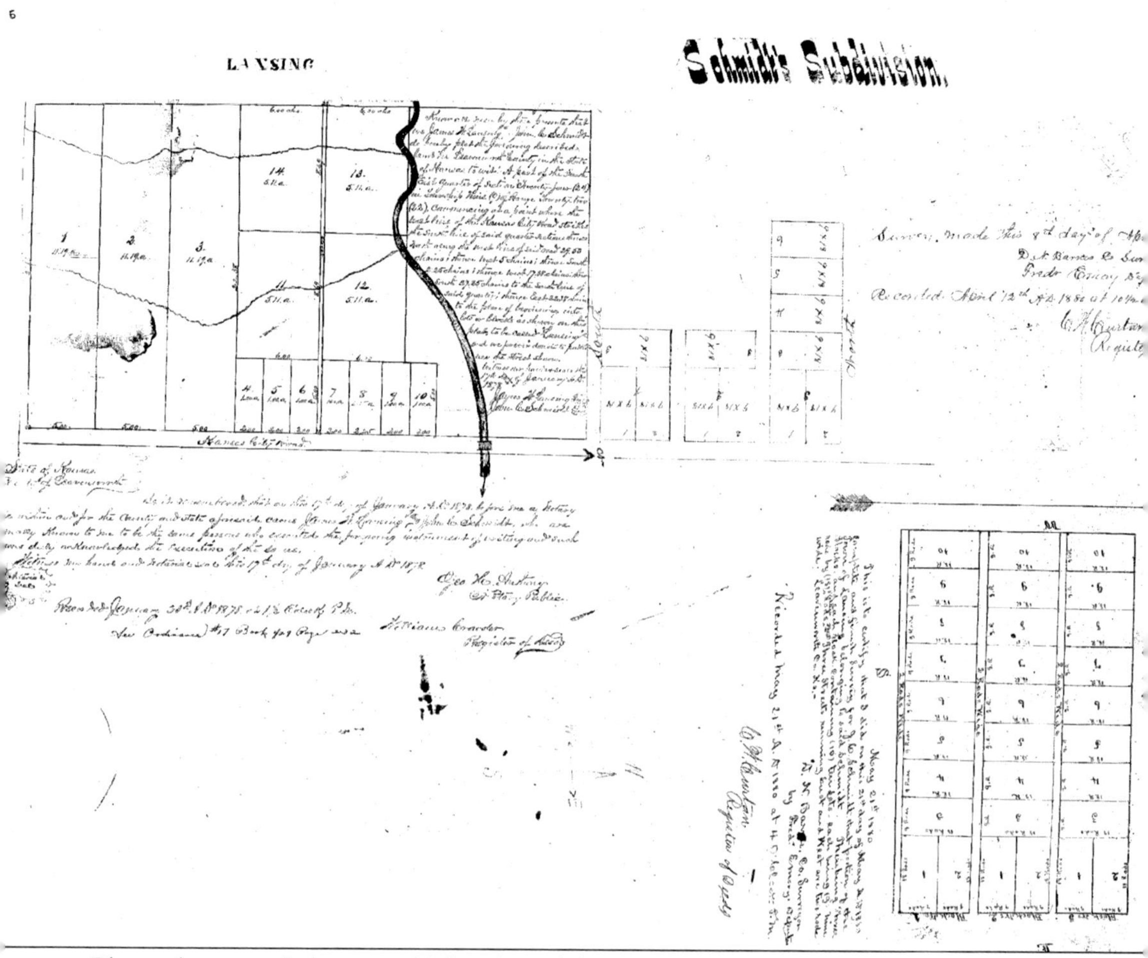

This is the original plat map of Schmidt's Subdivision, which became the city of Lansing. The Leavenworth County Register of Deeds recorded the map on January 23, 1878. (Courtesy of Jeff Culbertson.)

Born in October 1831, William Lansing Taylor studied law and medicine. During the Civil War, he served in the 7th Missouri Infantry and the Kansas Volunteer Cavalry. Then he became a hospital steward at the state penitentiary and later opened a general mercantile that held a post office and apothecary. Along with his friend John C. Schmidt, he founded what eventually became Lansing in 1878. (Courtesy of the Lansing Historical Museum.)

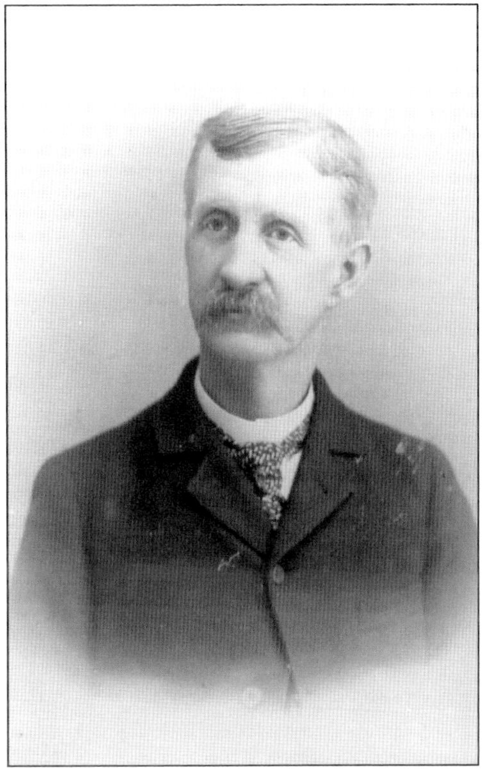

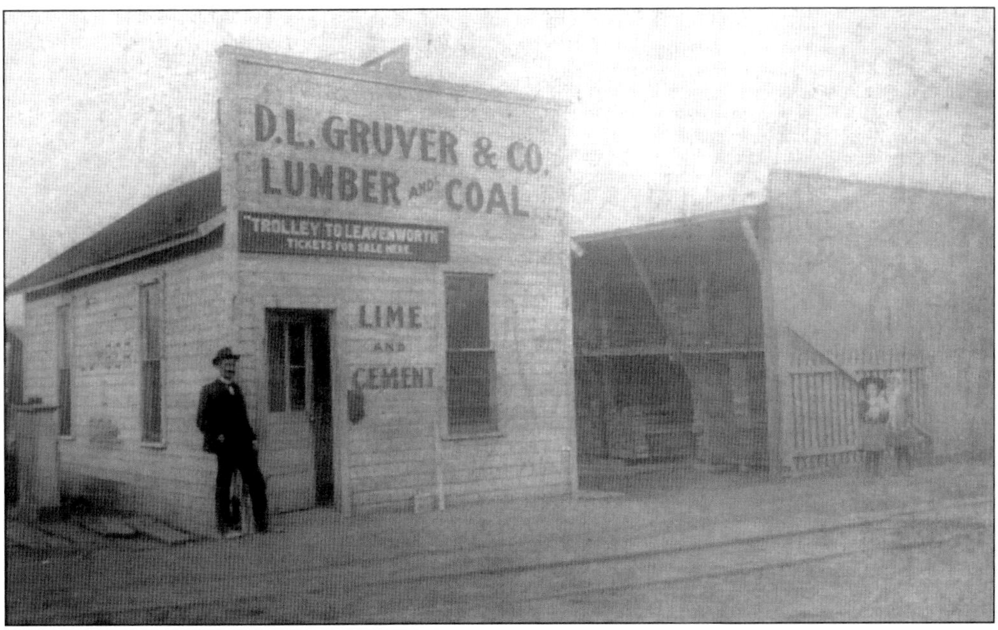

David Lincoln Gruver stands near his D. L. Gruver and Company Lumber and Coal business around 1901. Located on Kansas Avenue, the business sold trolley tickets to those wishing to travel on the interurban line. In addition to his business, Gruver was appointed Lansing's postmaster on March 3, 1905. He was born in May 1860 in Lee County, Illinois, and died in 1941 at the age of 81. (Courtesy of the Lansing Historical Museum.)

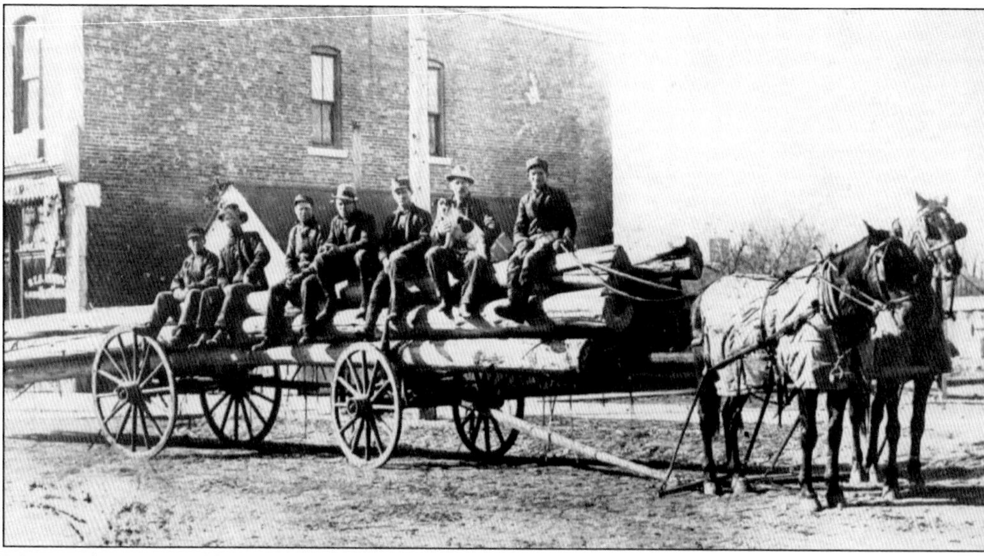

Men and a team of horses transport a load of lumber on Main Street. Lansing's Main Street remained unpaved south of Kay Street until the 1920s. As a child, Gene Young was told, "An Indian laid down all the bricks on Main Street." Whether the story is true or not remains to be proven. (Courtesy of the Lansing Historical Museum.)

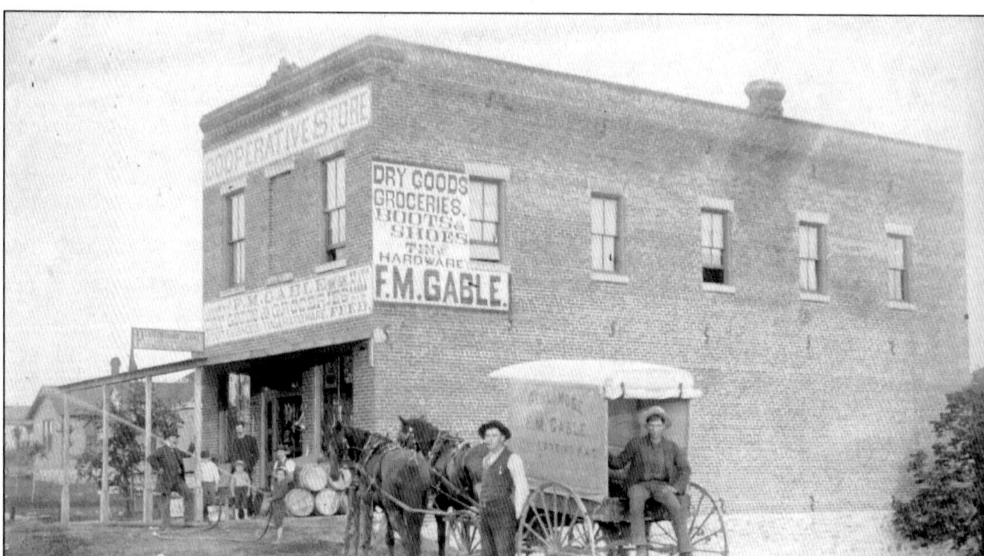

The F. M. Gable Store sold a variety of things, including dry goods, groceries, boots, shoes, feed, hardware, and "penitentiary coal." F. M. Gable is leaning against the post in front of the store, and Julian Gable is in front of the wagon in the foreground. (Courtesy of the Lansing Historical Museum.)

Here is the Lansing Baptist Church before 1909. (Courtesy of the Lansing Historical Museum.)

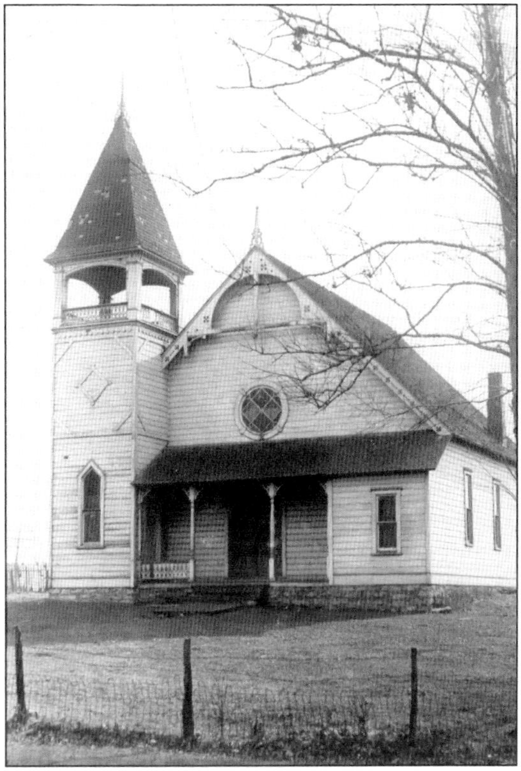

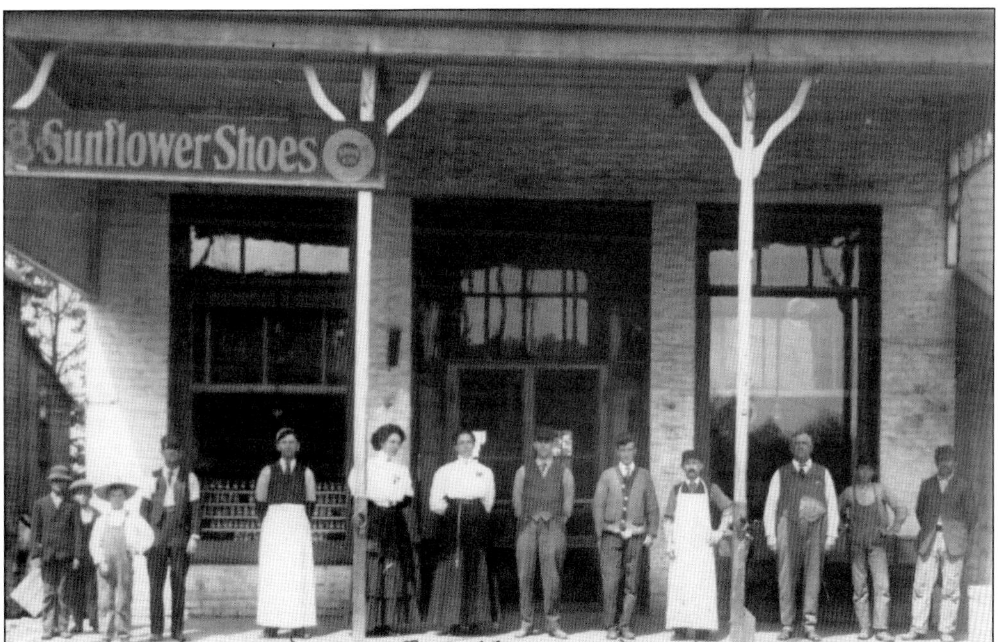

Brown's Store was formerly called Merritt's Store. From left to right are unidentified, unidentified, Audrey Campbell, Mort Brown, Herbert Walker, Emma Ernst, Isabel Brown, Jim Brown, Milton Scott, Joe Anthony, Mr. Brown, and Mr. Mathers. The photograph was taken during the second decade of the 20th century. (Courtesy of the Lansing Historical Museum.)

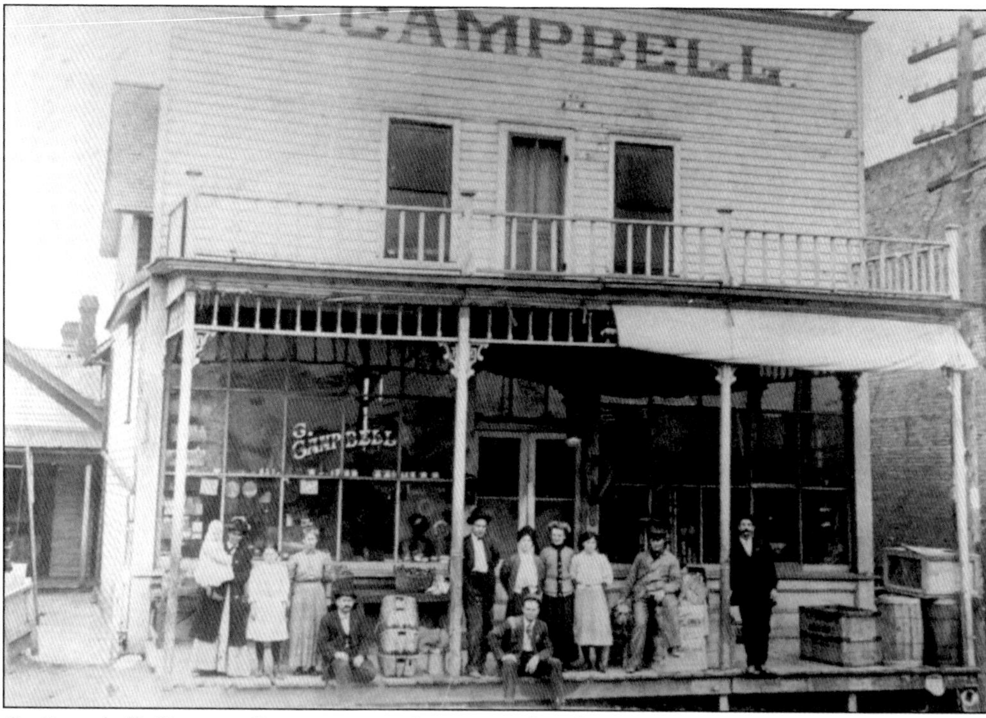

C. Campbell Grocery Store was on the west side of Lansing's Main Street. The building was destroyed by fire. This photograph was taken in the 1890s. (Courtesy of the Lansing Historical Museum.)

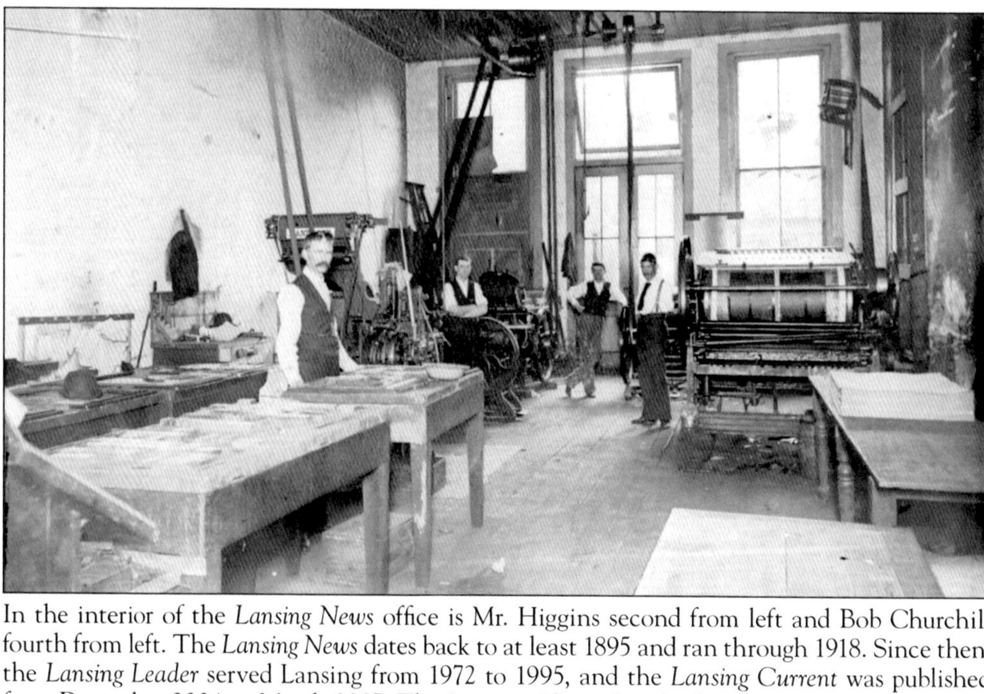

In the interior of the *Lansing News* office is Mr. Higgins second from left and Bob Churchill fourth from left. The *Lansing News* dates back to at least 1895 and ran through 1918. Since then, the *Lansing Leader* served Lansing from 1972 to 1995, and the *Lansing Current* was published from December 2004 to March 2007. The *Lansing Chronicle*, which is now called *Lansing This Week*, has been in publication since 2004. (Courtesy of the Lansing Historical Museum.)

Two

Kansas State Penitentiary

In 1859, the Kansas legislature authorized the creation of the Kansas State Penitentiary. Selecting the location of the penitentiary proved to be a challenge. One account said Topeka, Manhattan, Lawrence, and Leavenworth vied for the college that became the University of Kansas. Leavenworth agreed to drop out of the running if it could have the penitentiary.

The *Leavenworth Times* published "Plot to 'Steal' Penitentiary at Lansing Related." The paper reported that Gov. Charles Robinson delayed work on the construction of the prison in an attempt to move the prison elsewhere. The Kansas state legislators from Leavenworth County persevered and secured the location of the prison five miles south of Leavenworth.

With the location determined, a delegation from Kansas visited prisons in Ohio, New York, Michigan, and Illinois to find an ideal prison to use as a model for the Kansas penitentiary. The group decided that the prison in Joilet, Illinois, would serve as a model and chose Erasmus Carr as the architect for the project.

Construction on the prison began in 1864 with the use of inmate labor; however, the Civil War delayed the project. In 1867, workers finished the construction of the main building, and the first inmates were relocated to the building in July 1868. At first, the prison housed state and federal convicts. Until 1909, prisoners from the Oklahoma Territory served their sentences in Lansing.

The population of the prison has grown throughout the years. In 1875, 26 officers guarded 379 inmates. Today approximately 2,500 prisoners are serving sentences in Lansing. The prison has 700 staff members with an additional 300 contract workers. The prison has changed throughout the years. Originally, female inmates served their sentences in the same complex as the men. Later the women were moved to a separate facility on Highway 5. The minimum- and medium-security female inmates moved to the Topeka Correctional Facility in 1988, and the maximum security women moved there in 1995.

Overall, the field of corrections has changed from the harsh treatment of the 1800s to a more humane treatment of prisoners that places an emphasis on rehabilitation and education.

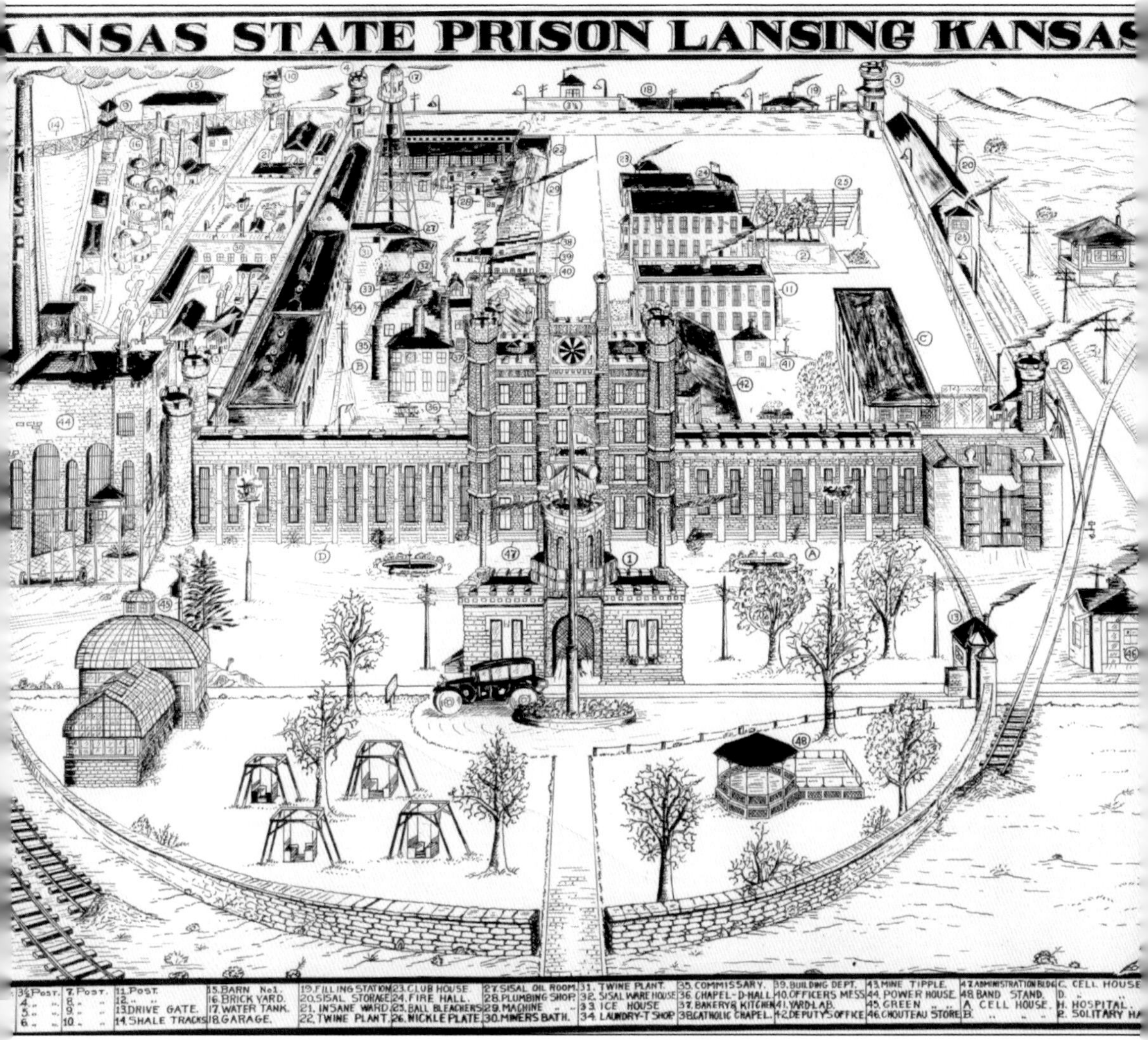

This map shows the Kansas State Penitentiary.

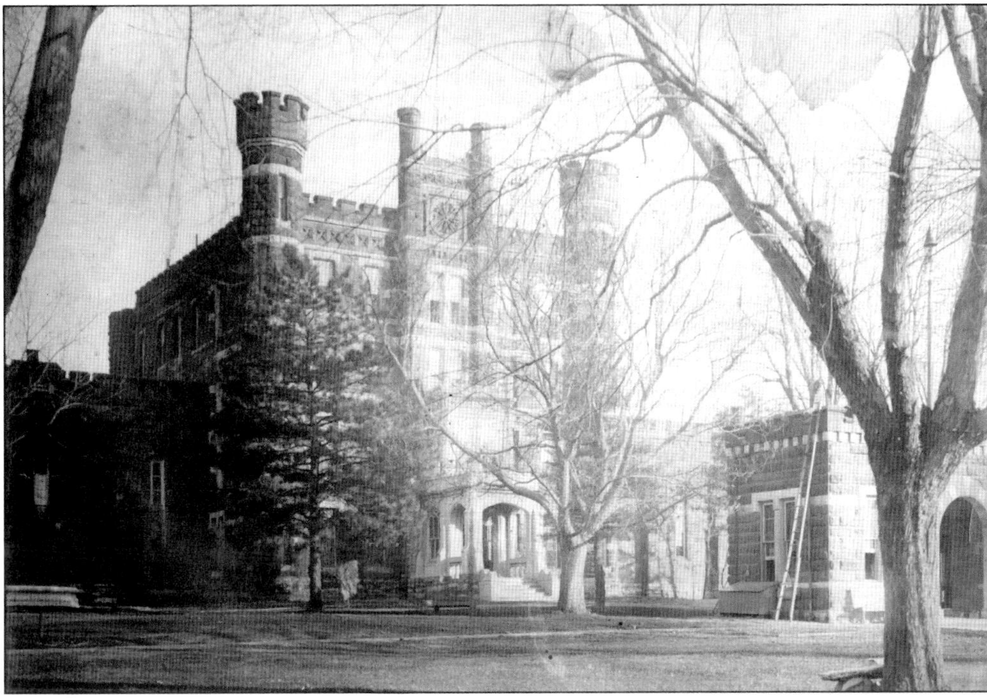

Established by the Kansas legislature in 1859, the Kansas State Penitentiary is the oldest prison in the state of Kansas. The small structure in the foreground contained an office where a guard checked prison visitors for weapons. The prison entrance faces the west. Completed in 1867, the Gothic-style main building is made of sandstone. The lawn outside the prison walls featured flower beds and fountains. (Courtesy of the Lansing Historical Museum.)

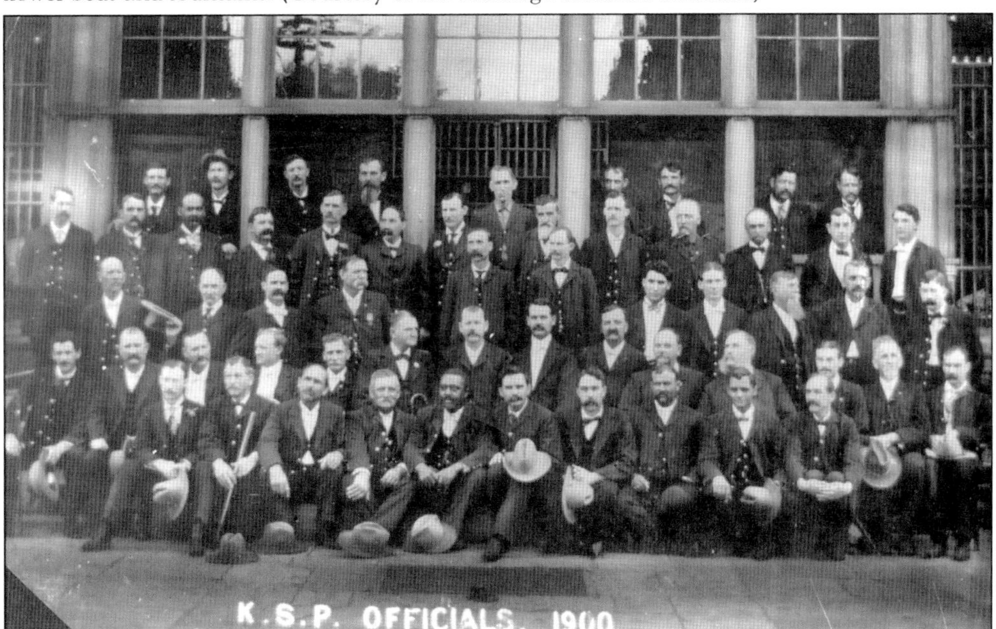

Here is a group photograph of Kansas State Penitentiary officials in 1900. (Courtesy of the Lansing Historical Museum.)

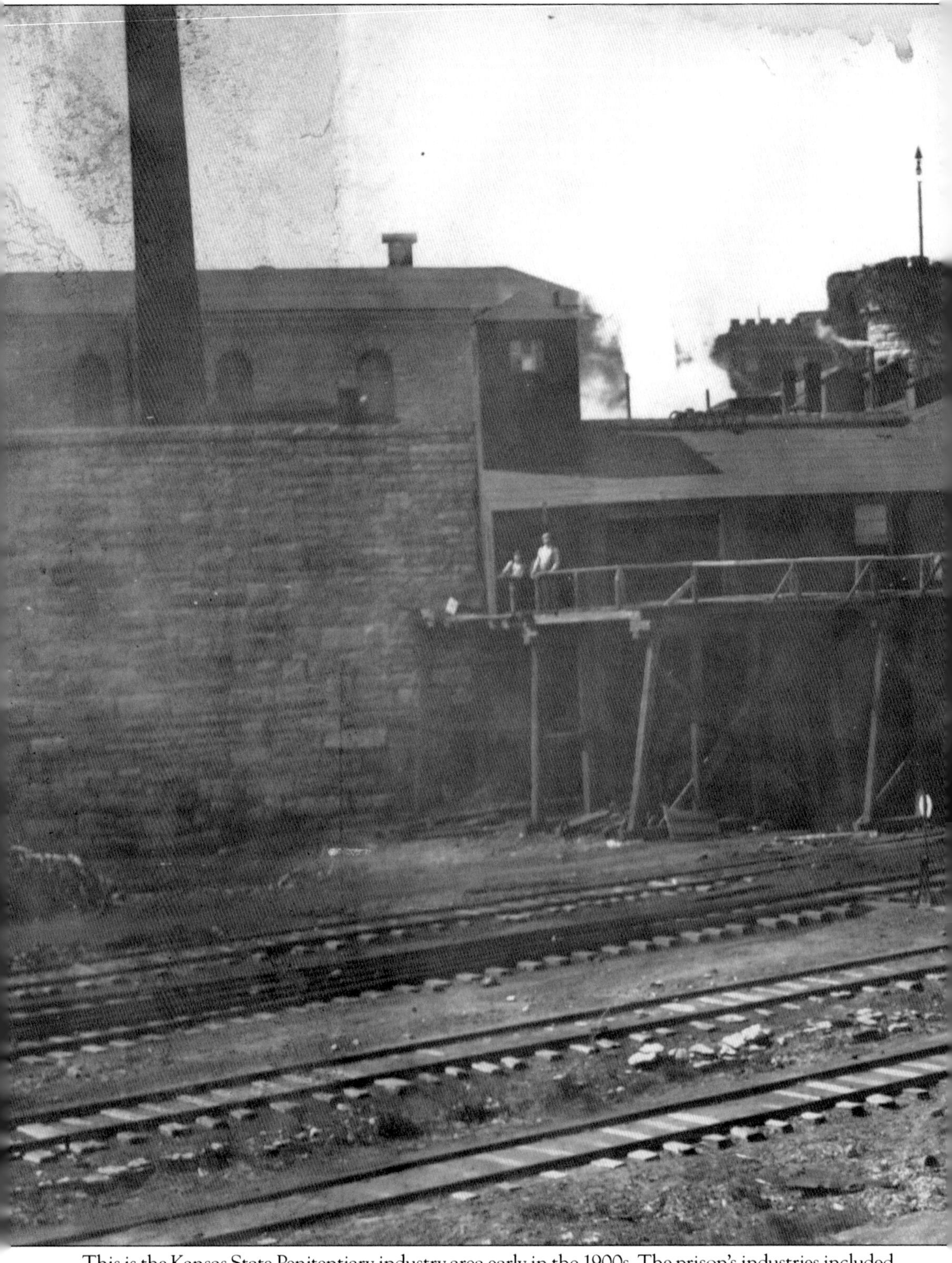

This is the Kansas State Penitentiary industry area early in the 1900s. The prison's industries included

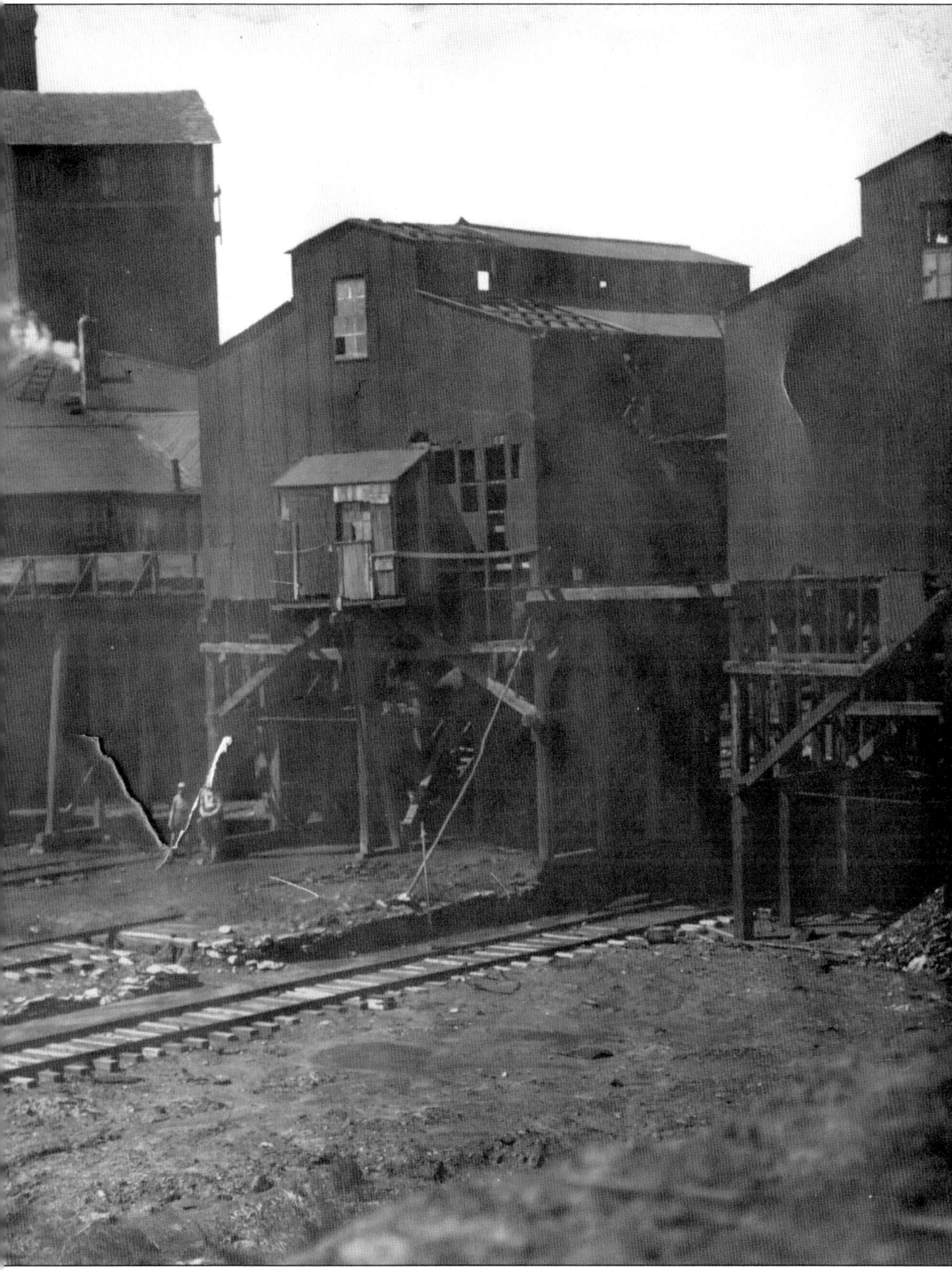

a coal mine, brickyard, twine plant, and tinker shop. (Courtesy of the Lansing Historical Museum.)

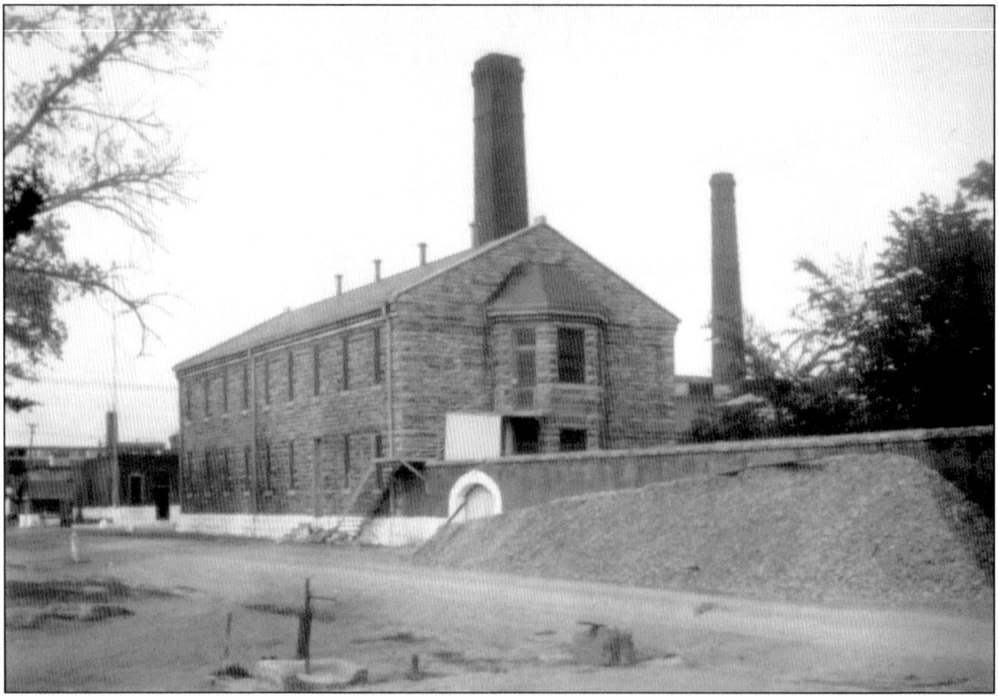

Above is the brickyard plant building in the second decade of the 20th century. (Courtesy of the Lansing Historical Museum.)

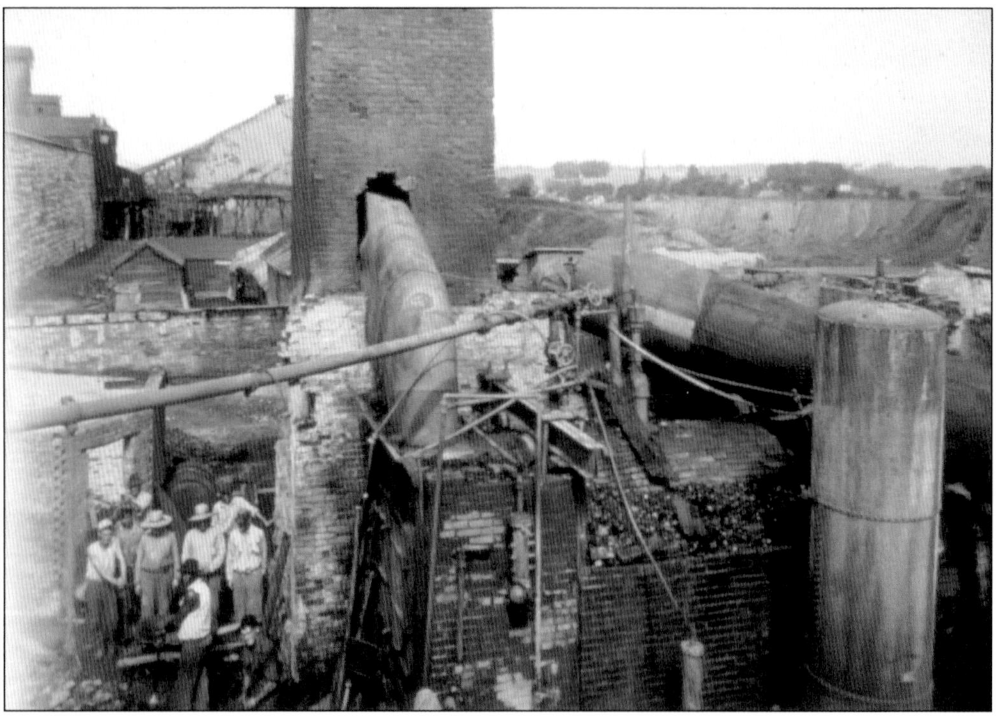

Possible machinery for making bricks is shown at the Kansas State Penitentiary brickyard in the second decade of the 20th century. (Courtesy of the Lansing Historical Museum.)

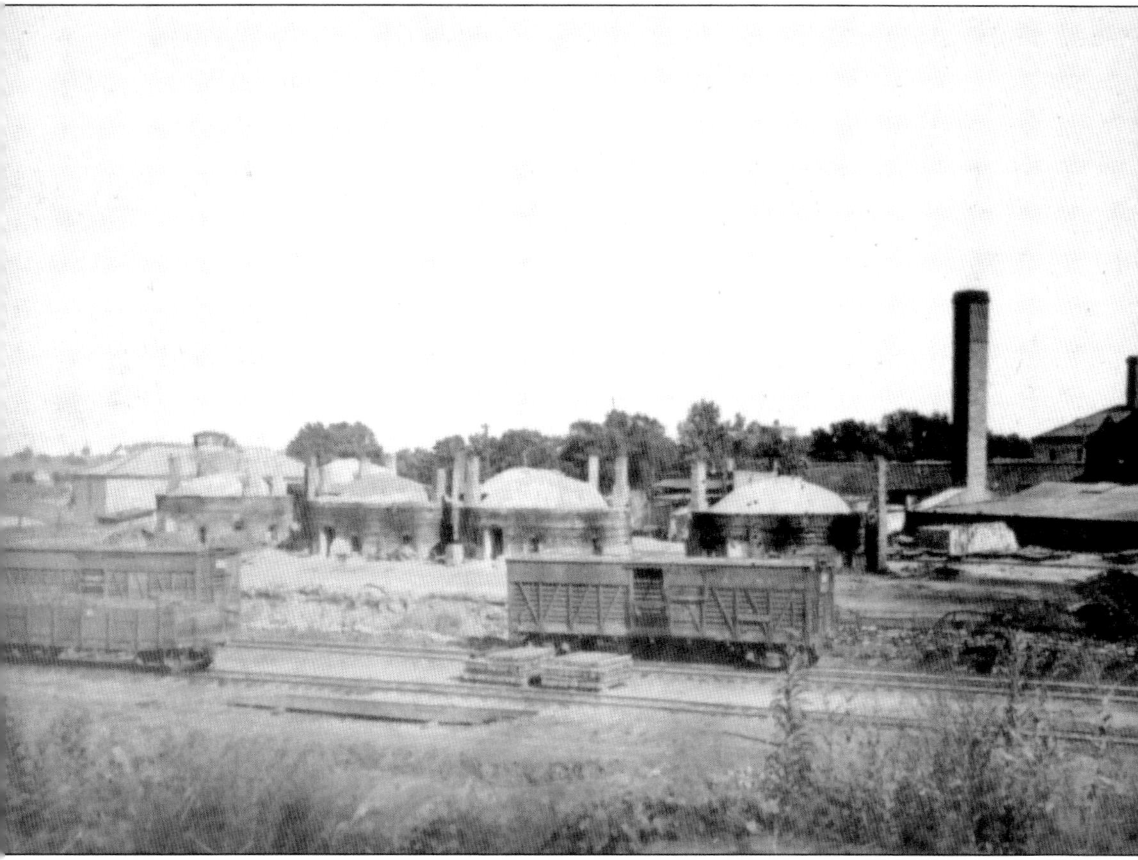

Three Atchison, Topeka, and Santa Fe Railway cars in the Kansas State Penitentiary brickyard wait to transport goods. (Courtesy of the Lansing Historical Museum.)

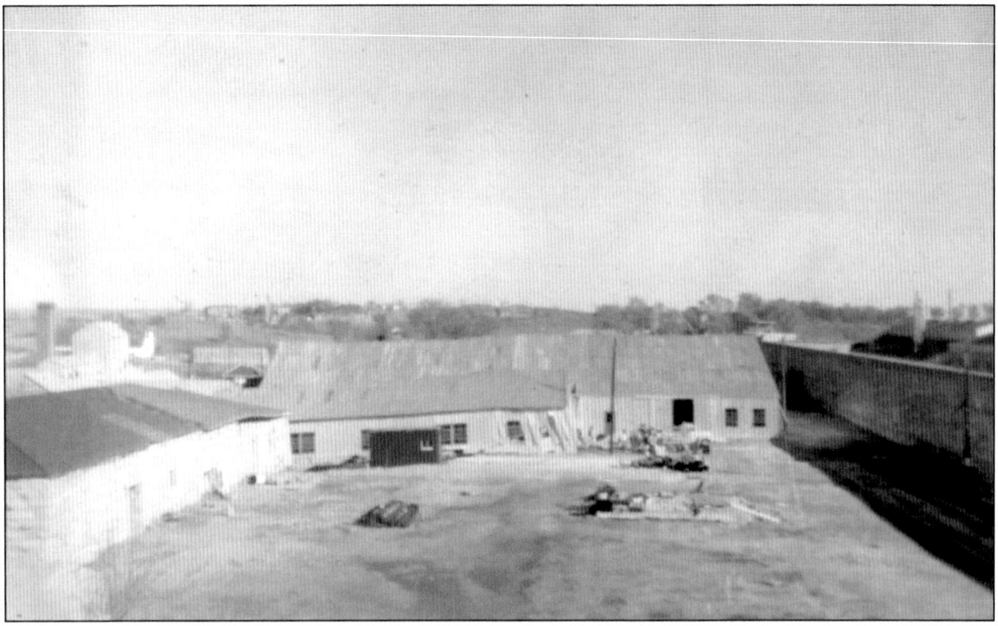

A mine cave-in damaged this brickyard building. Today core samples are taken in certain areas of Lansing before constructing new buildings to ensure there are no old coal mine tunnels that could cave in and damage a building. (Courtesy of the Lansing Historical Museum.)

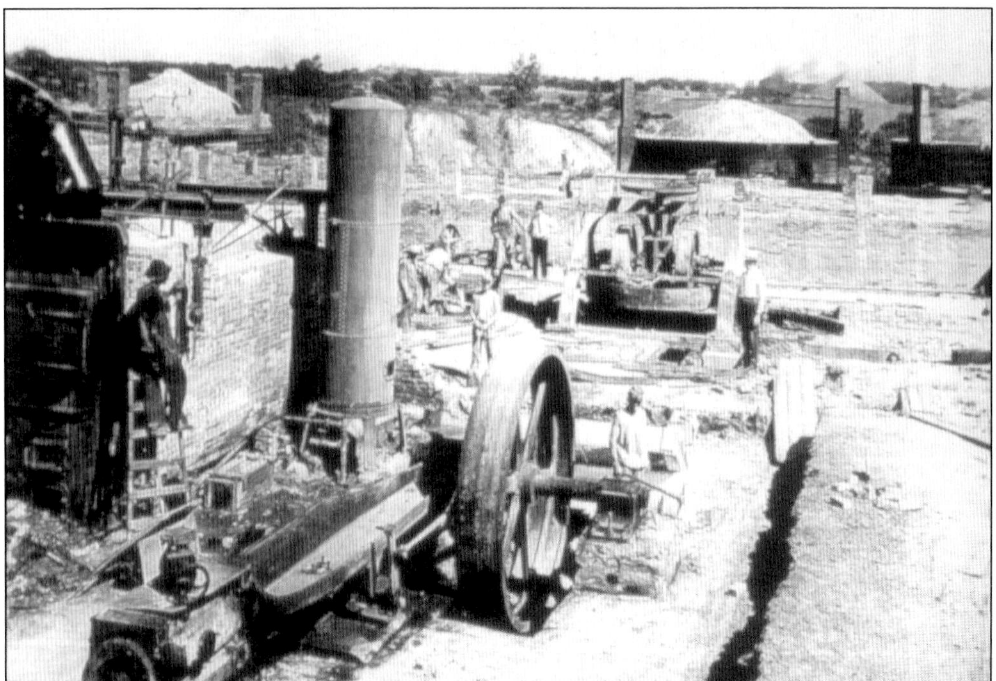

This may be a brick-manufacturing machine in the Kansas State Penitentiary brickyard. The domed building in the background is probably a kiln for firing the bricks. (Courtesy of the Lansing Historical Museum.)

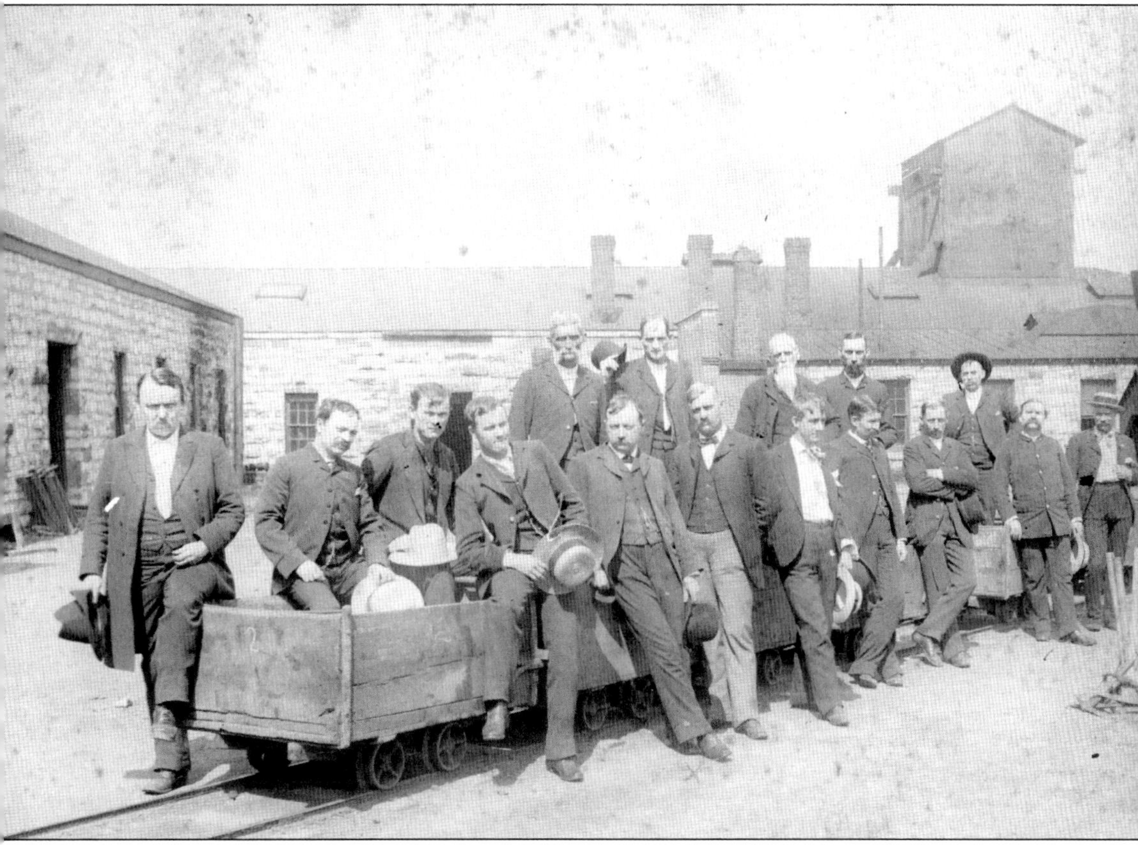

John Higgins and 13 other officials pause for a photograph on coal mine cars. The Kansas State Penitentiary coal mine provided coal for state institutions and the local schools. At one point in history, Kansas ranked third in coal production in the United States. During the height of coal production, almost 500 inmates worked in the mine. The mine closed in 1947 due to high costs and low demand. (Courtesy of the Lansing Historical Museum.)

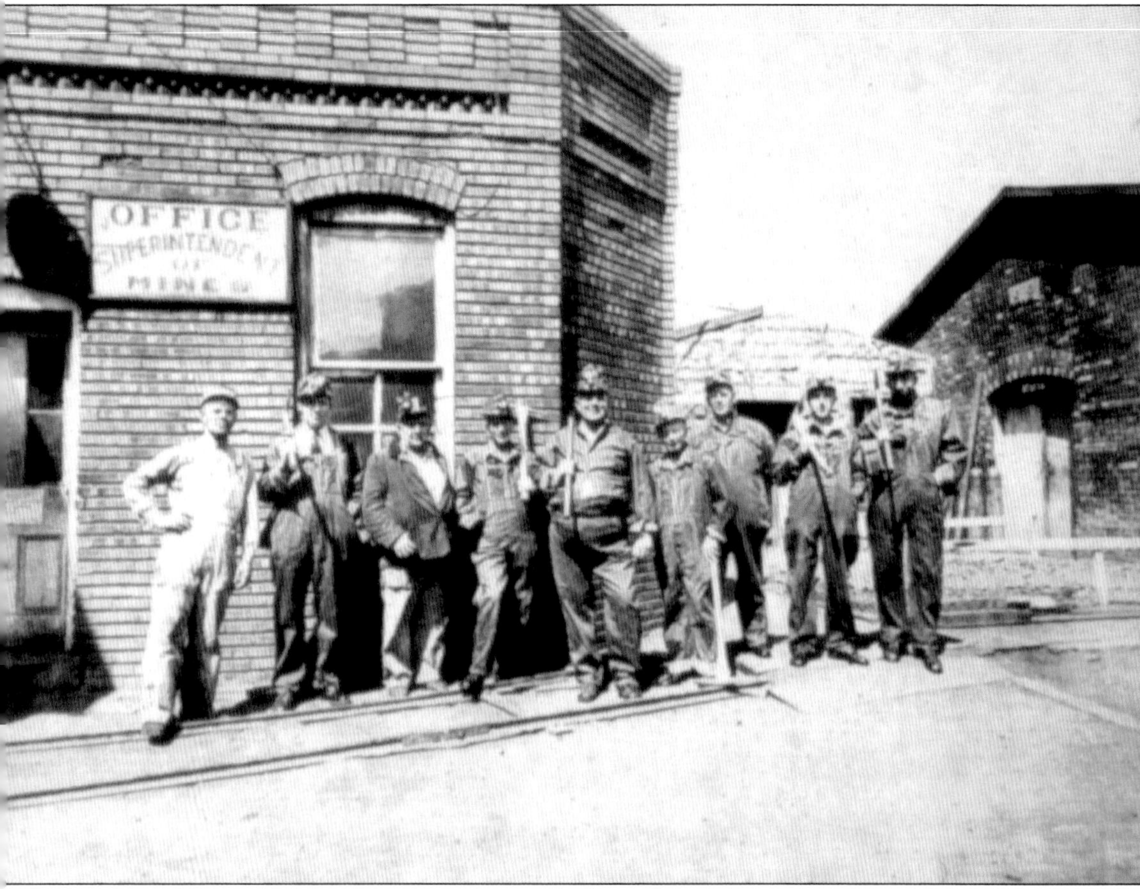

A group of men in front of the Kansas State Penitentiary coal mine superintendent's office pose for a photograph. The superintendent had to make sure that ventilation equipment and water pumps were in good working condition to help ensure the safety of the officers and inmates in the mine. On occasion, accidents did happen, such as a gas explosion in December 1929 that mortally wounded two inmate miners. (Courtesy of the Lansing Historical Museum.)

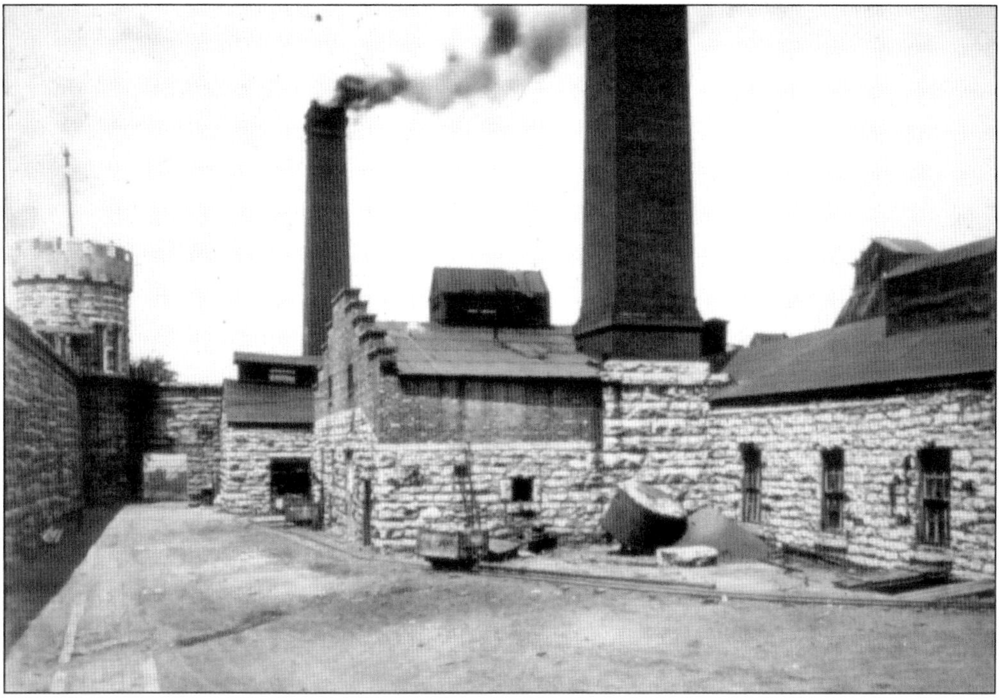

A coal car is stopped near the Kansas State Penitentiary coal mine tunnels. A guard turret is in the background on the left. (Courtesy of the Lansing Historical Museum.)

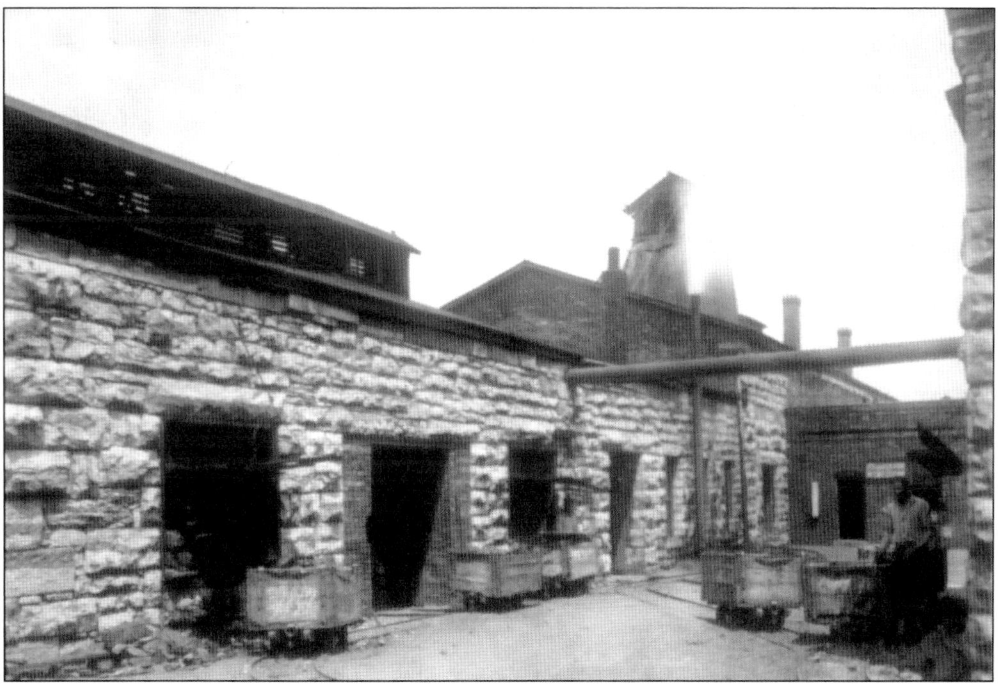

The tunnels here are leading to the Kansas State Penitentiary coal mine. (Courtesy of the Lansing Historical Museum.)

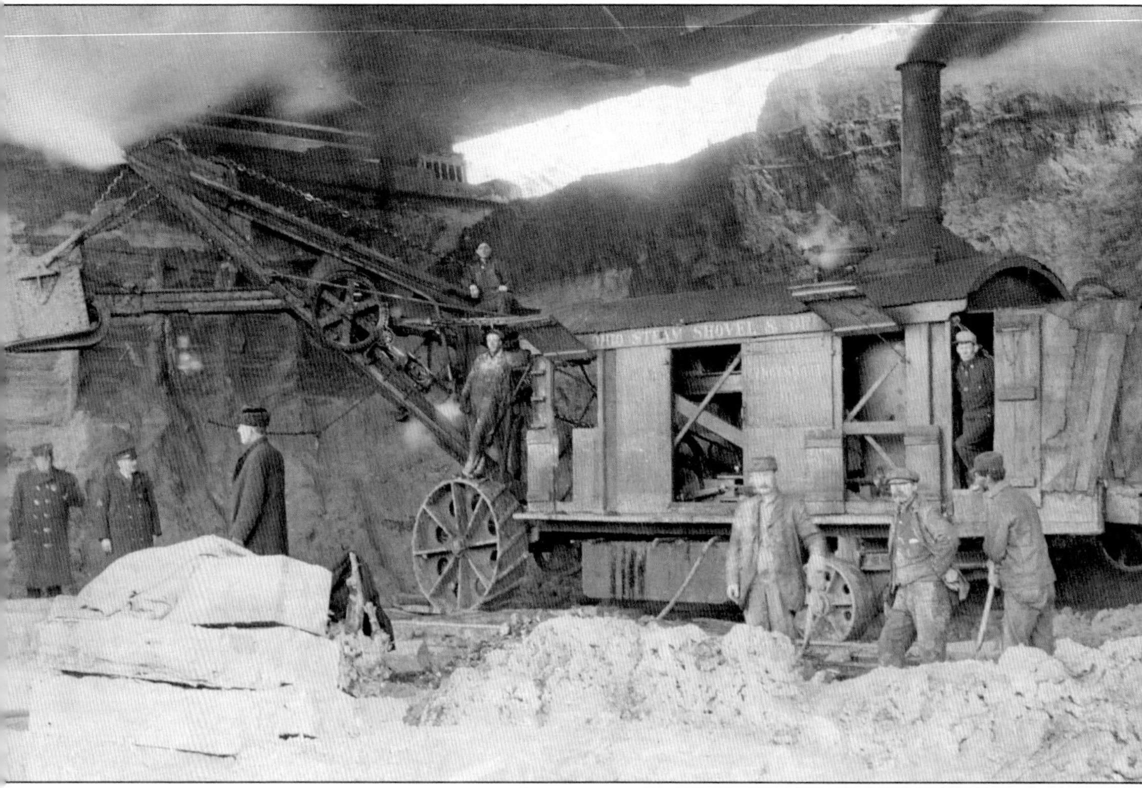

Joseph Walters (far left) assists in the supervision of inmates using a steam-powered shovel to move earth and rock at the Kansas State Penitentiary. (Courtesy of the Lansing Historical Museum.)

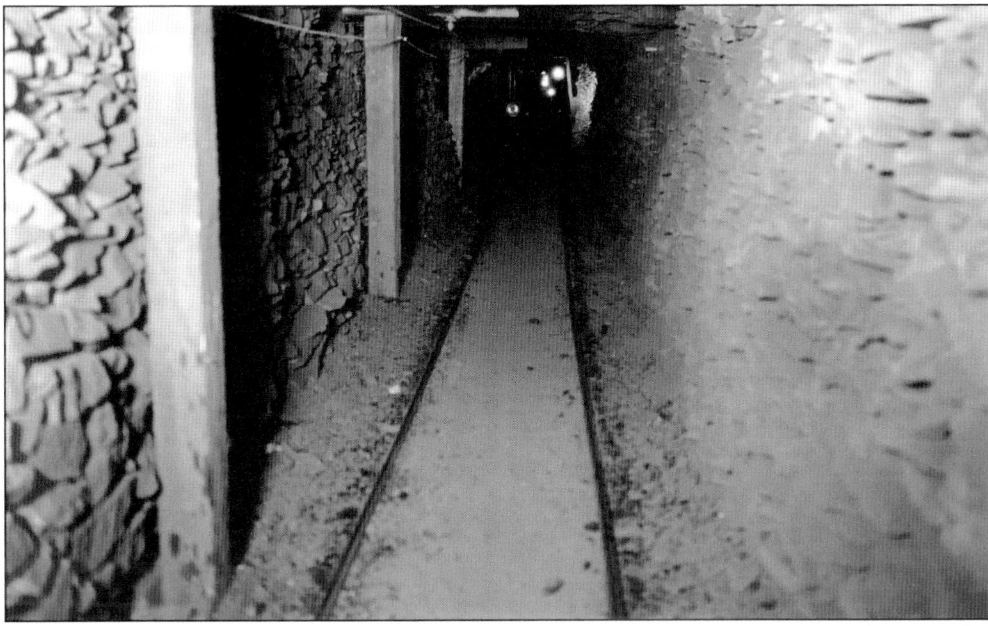

In 1881, prison officials and inmates excavated the coal shaft at the prison. The mine proved to be a dangerous place at times, with cave-ins and four mutinies, such as the one in 1901. On that day, 356 inmates rebelled and overpowered 18 guards in the mine. In a daring rescue, William Duckett led seven men down into the mine. A fight ensued that left 5 dead and 25 wounded. (Courtesy of the Lansing Historical Museum.)

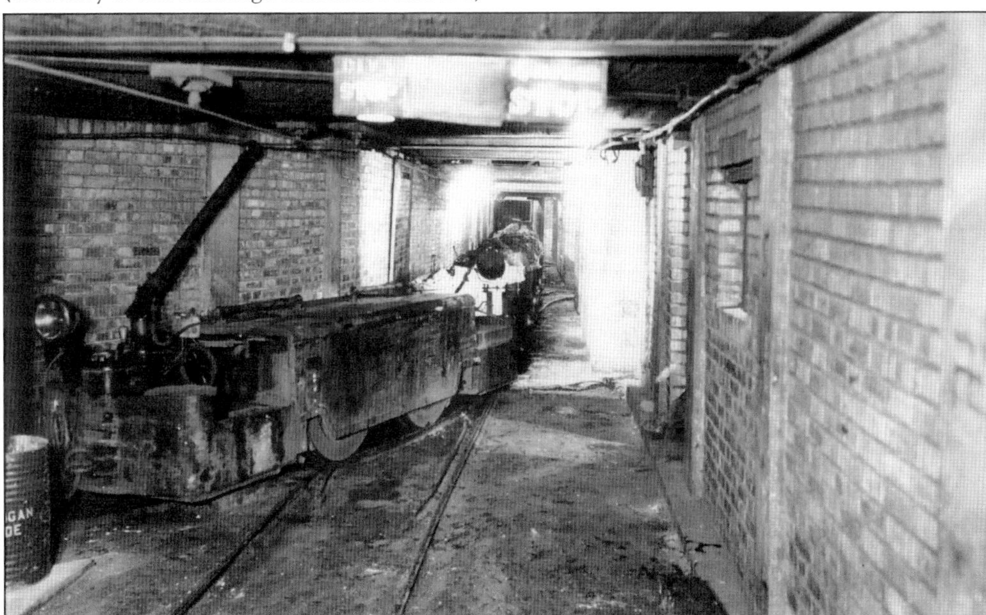

Kansas State Penitentiary coal mine cars transported coal to the surface. Inmates had to dig a quota of coal to "earn their keep." In 1927, an inmate had to dig 10 tons of coal a week for his quota. For each ton above the quota, an inmate received $1.50 for his effort. One inmate used the money he made from mining extra coal to buy his mother a house in Coffeyville. (Courtesy of the Lansing Historical Museum.)

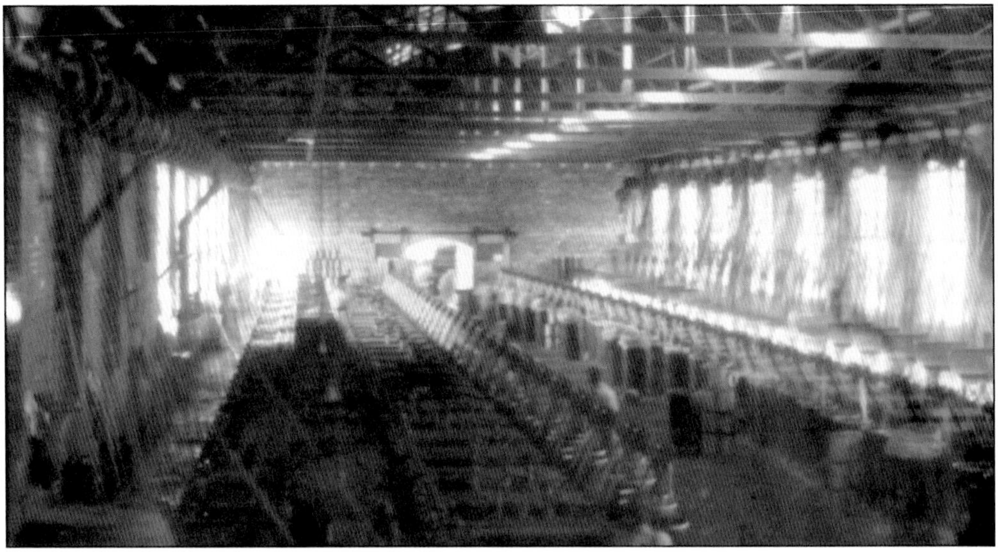

The Kansas State Penitentiary twine plant began taking twine orders in April 1900. Within 10 days, the plant shipped one-tenth of its total output (100,000 pounds) to farmers. Farmers ordered by mail between 100 and 500 pounds of twine to use during the harvest season. (Courtesy of the Lansing Historical Museum.)

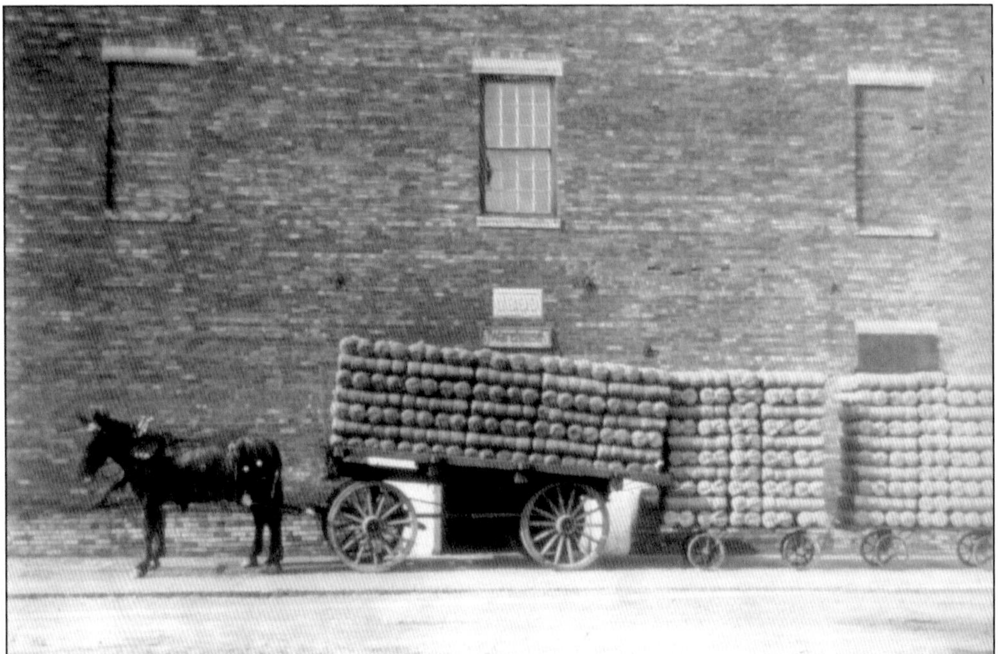

A horse pulls wagonloads of twine manufactured at the Kansas State Penitentiary. The horse and wagons are standing in front of a warehouse built in 1899. (Courtesy of the Lansing Historical Museum.)

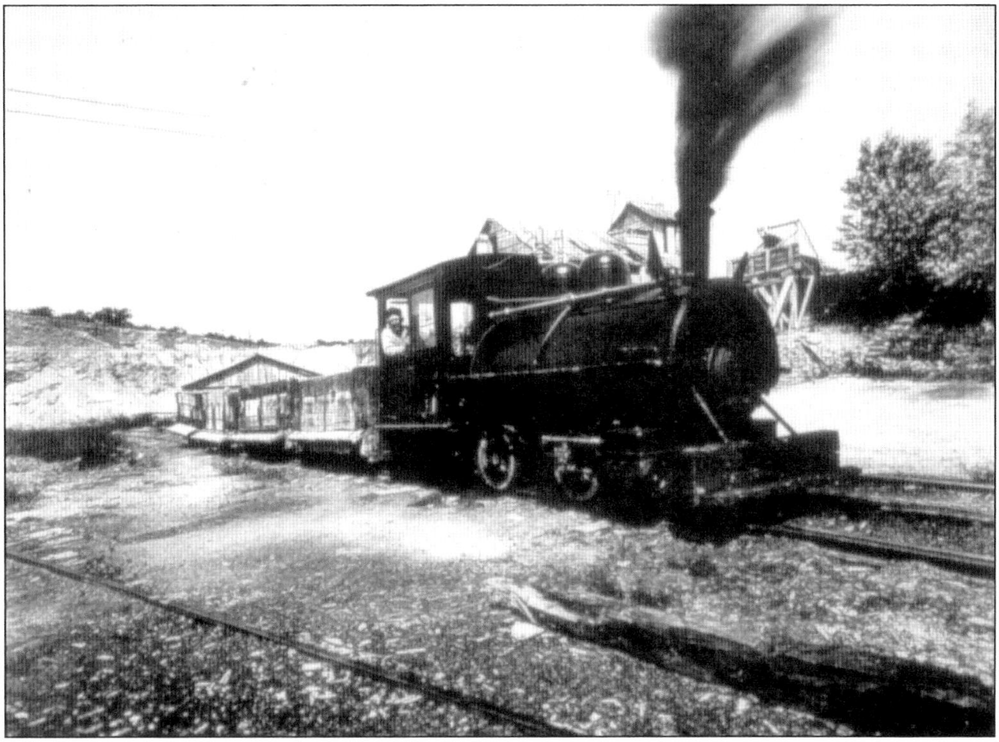

This train engine is on its way to the Kansas State Penitentiary. (Courtesy of the Lansing Historical Museum.)

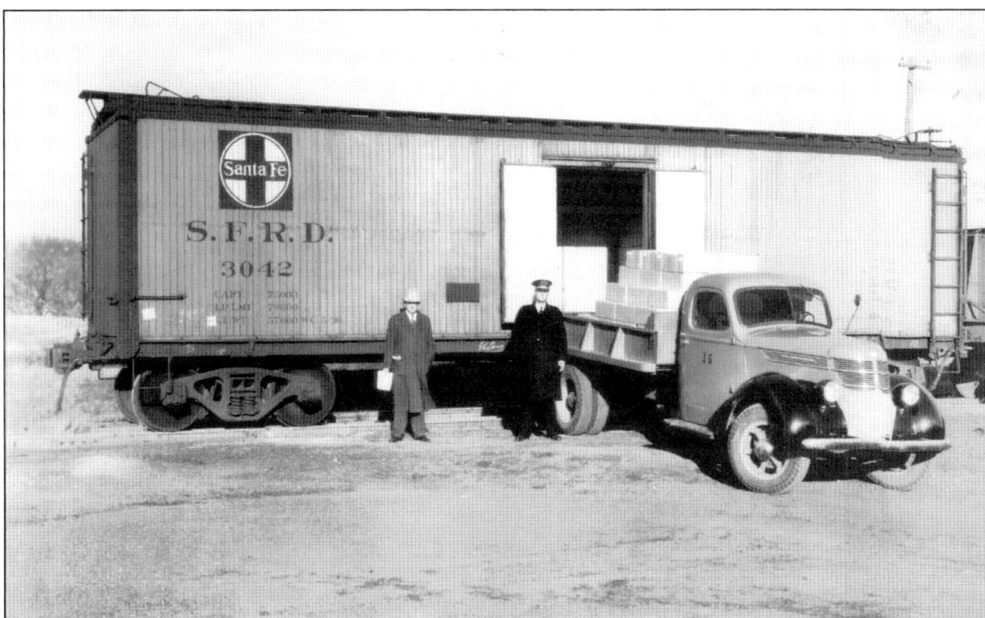

The Atchison, Topeka, and Santa Fe Railway built a railroad spur directly to the Kansas State Penitentiary. This spur enabled operation supplies to be shipped in easily and items produced by the prison's industries to be shipped out. (Courtesy of the Lansing Historical Museum.)

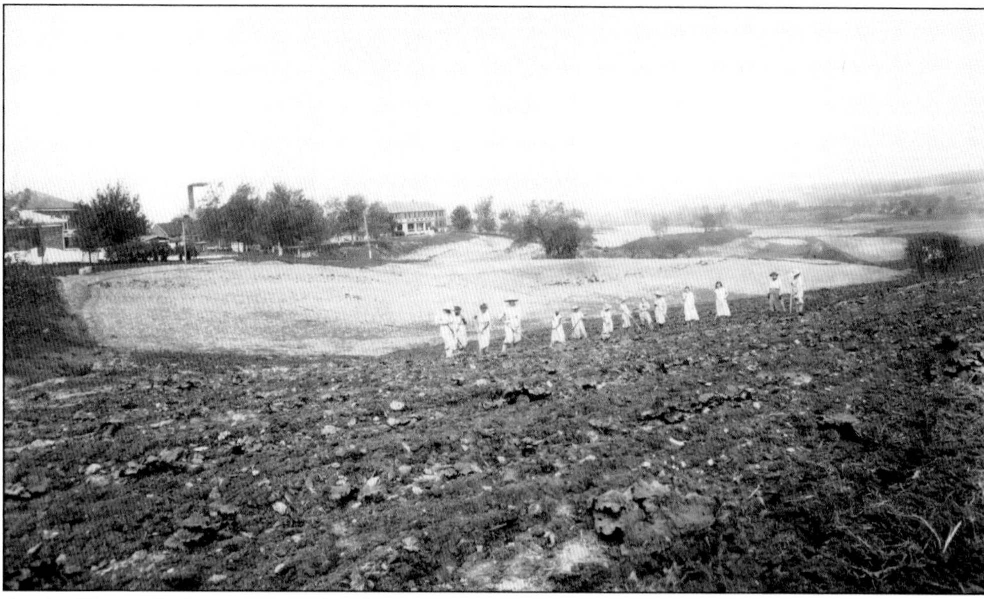

At the Kansas Industrial Farm for Women, inmates are working a field. In the beginning, female inmates were housed at the Kansas State Penitentiary. This created problems, so the women were moved to tents at a separate location until permanent buildings could be constructed. Originally only women who had committed crimes were sent to the farm. However, with the onset of World War I, women who contracted venereal diseases came to the farm for treatment. (Courtesy of the Lansing Historical Museum.)

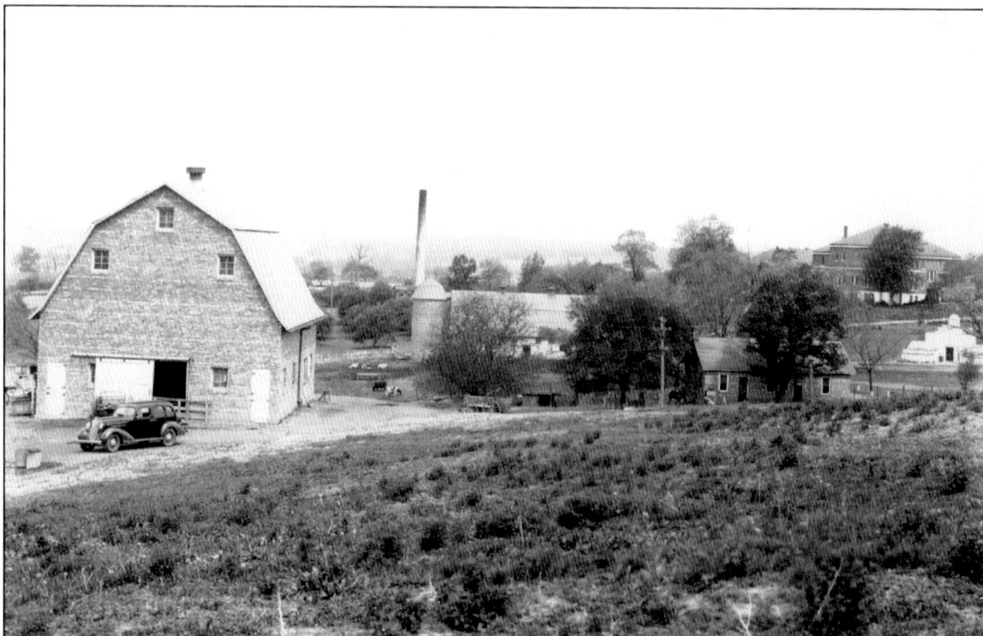

The Kansas State Penitentiary's eastern border lies on the Missouri River. The area is fertile farmland, and the prison utilized the land to grow crops and practice animal husbandry. The food produced by the farm went to feed the inmates and made the institution more self-sufficient. (Courtesy of the Lansing Historical Museum.)

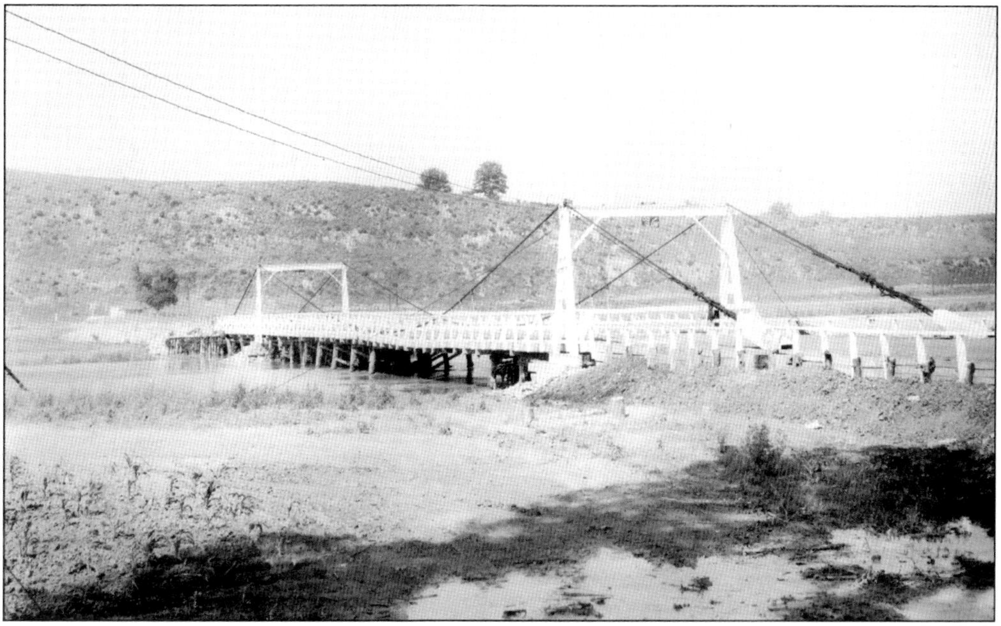

This suspension bridge crossed the Missouri River to connect with the prison's property. It appears that the bridge is either under construction or possibly being repaired from flood damage. There is a railroad crossing on the far side of the bridge and what appears to be a corn crop in the foreground. The photograph is from 1931 or 1932. (Courtesy of the Lansing Historical Museum.)

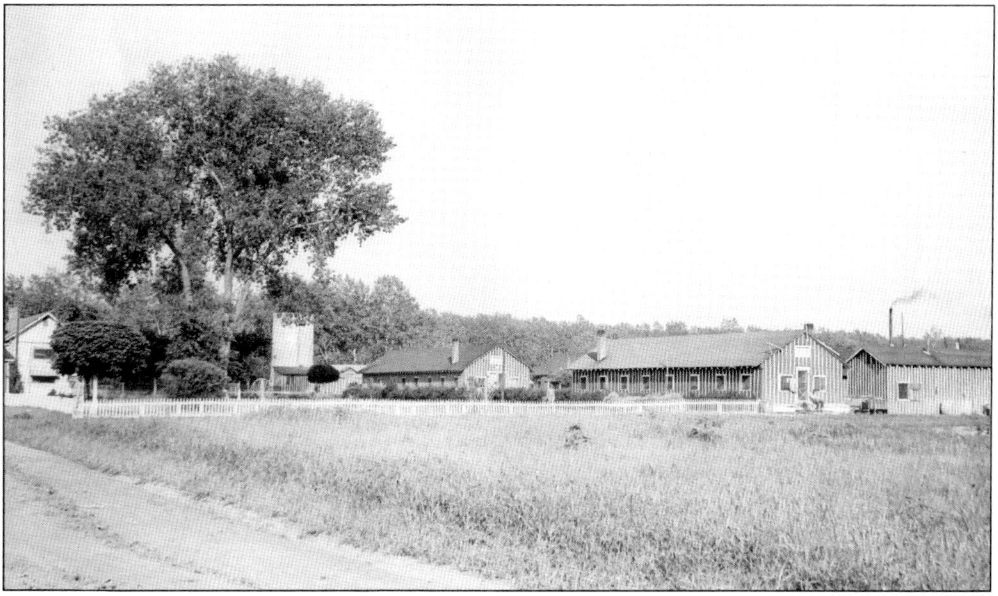

Kansas State Penitentiary established Island Camp No. 2 for inmates working at the sawmills and clearing timber for new land. The camp could accommodate 150 men. These first-time offenders were on their honor not to run off, and few broke their promise not to escape. The inmates harvested cottonwood trees to build the camp's buildings. From June 1931 to June 1932, the sawmill processed over 400,000 feet of timber for institutional use. (Courtesy of the Lansing Historical Museum.)

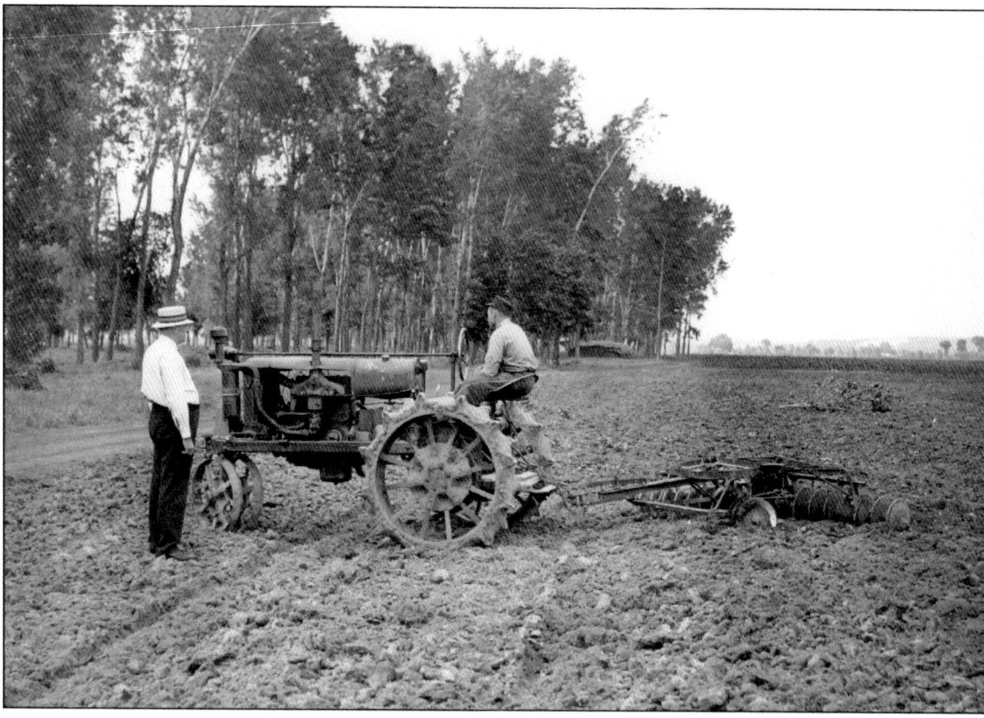

A Kansas State Penitentiary inmate plows a field at the prison farm in the 1930s. (Courtesy of the Lansing Historical Museum.)

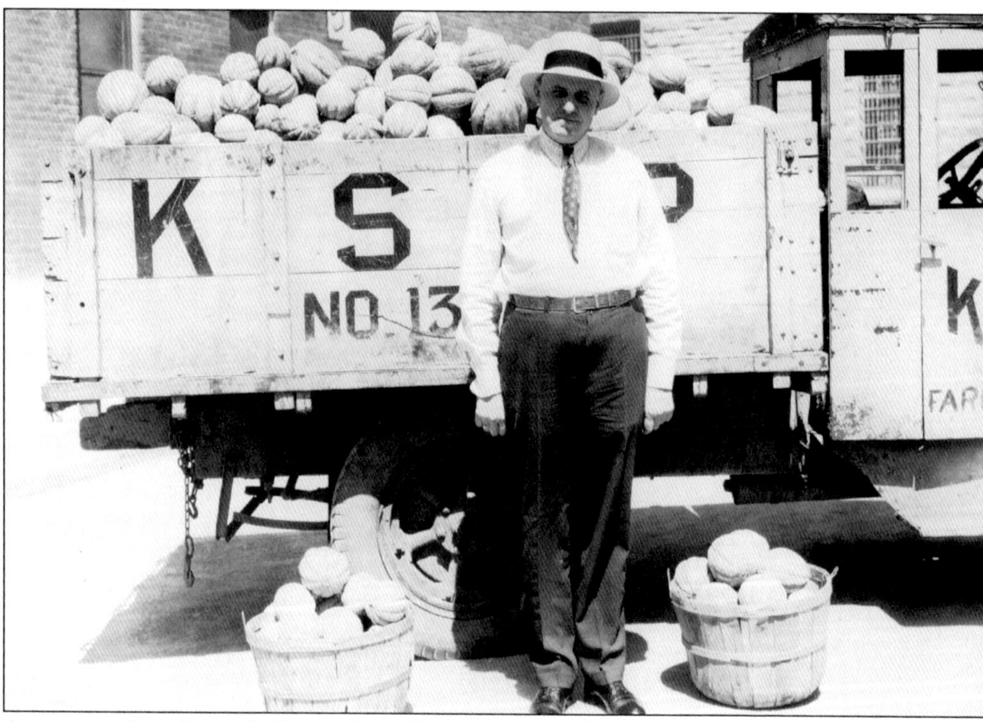

A man stands in front of a Kansas State Penitentiary truck loaded with cantaloupe grown on the prison's farm in the 1930s. (Courtesy of the Lansing Historical Museum.)

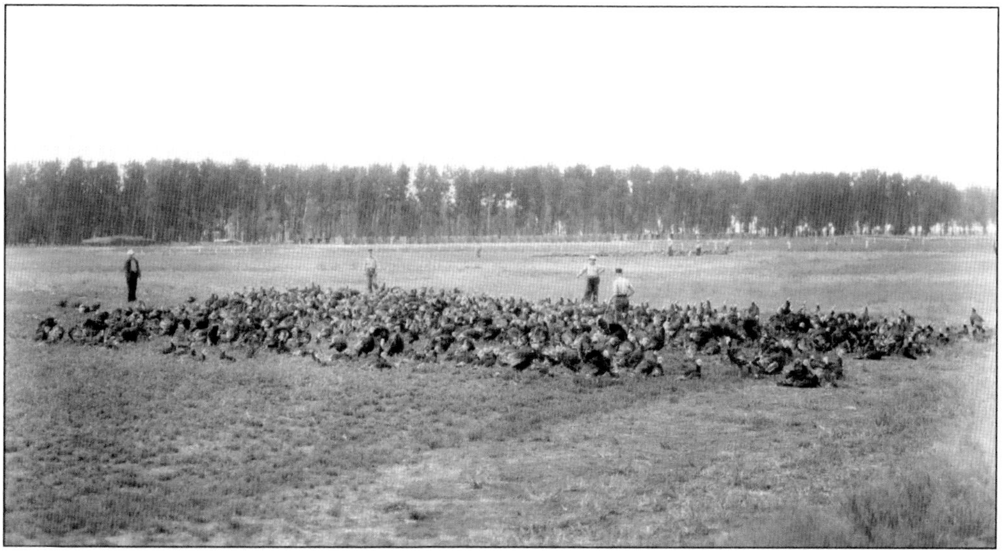

Men herd turkeys at the Kansas State Penitentiary farm in the 1930s. The farm raised turkeys to feed the inmates at Thanksgiving and Christmas. The women from the Kansas Industrial Farm for Women prepared the turkeys for these special occasions. (Courtesy of the Lansing Historical Museum.)

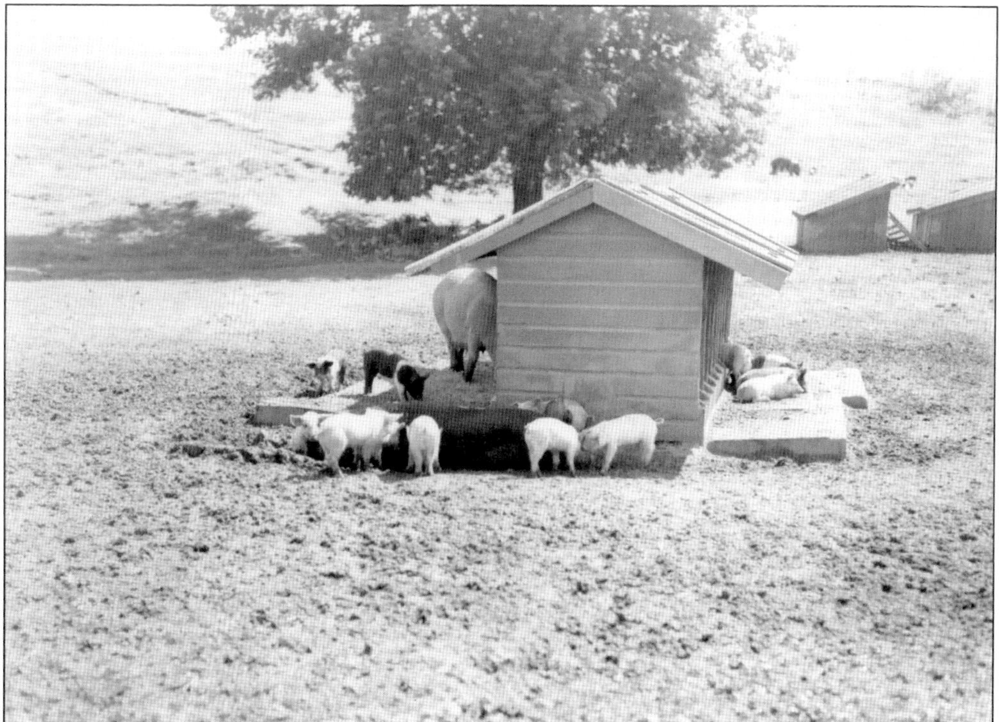

A sow and her piglets gather at the Kansas State Penitentiary farm in the 1960s. Pigs are no longer raised on prison grounds, but visitors will find cattle and goats still being raised. (Courtesy of the Lansing Historical Museum.)

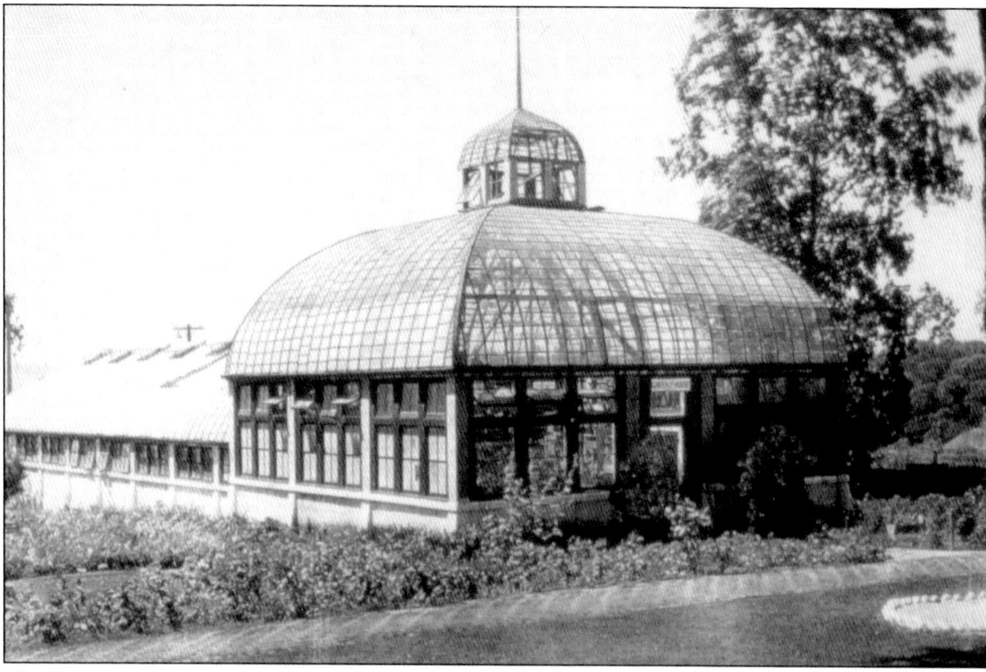

The Kansas State Penitentiary used greenhouse plants for the prison's flower beds. (Courtesy of the Lansing Historical Museum.)

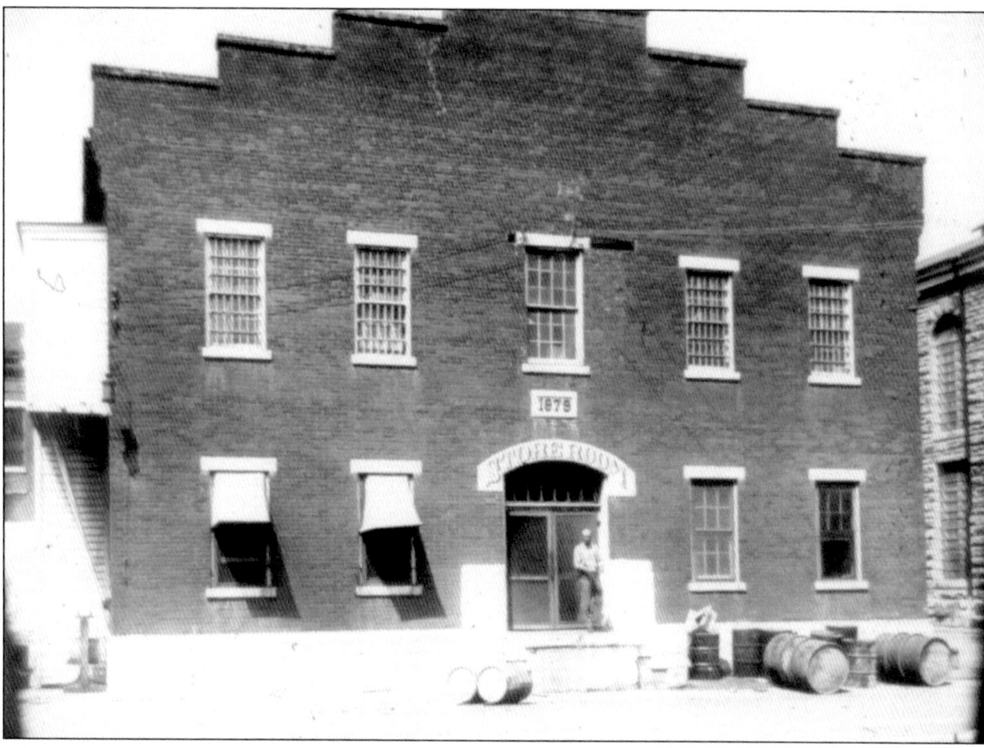

The Kansas State Penitentiary warehouse was built in 1879. (Courtesy of the Lansing Historical Museum.)

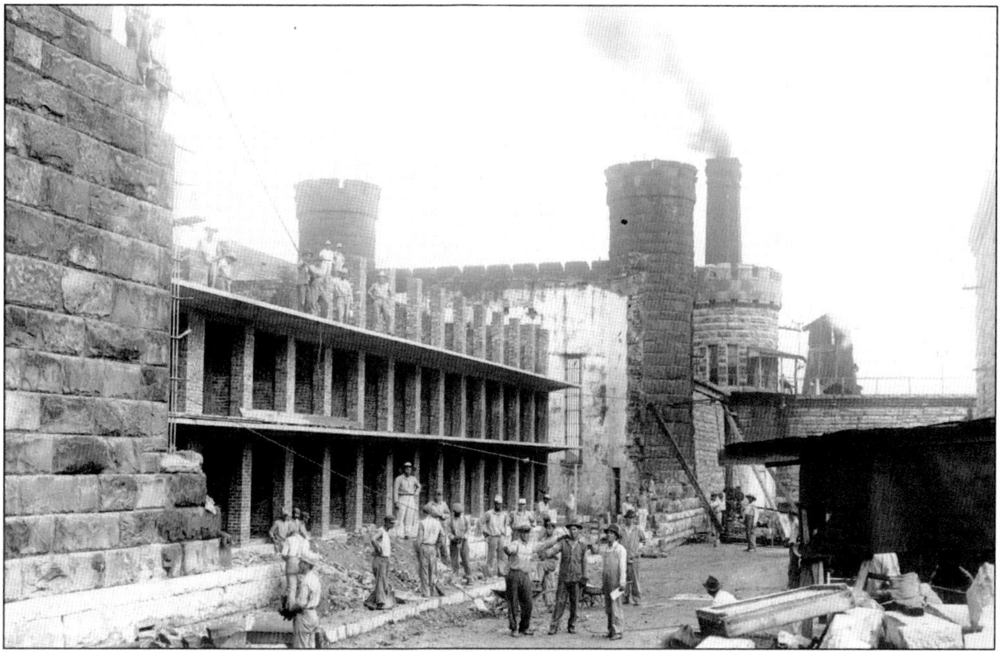

Construction occurs at the Kansas State Penitentiary in the second decade of the 20th century. Inmate labor has always been utilized by the prison to carry out projects and day-to-day operations. Inmates complete construction projects on prison grounds and in the community, such as the concession stand at City Park. (Courtesy of the Lansing Historical Museum.)

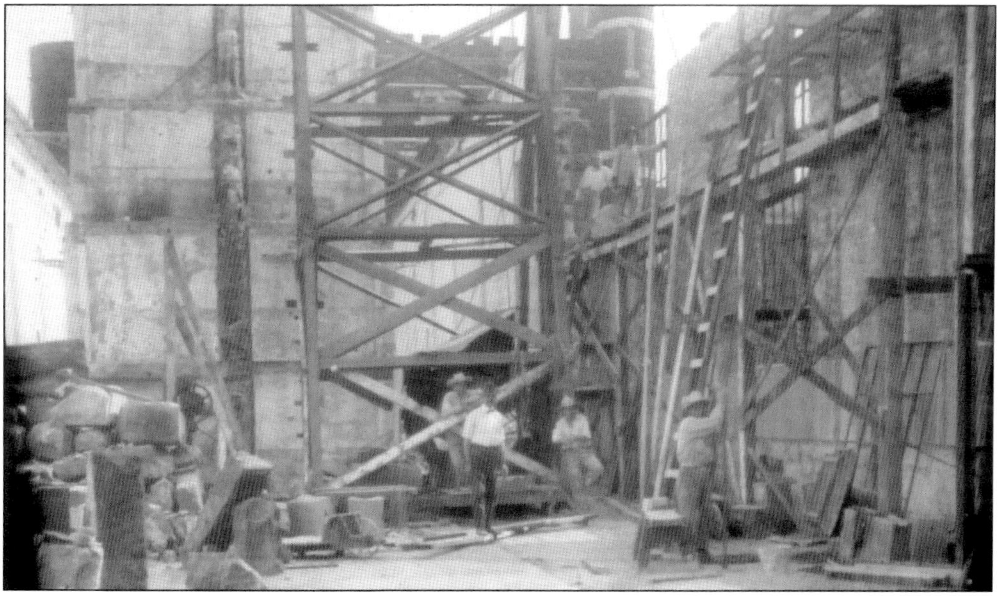

On November 7, 1916, a new electric motor attached to the ventilation fan caused a fire that sent clouds of suffocating smoke into the north wing cells. Guard A. C. Taylor single-handedly had to open each cell to let the inmates out to safety. Inmate firemen along with Leavenworth firemen fought the blaze that heavily damaged the roof, fan room, and north end of the cell tiers. This photograph depicts the restoration of the north wing. (Courtesy of the Lansing Historical Museum.)

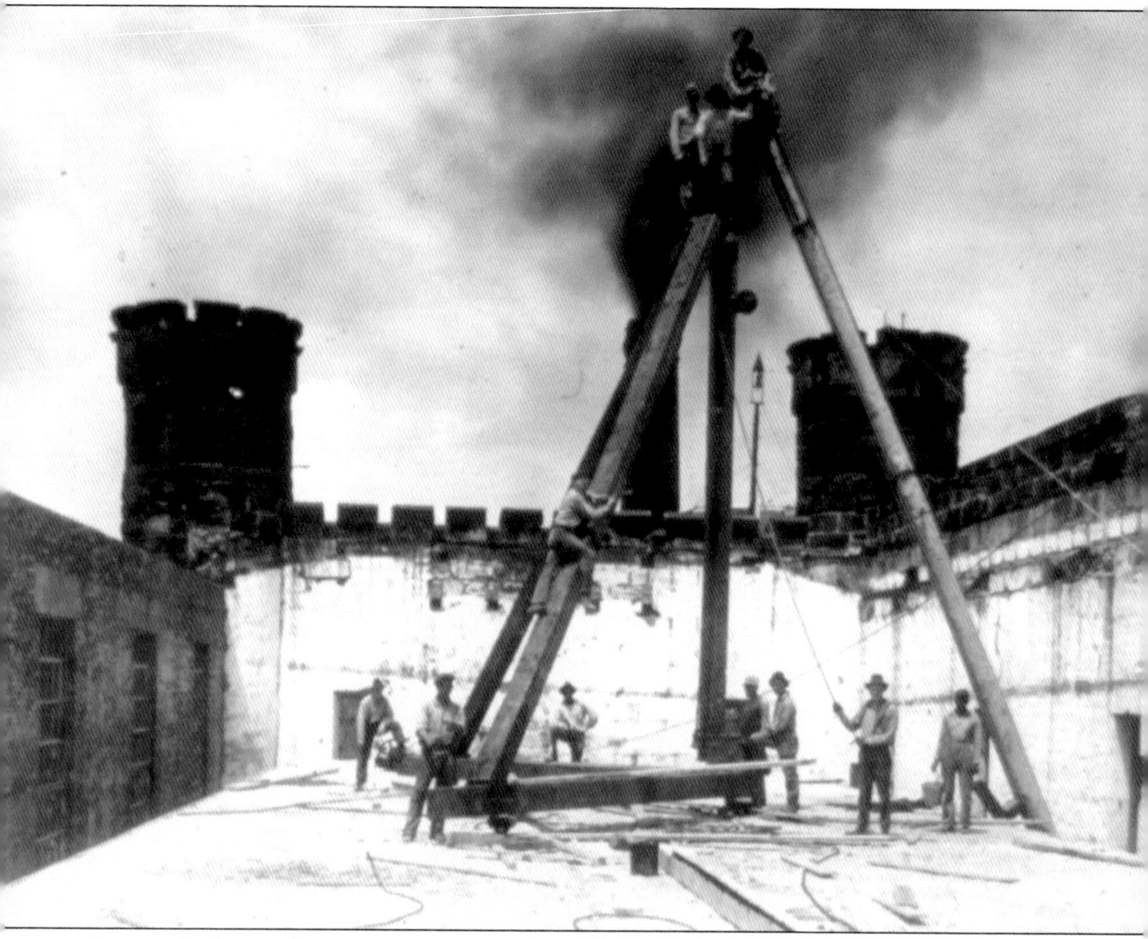

Inmates in the north wing attempt to raise a roof beam with scaffolding after the fire. (Courtesy of the Lansing Historical Museum.)

Kansas State Penitentiary inmates line up in front of their cells during the second decade of the 20th century. (Courtesy of the Lansing Historical Museum.)

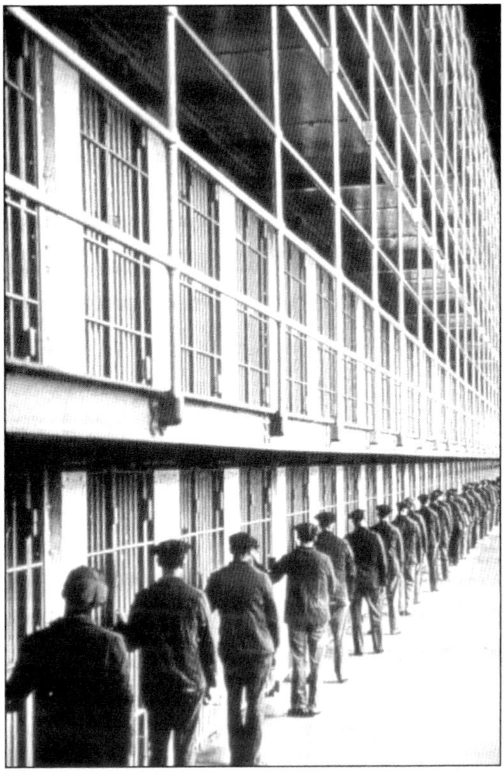

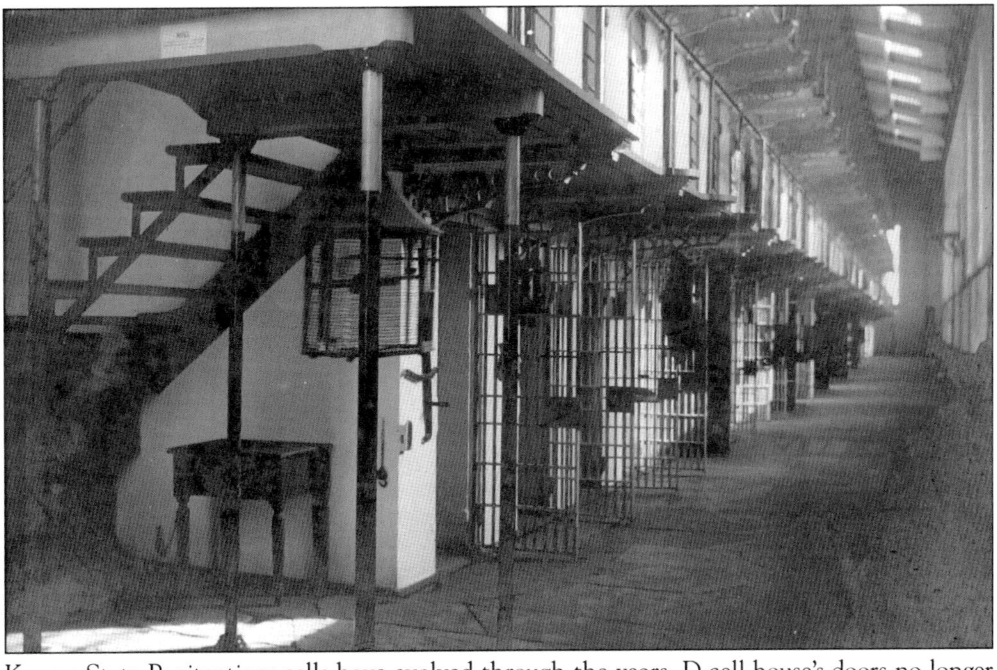

Kansas State Penitentiary cells have evolved through the years. D cell house's doors no longer have the traditional bars. Instead, they have a woven metal mesh that prevents people from reaching out of or into the cell. Inmates in wheelchairs have modified cell doors so there is enough clearance for the wheelchair to pass through. (Courtesy of the Lansing Historical Museum.)

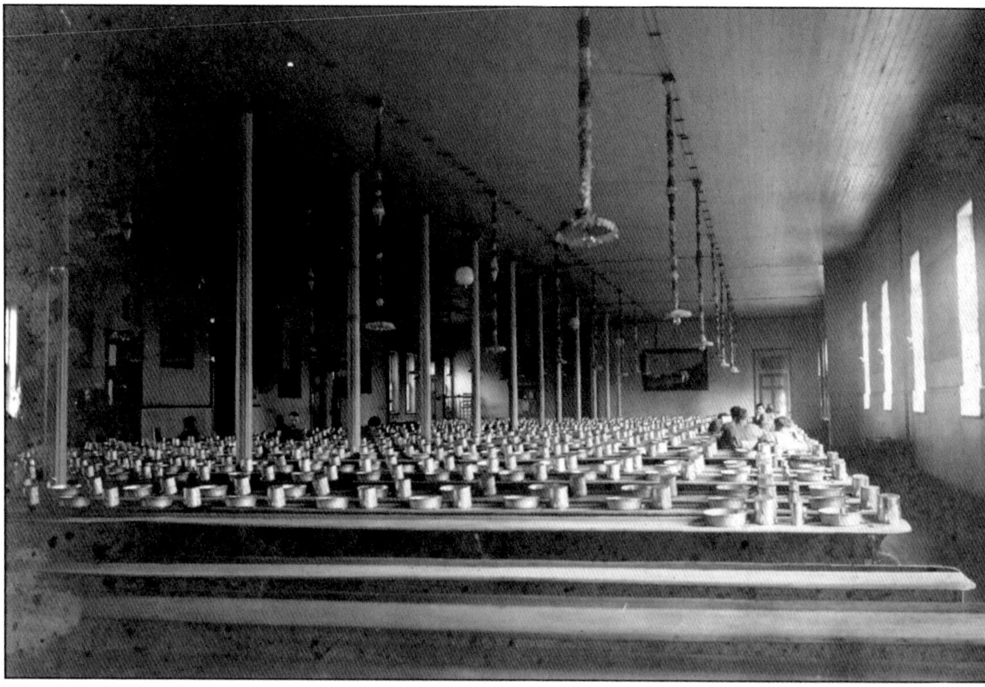

The Kansas State Penitentiary dining hall had long tables for decades until warden Sherman Crouse changed the seating to four-man tables in the 1960s. (Courtesy of the Lansing Historical Museum.)

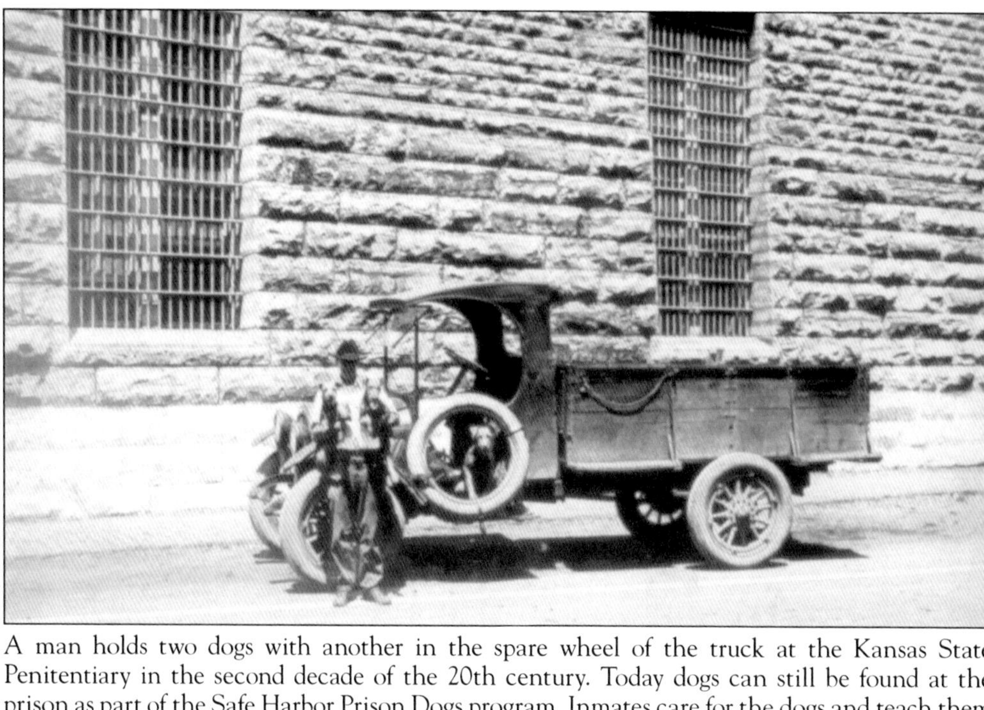

A man holds two dogs with another in the spare wheel of the truck at the Kansas State Penitentiary in the second decade of the 20th century. Today dogs can still be found at the prison as part of the Safe Harbor Prison Dogs program. Inmates care for the dogs and teach them basic commands to make them ready for adoption into loving homes. (Courtesy of the Lansing Historical Museum.)

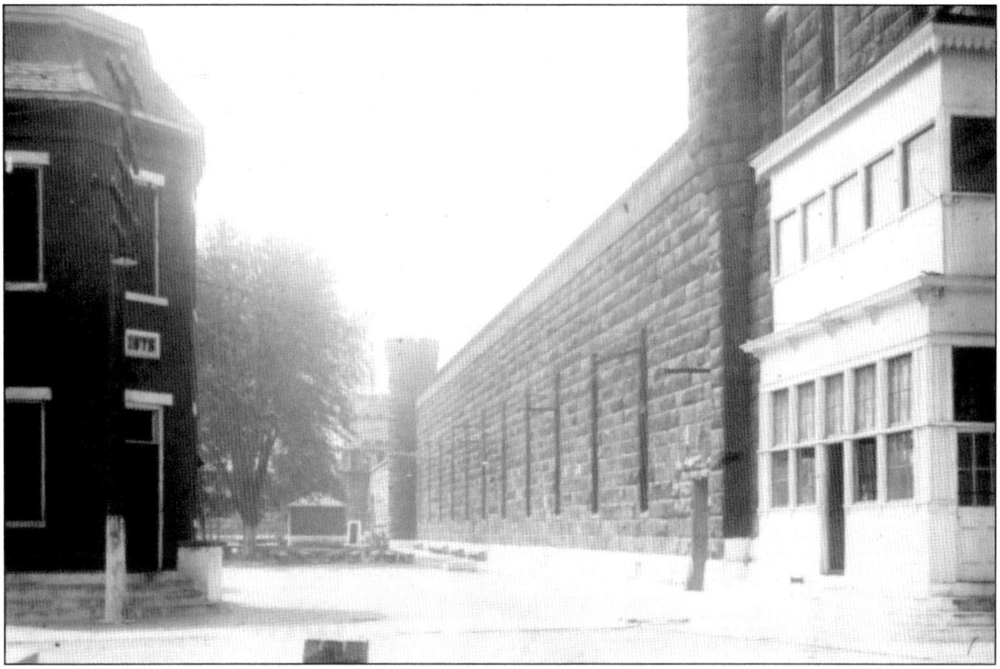

The Kansas State Penitentiary deputy warden's office is the building on the left side of the photograph. It was known as the "bell tower" because of the bell on top that officials used to signal the inmates. (Courtesy of the Lansing Historical Museum.)

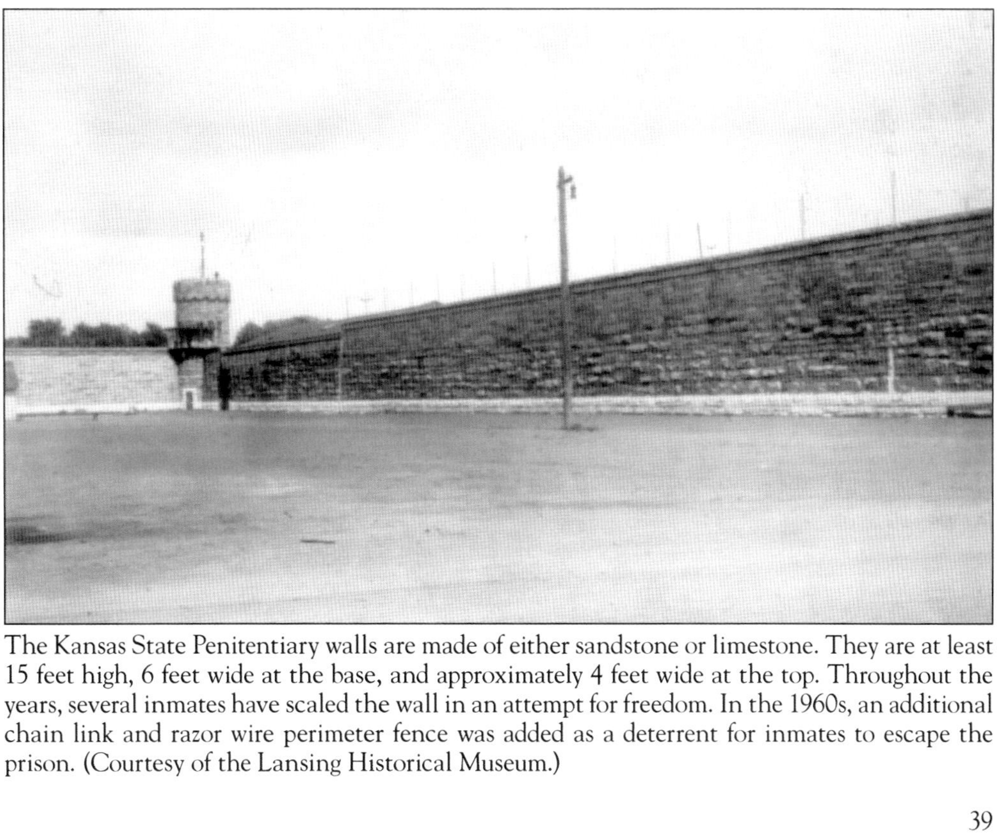

The Kansas State Penitentiary walls are made of either sandstone or limestone. They are at least 15 feet high, 6 feet wide at the base, and approximately 4 feet wide at the top. Throughout the years, several inmates have scaled the wall in an attempt for freedom. In the 1960s, an additional chain link and razor wire perimeter fence was added as a deterrent for inmates to escape the prison. (Courtesy of the Lansing Historical Museum.)

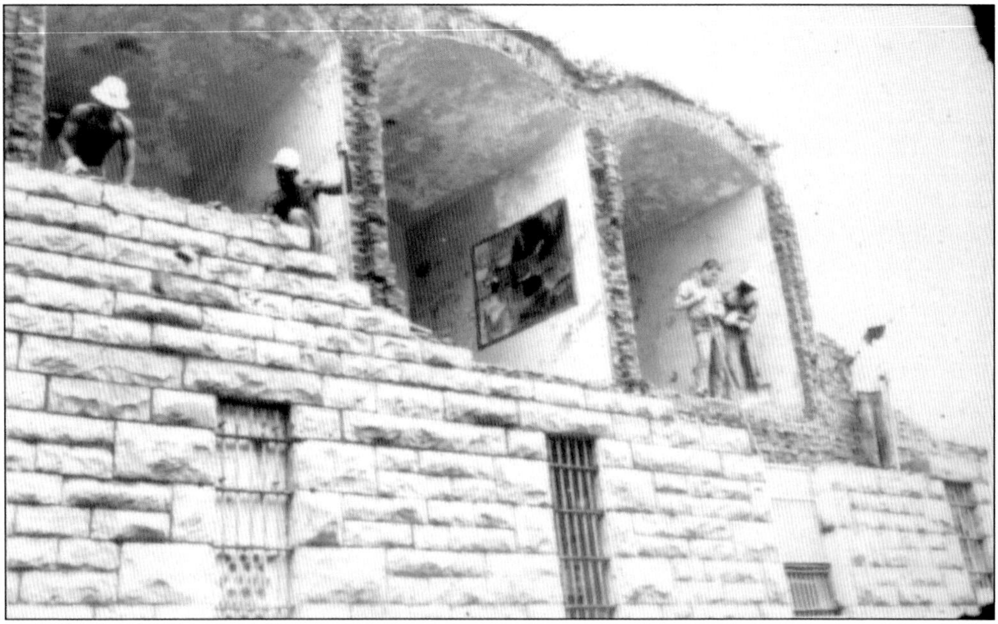

The security and isolation building was a precursor to the adjustment and treatment building at the Kansas State Penitentiary. The building is used to house inmates who have to be separated from the general population for serious violations of the rules. (Courtesy of the Lansing Historical Museum.)

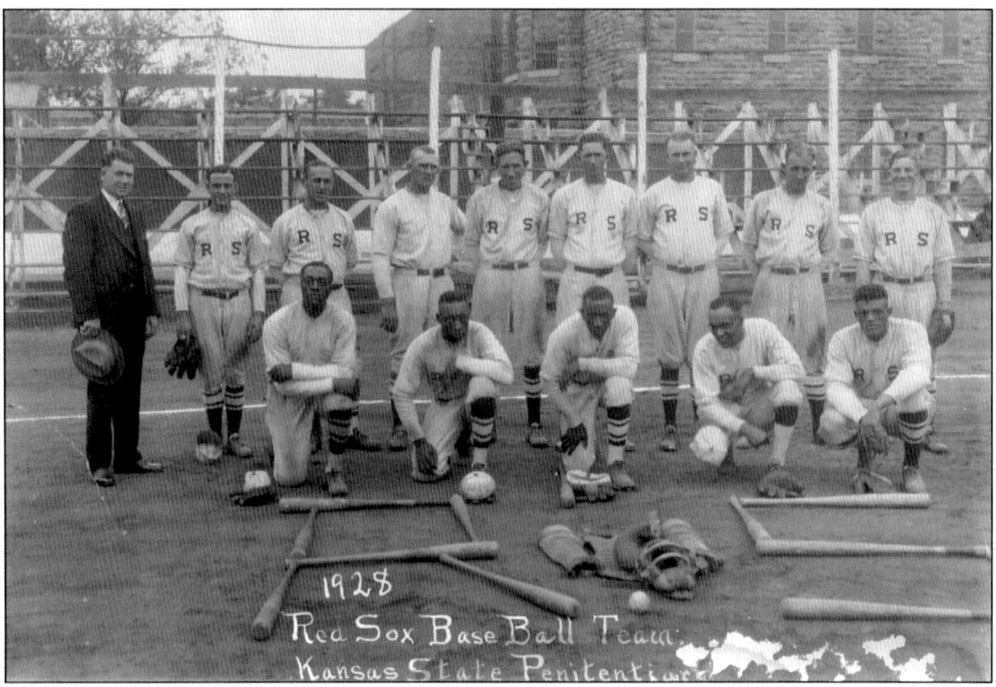

The Kansas State Penitentiary 1928 Red Sox baseball team played community baseball teams at the prison in a friendly competition. Baseball benefited the inmates by providing exercise and fostering sportsmanship among the inmates. The tradition between the prison and community teams lasted for many years. (Courtesy of the Lansing Historical Museum.)

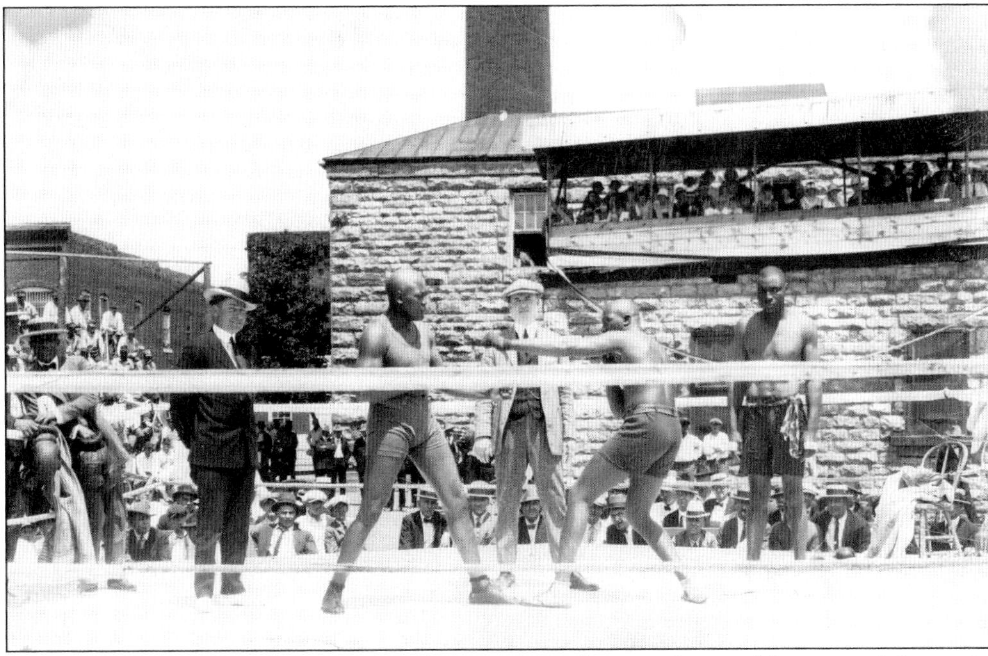

On April 26, 1928, warden W. H. Mackey announced a wrestling and boxing exhibition for that Saturday at 2:00 p.m. These exhibitions provided entertainment for the inmates and the community. Seven boxing bouts between inmates in different weight classes were scheduled to go three to five rounds. (Courtesy of the Lansing Historical Museum.)

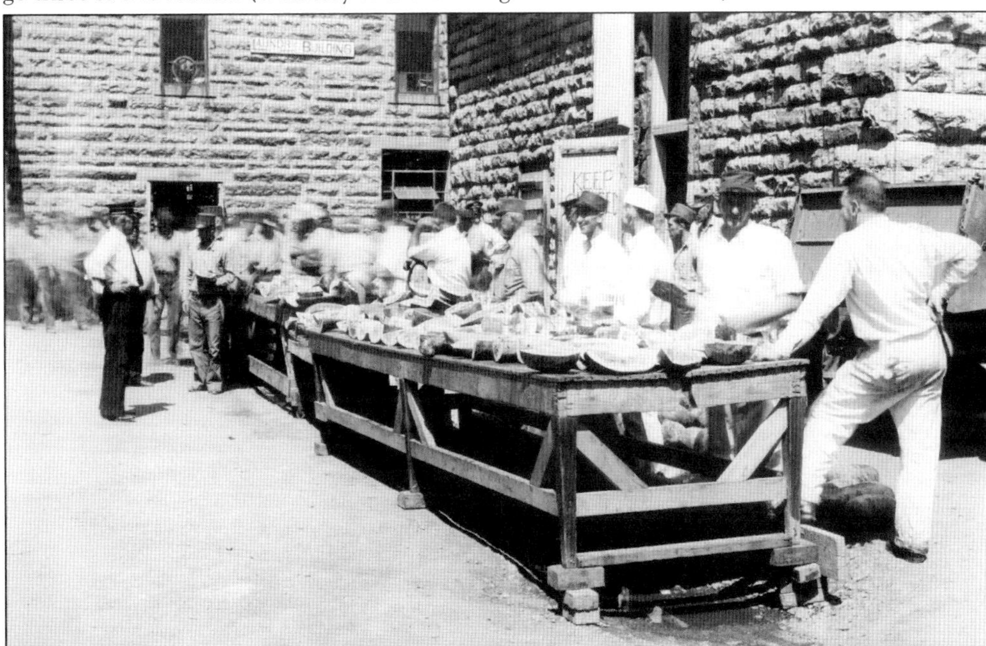

The Kansas State Penitentiary grew its own produce to feed the inmates. Here the inmates are treated to a watermelon feed. In his 1954–1956 biennial report, farm superintendent J. N. Bieri reported that the prison farm inmates harvested 392,265 pounds of watermelon. (Courtesy of the Lansing Historical Museum.)

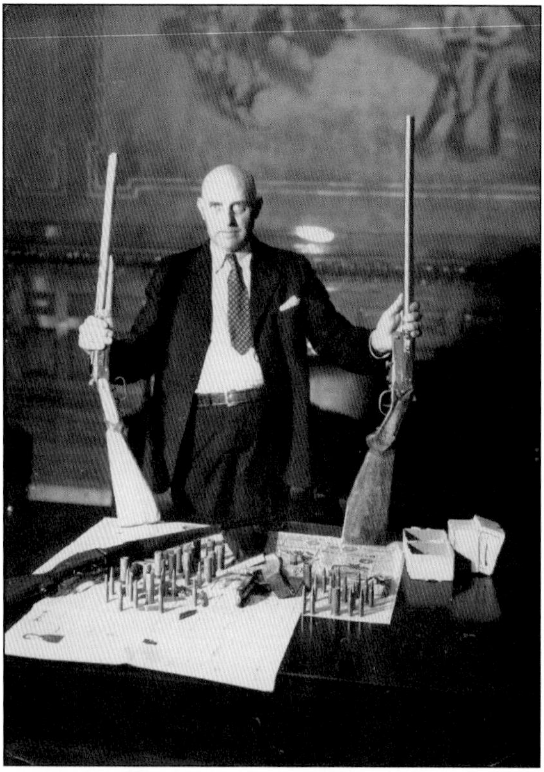

Kirk Prather served as Kansas State Penitentiary warden in the 1930s. Inmates took Prather and guards hostage during a Memorial Day baseball game. One of the bank robbers in the escape ensured the hostages' safety and freed them when the group reached Oklahoma. The man in this picture is believed to be Prather. He is holding two shotguns, and a Savidge 99 rifle is on the table. (Courtesy of the Lansing Historical Museum.)

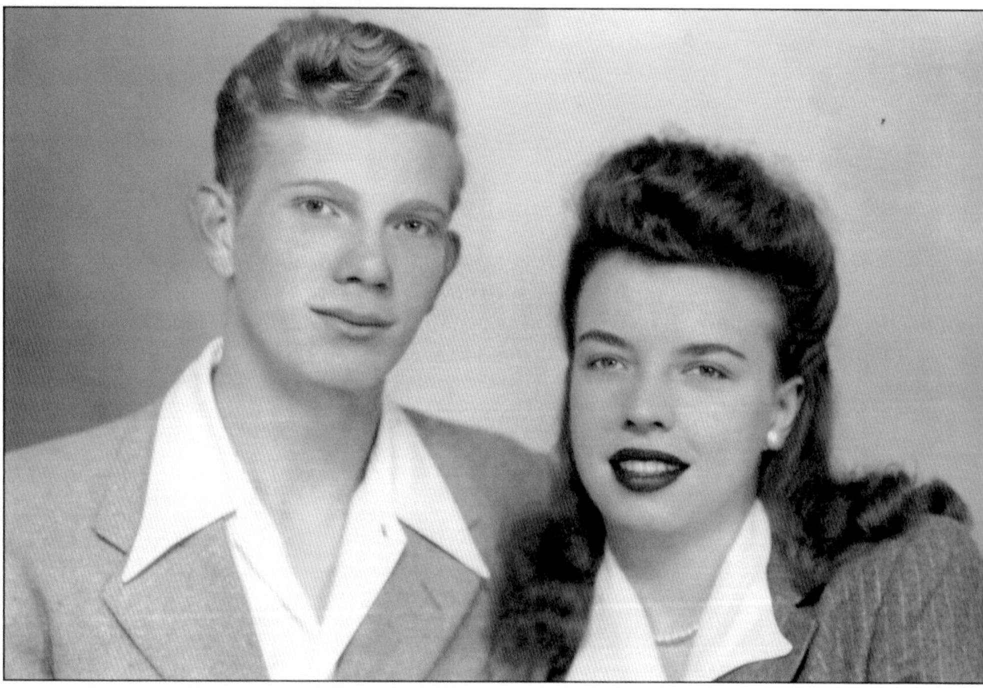

Siblings J. T. and Grace Brown pose for a photograph taken by a Kansas State Penitentiary inmate photographer. Their grandfather Jesse Crouch worked at the prison. (Courtesy of the Lansing Historical Museum.)

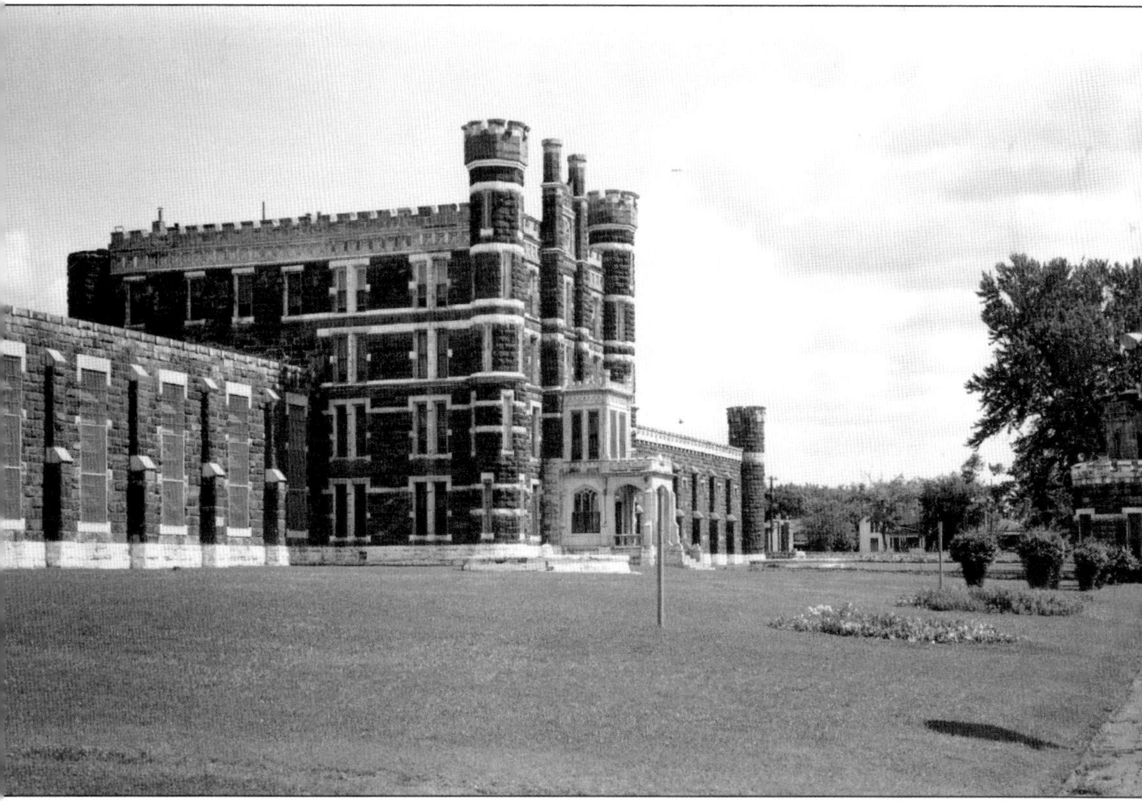

Here is the Kansas State Penitentiary in the 1950s before the chain-link fence and razor wire were built around the perimeter. For decades, the prison has maintained a beautiful lawn with flower beds. (Courtesy of the Lansing Historical Museum.)

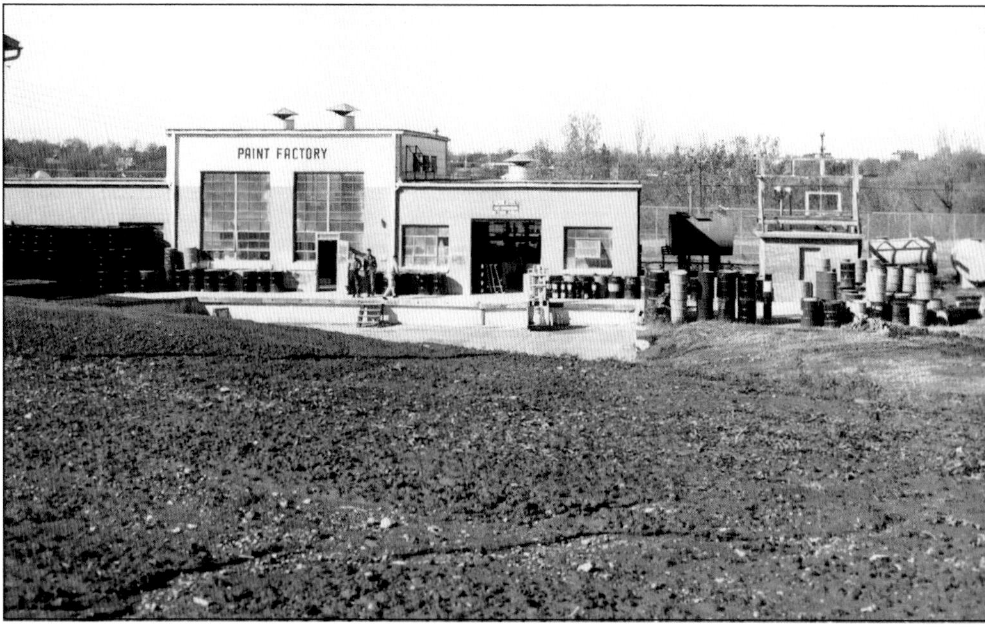

During a riot in 1969, the Kansas State Penitentiary paint factory sustained damage from a fire. Today the prison continues to manufacture paint that is used by the State of Kansas and other government institutions such as school districts. The prison also makes cleaning chemicals and street signs, but it no longer makes license plates. (Courtesy of the Lansing Historical Museum.)

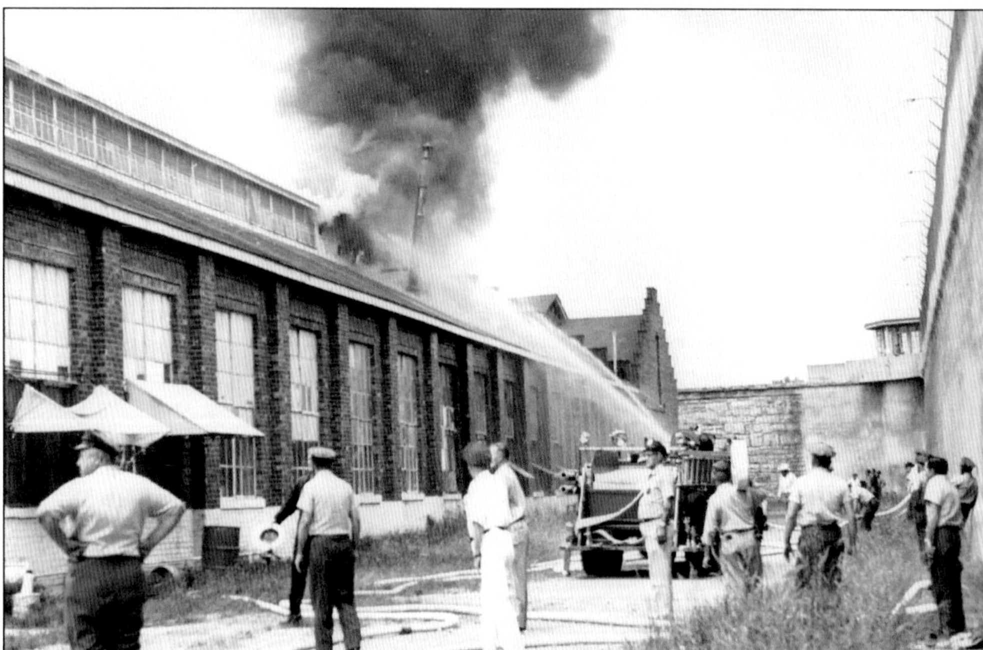

In 1969, a riot occurred at the Kansas State Penitentiary. The highway patrol sent 200 men in to help restore order at the prison. Here firefighters battle a blaze set by the inmates. (Courtesy of the Lansing Historical Museum.)

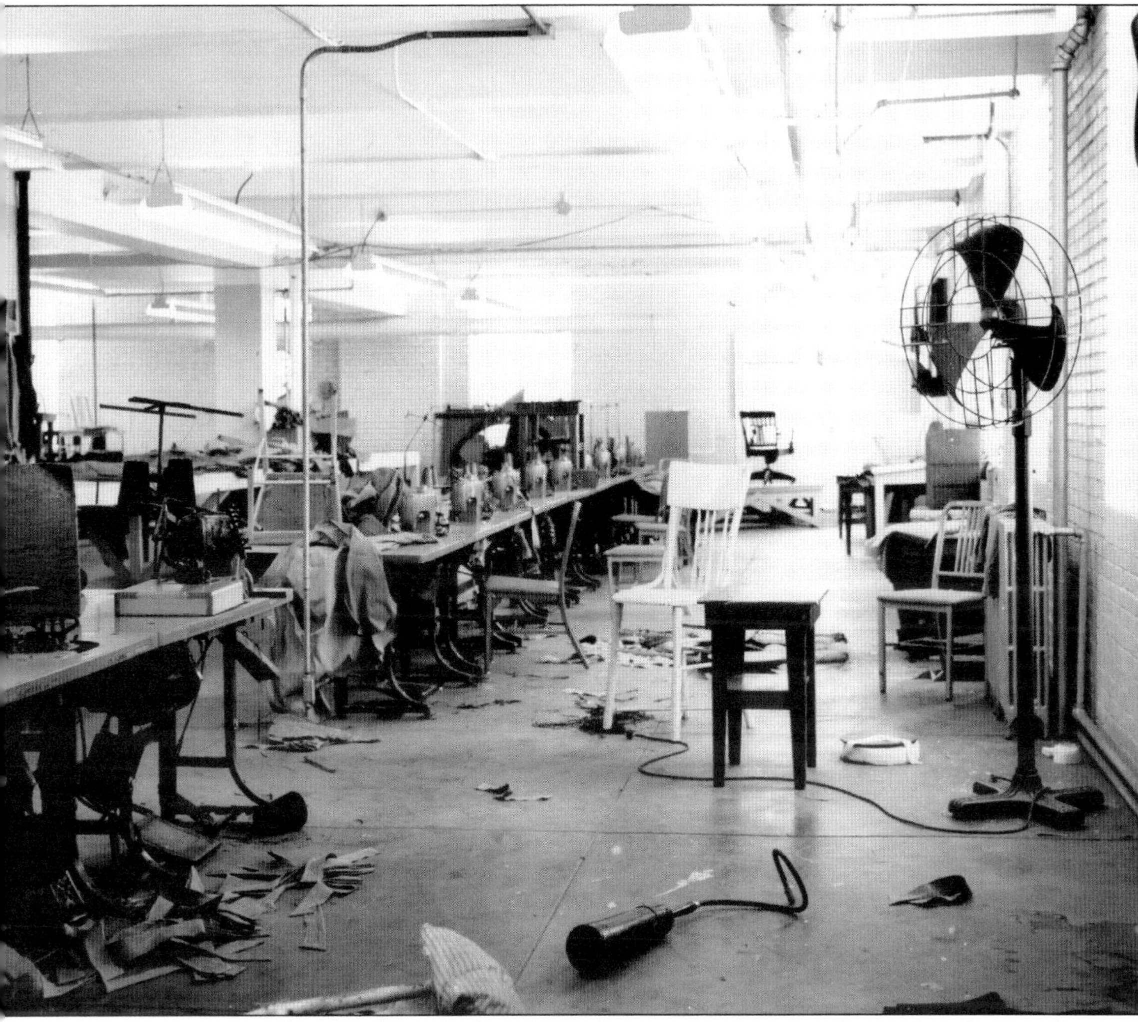

The tailor shop was located above the laundry at the prison. Inmates made guard uniforms and other items. This photograph was taken in the aftermath of the riot in 1969. While there is currently no tailor shop in existence, a group of protective custody inmates hem and repair inmate uniforms. Today Impact Design, a private company with a factory on the prison grounds, employs inmates to embroider logos onto clothing. (Courtesy of the Lansing Historical Museum.)

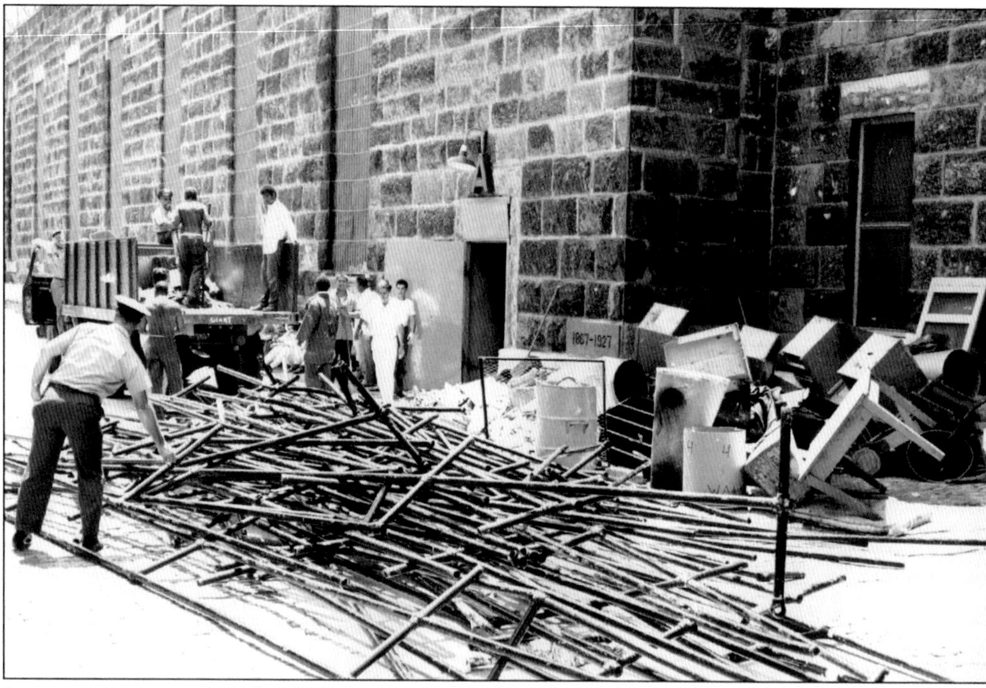

Inmates clean up after the 1969 riot at the Kansas State Penitentiary. The rails from inside A cell house had to be removed so repairs could be made to the interior. (Courtesy of the Lansing Historical Museum.)

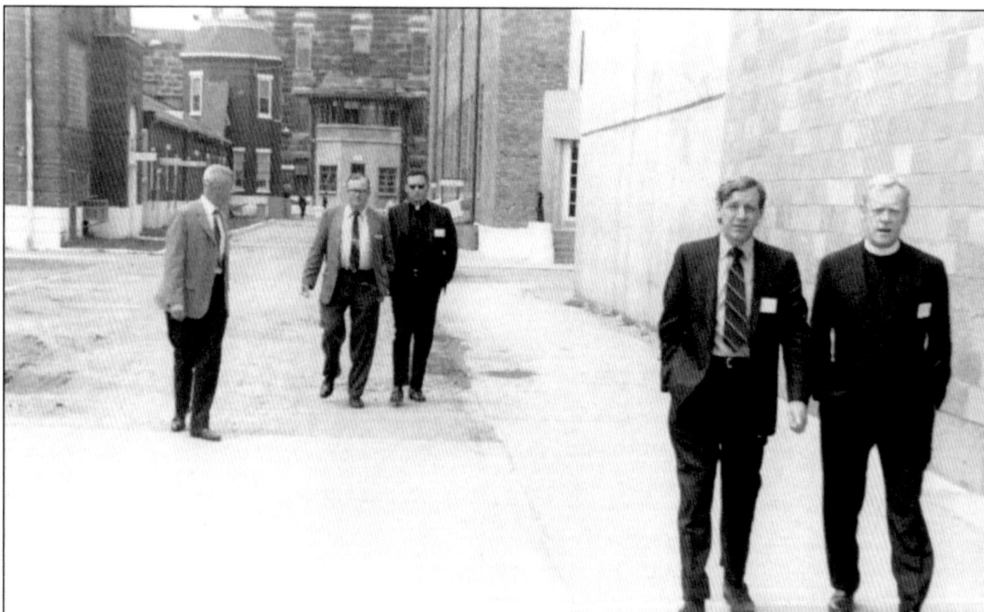

Five men wait in the maximum-security area at the Kansas State Penitentiary. Fr. Ed Simons (third from left) served as the Catholic chaplain at the prison from 1970 to 1976. He also led the congregation at St. Frances de Sales for two years. Presbyterian minister Al Davies (far right) served as a chaplain at the Kansas Reception and Diagnostic Center in Topeka. (Courtesy of the Lansing Historical Museum.)

Warden Sherman Crouse and his wife, Bonnie, enjoy his retirement party. Crouse served as warden from 1963 to 1970. He also served as Lansing's mayor from 1977 to 1978. (Courtesy of the Lansing Historical Museum.)

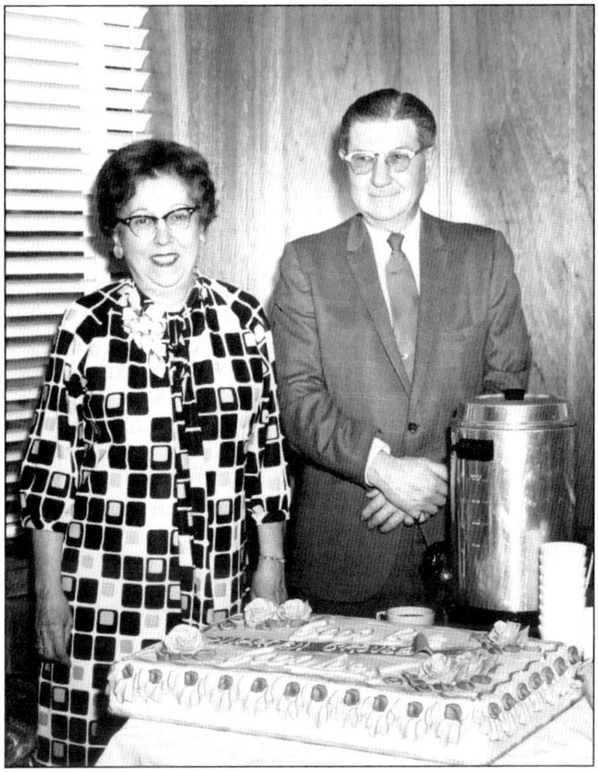

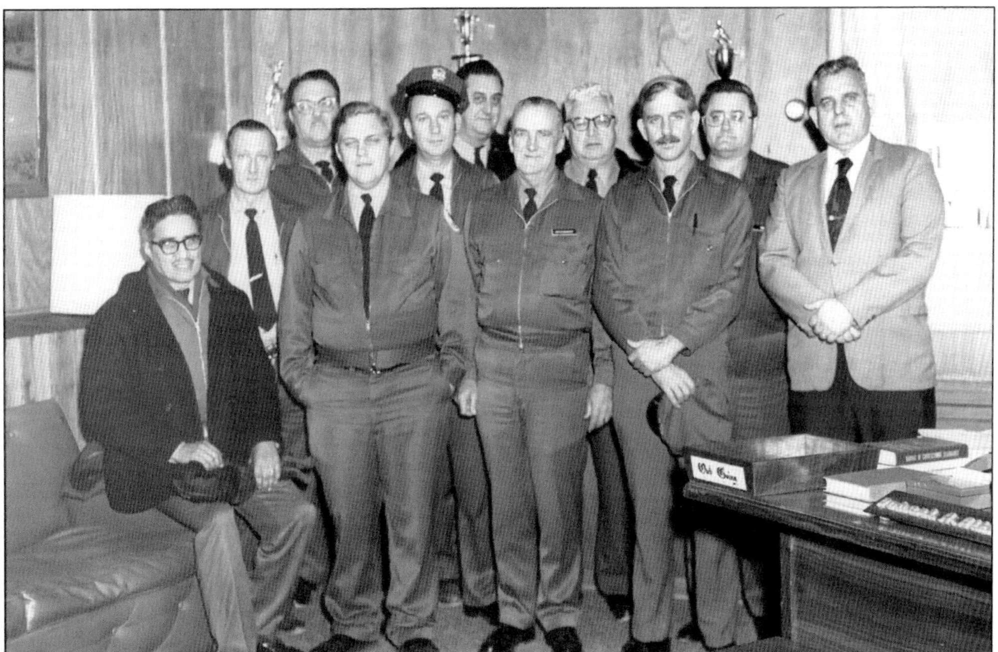

Kansas State Penitentiary officers in warden R. A. Adkins office pose for a group photograph. Adkins served as acting warden from 1974 to 1975 and then as warden from 1979 to 1981. (Courtesy of the Lansing Historical Museum.)

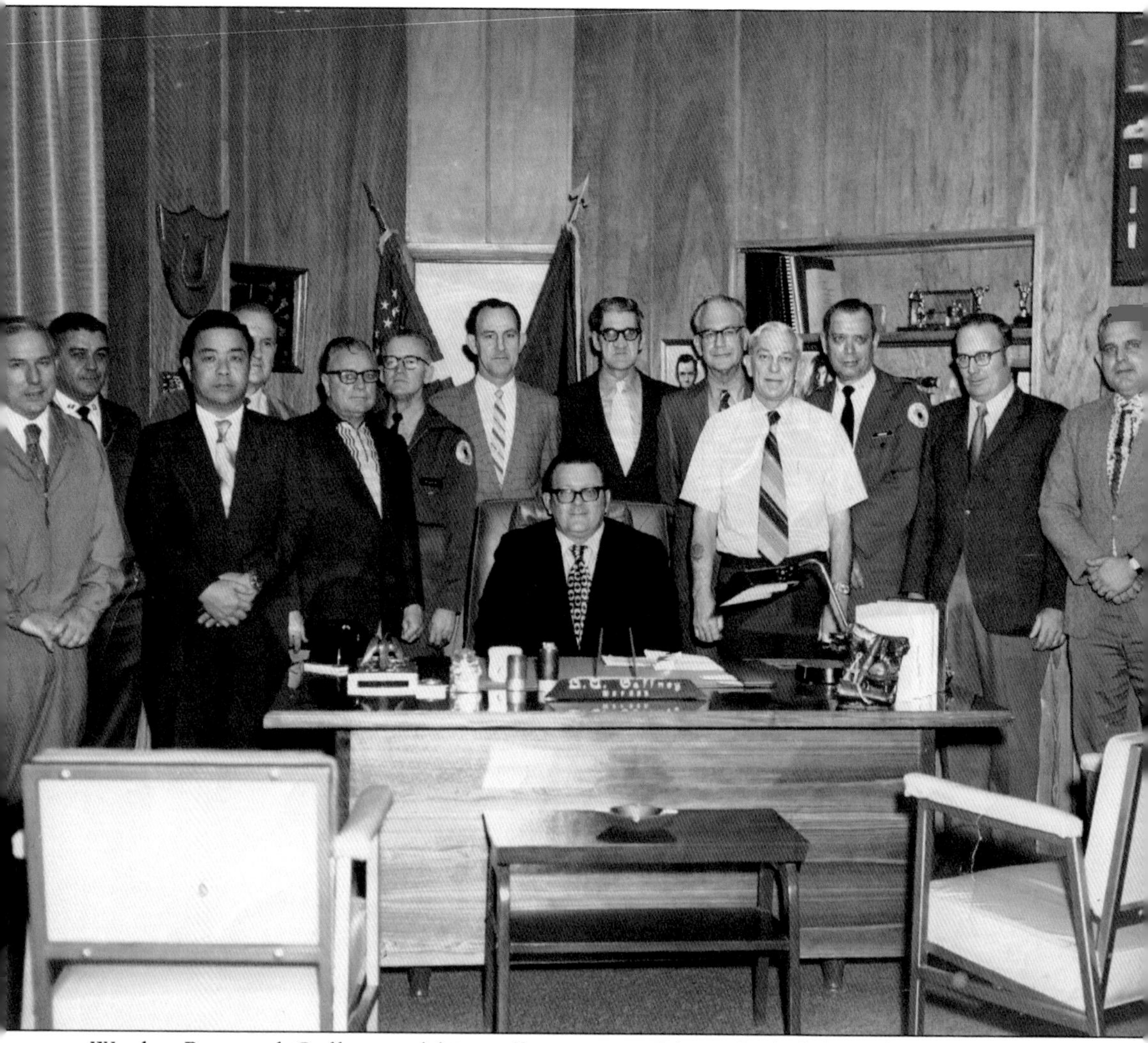

Warden Raymond Gaffney and his staff are pictured here. Included in this image are Bill Barker, R. J. Gaffney, Bob Bachtel, Captain Wetzel, George Clark, Roy Earls, Chester Wheatley, R. V. Oliver, Alspaugh, Major Johnson, Robert Adkins. (Courtesy of the Lansing Historical Museum.)

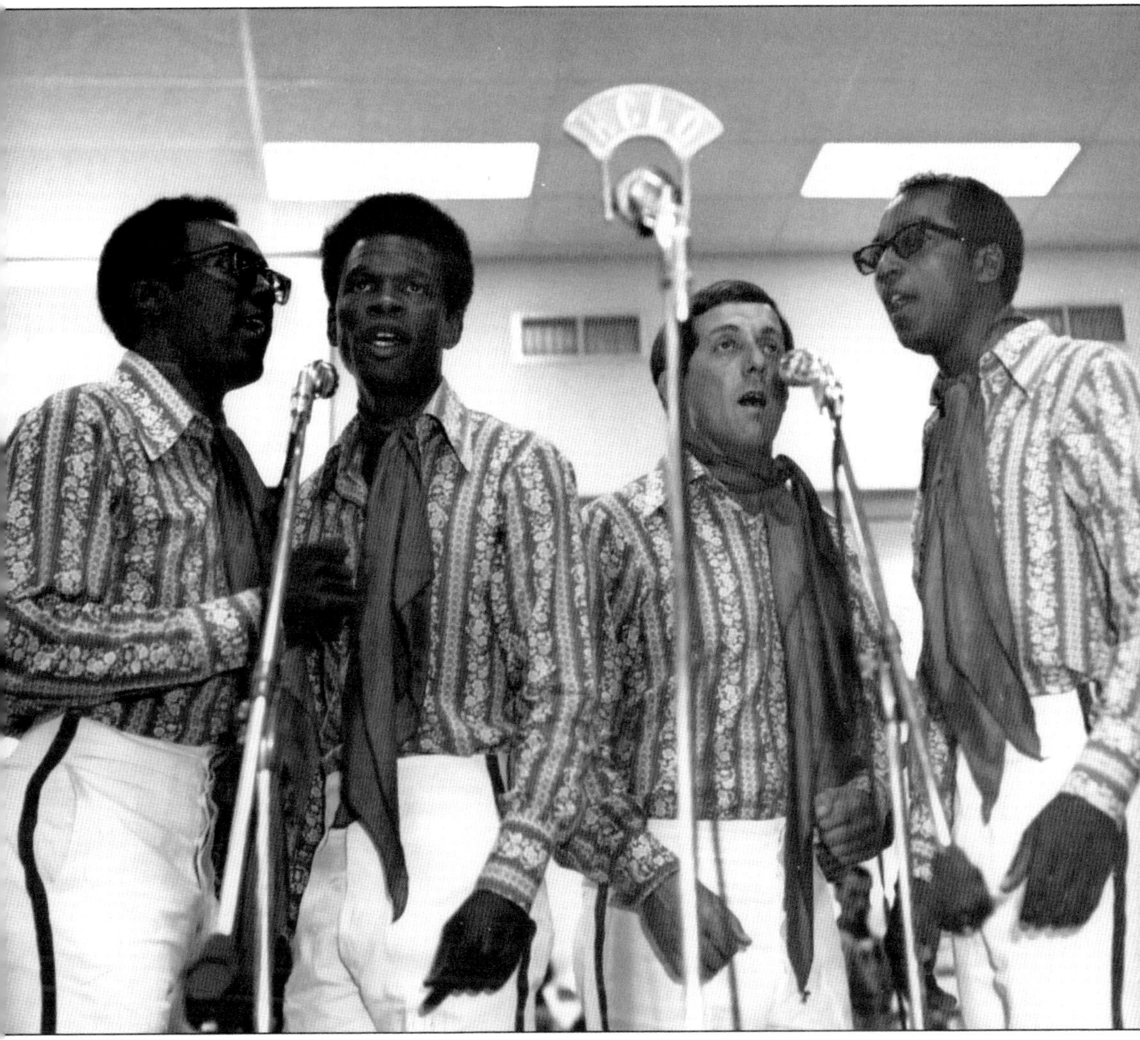

The Kansas State Penitentiary inmates formed the Beacon of Hope Chapel Singers to raise money for a prison chapel. The group gave choir concerts across the state of Kansas during warden Gaffney's tenure in the early 1970s. The group even recorded an album at the Cavern Sound Corporation in Independence, Missouri. The record, titled *Over the Walls*, features hymns, such as "He's My Light" and the more contemporary "Let the Sunshine In." (Courtesy of the Lansing Historical Museum.)

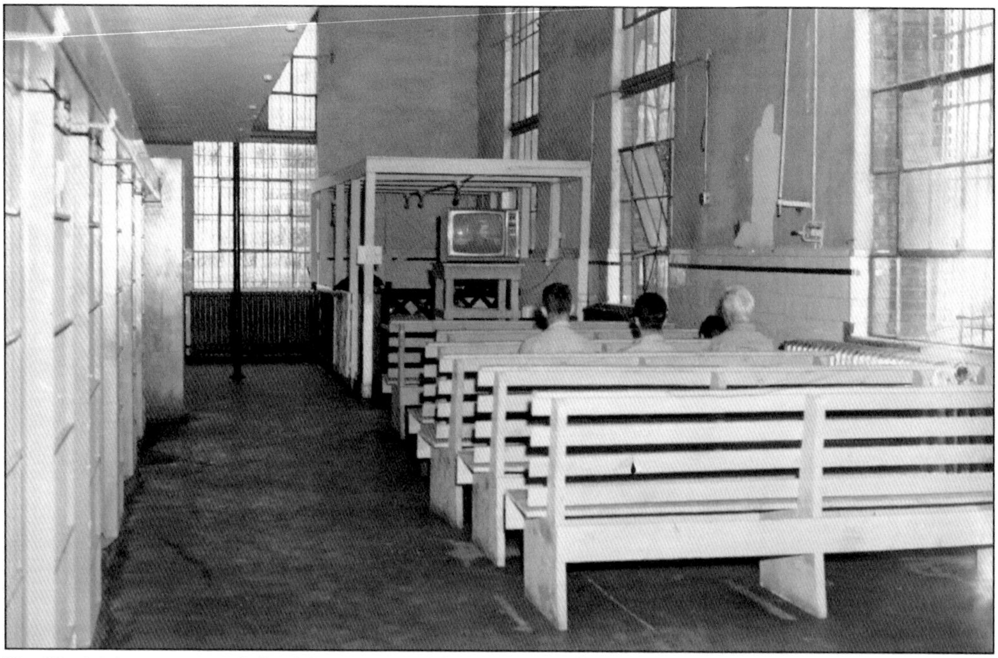

Dr. Karl Menninger of the Menninger Clinic in Topeka was a national leader in the field of psychiatry. In 1971, he visited the Kansas State Penitentiary as an advisor to Gov. Robert Docking on state prisons. One of the positive changes he noted in the prison was the introduction of television in the cell blocks. (Courtesy of the Lansing Historical Museum.)

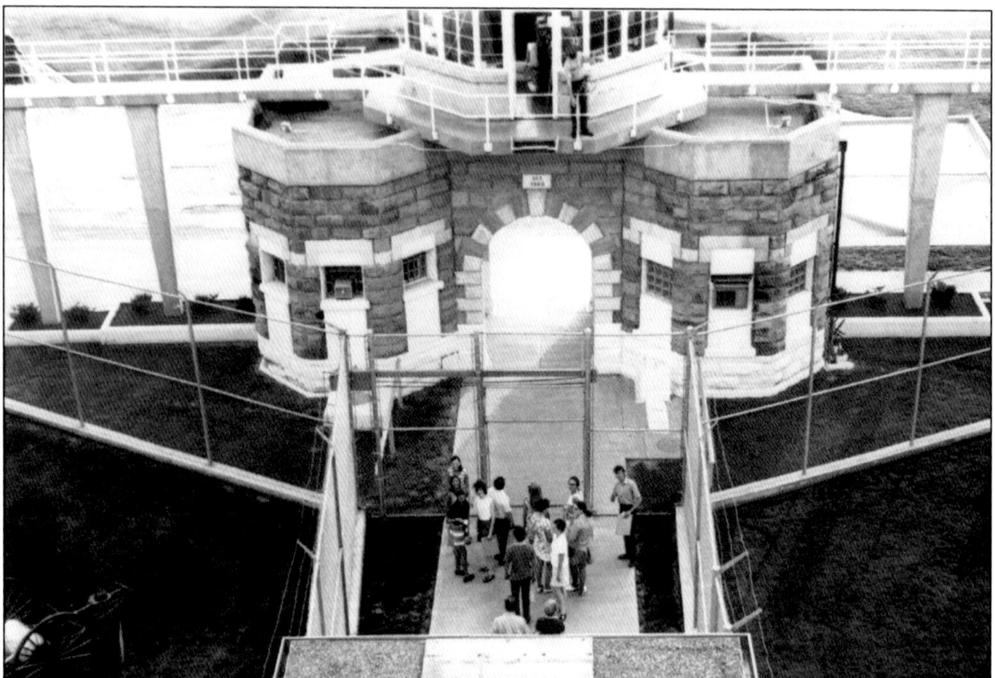

A group of visitors wait to enter the Kansas State Penitentiary through tower No. 1 in the 1960s. (Courtesy of the Lansing Historical Museum.)

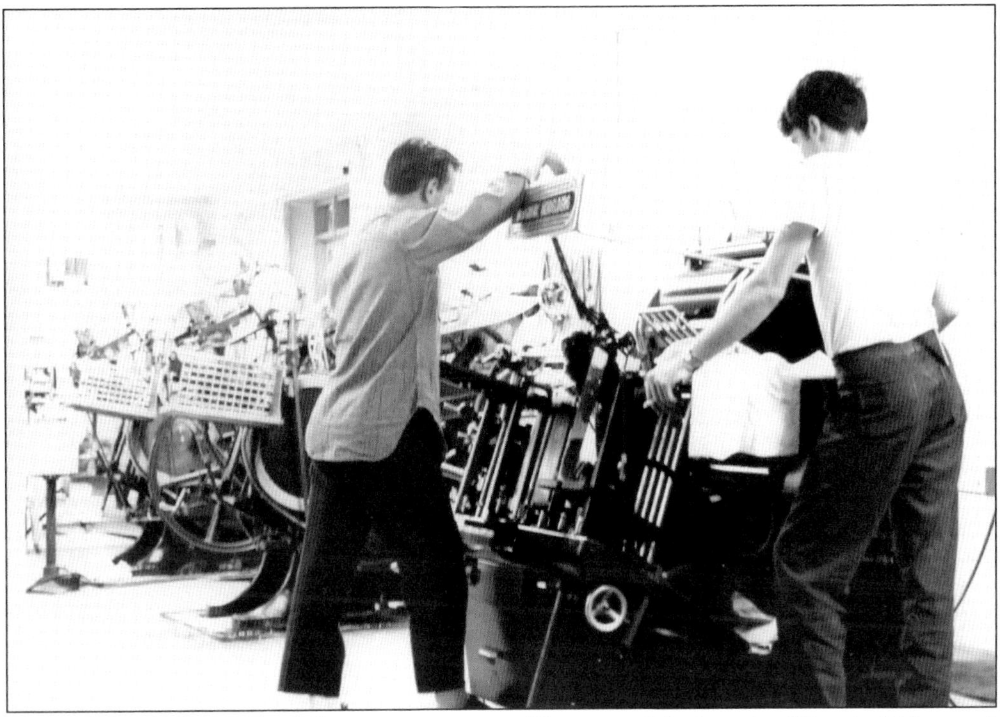

Two inmates work on a Heidelberg printing press. (Courtesy of the Lansing Historical Museum.)

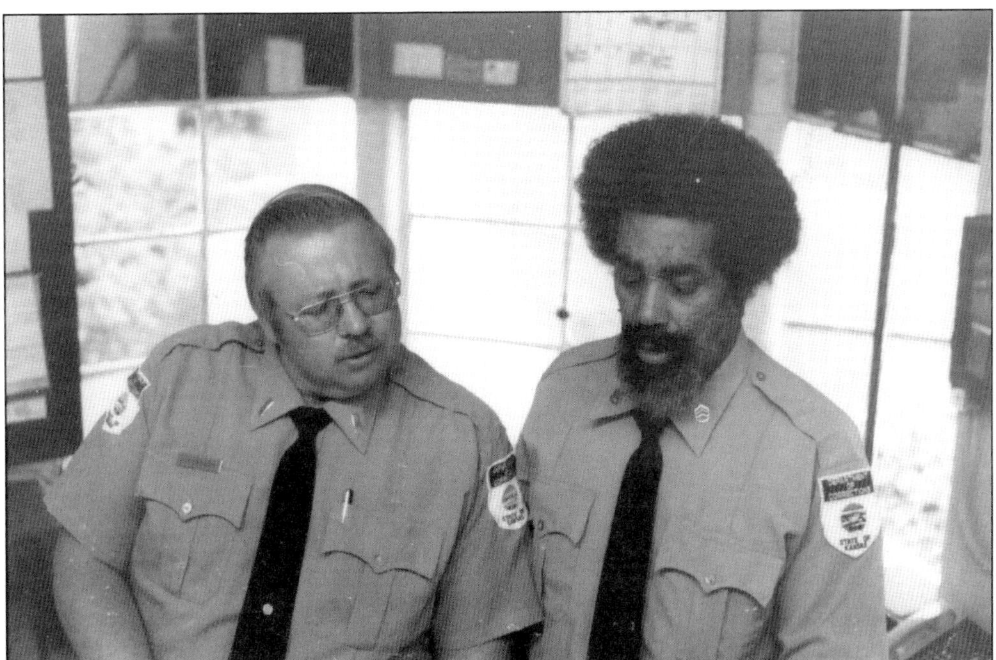

Lt. William Randolph (left) and corrections specialist I Tom Lewis are pictured here. (Courtesy of the Lansing Historical Museum.)

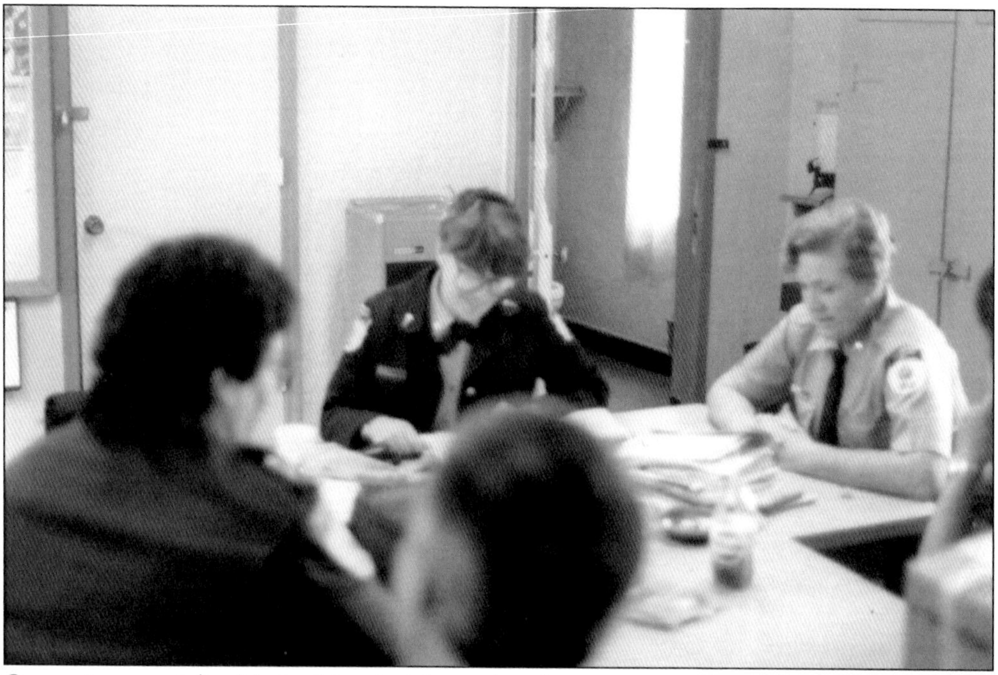

Corrections specialist I Luisa Mangieri (center) and corrections officer I Peggy Teeters (right) are pictured above. (Courtesy of the Lansing Historical Museum.)

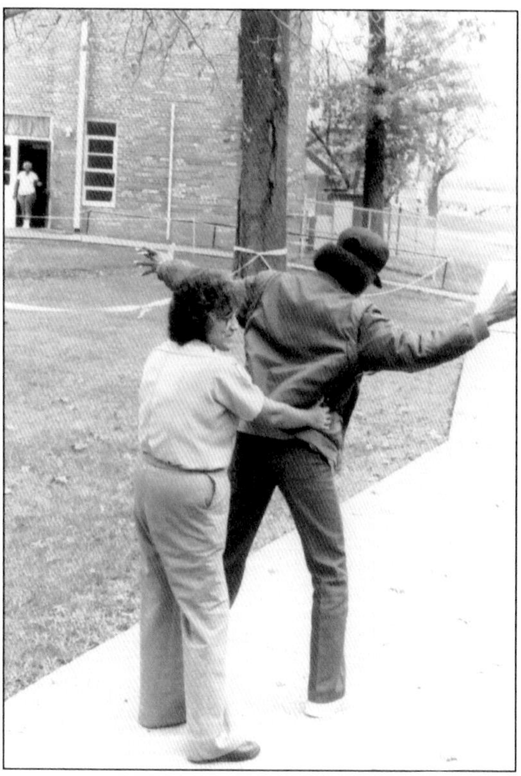

Beatrice (Bea) Wardlow is checking an inmate for contraband. (Courtesy of the Lansing Historical Museum.)

Three

RAILROADS

In the 1800s, railroads provided an efficient way to transport agricultural commodities from rural areas to the cities. In turn, locomotives transported manufactured goods from the cities to the rural areas. Without the services of railroads, the transportation of commodities slowed down and the cost of the commodities increased. Many small towns vied for a railroad depot to ensure their survival.

Lansing had a Union Pacific Railroad depot located north of East Mary Street and an Atchison, Topeka and Santa Fe Railway depot. Originally a Leavenworth, Northern and Southern Railroad depot, the Atchison, Topeka and Santa Fe Railway company purchased the depot located near present-day 211 North Main Street. In addition to transporting freight and passengers, the depot offered Western Union telegraph service. The depot served the Lansing community until the 1960s, when it ceased operations. Afterward, the Leavenworth County Cooperative stored fertilizer in the 1887 building for years. In 1989, the building faced demolition. Citizens concerned about losing one of the last original buildings connected to downtown Lansing came together and formed the Lansing Historical Society.

The Lansing Historical Society made saving the depot from destruction its mission. After many fund-raisers and with a donation from the City of Lansing, workers hoisted the building onto a truck and transported the historic depot south on Main Street to Kansas Avenue. The Lansing Correctional Facility agreed to give the depot a home on prison grounds next to Leavenworth County Fire District No. 1. The building has resided there since 1992, and volunteers restored the building to become the Lansing Historical Museum. The depot is a classic example of a standardized rural–small town combination station.

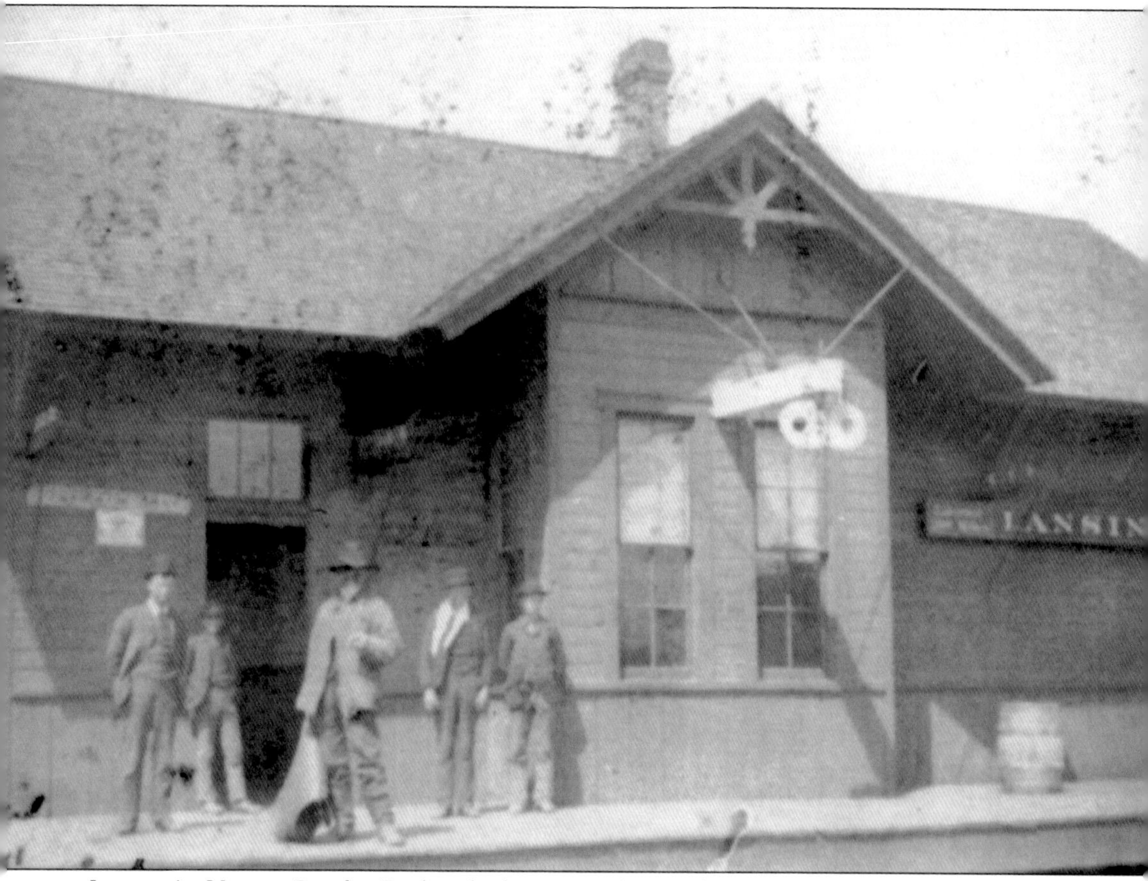

Lansing's Union Pacific Railroad depot is shown here. (Courtesy of the Lansing Historical Museum.)

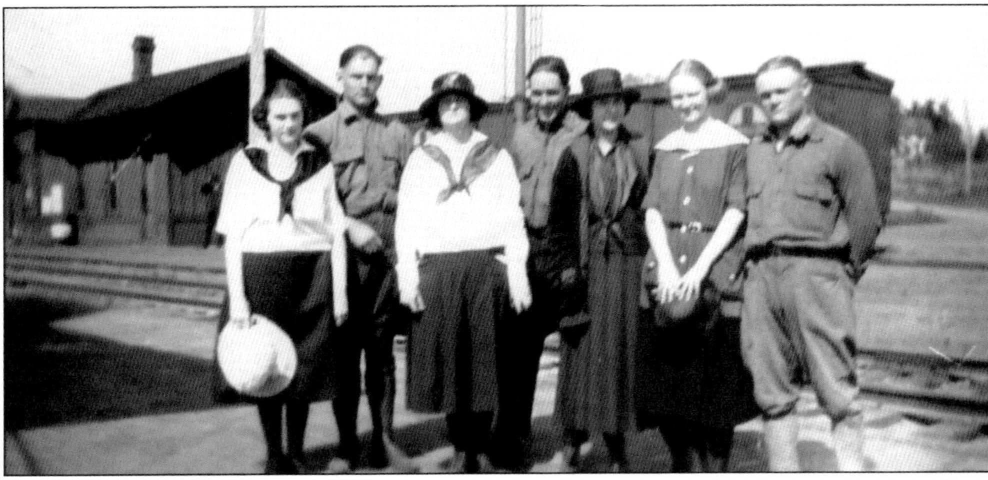

This 1920s photograph shows Lansing's Santa Fe Railroad depot in the background. William Cherrie chose the original site and design of the building. He served as the first station agent for the 1887 depot for 44 years. (Courtesy of the Lansing Historical Museum.)

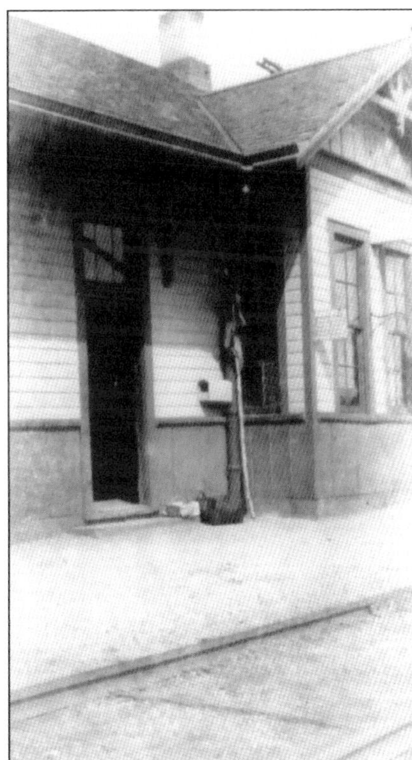

Here is another view of Lansing's Union Pacific Railroad depot. The depot was located north of East Mary Street and no longer exists. (Courtesy of the Lansing Historical Museum.)

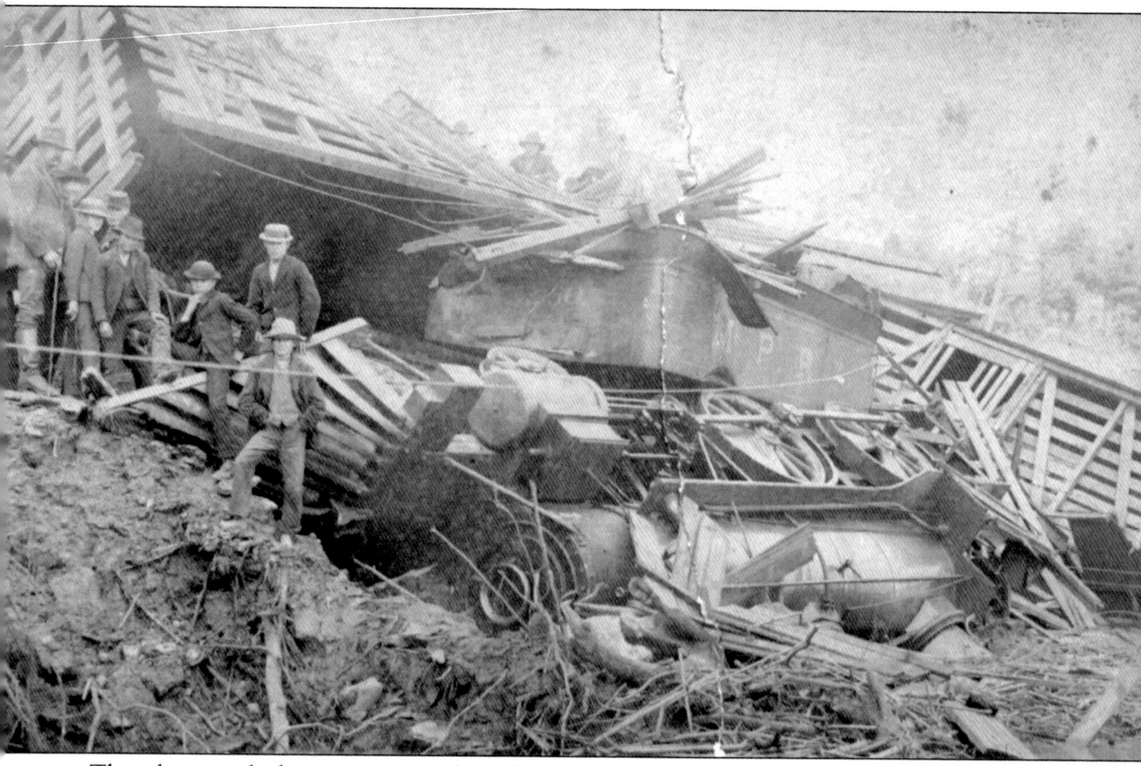

This photograph shows a train crash and wreckage south of Lansing. (Courtesy of the Lansing Historical Museum.)

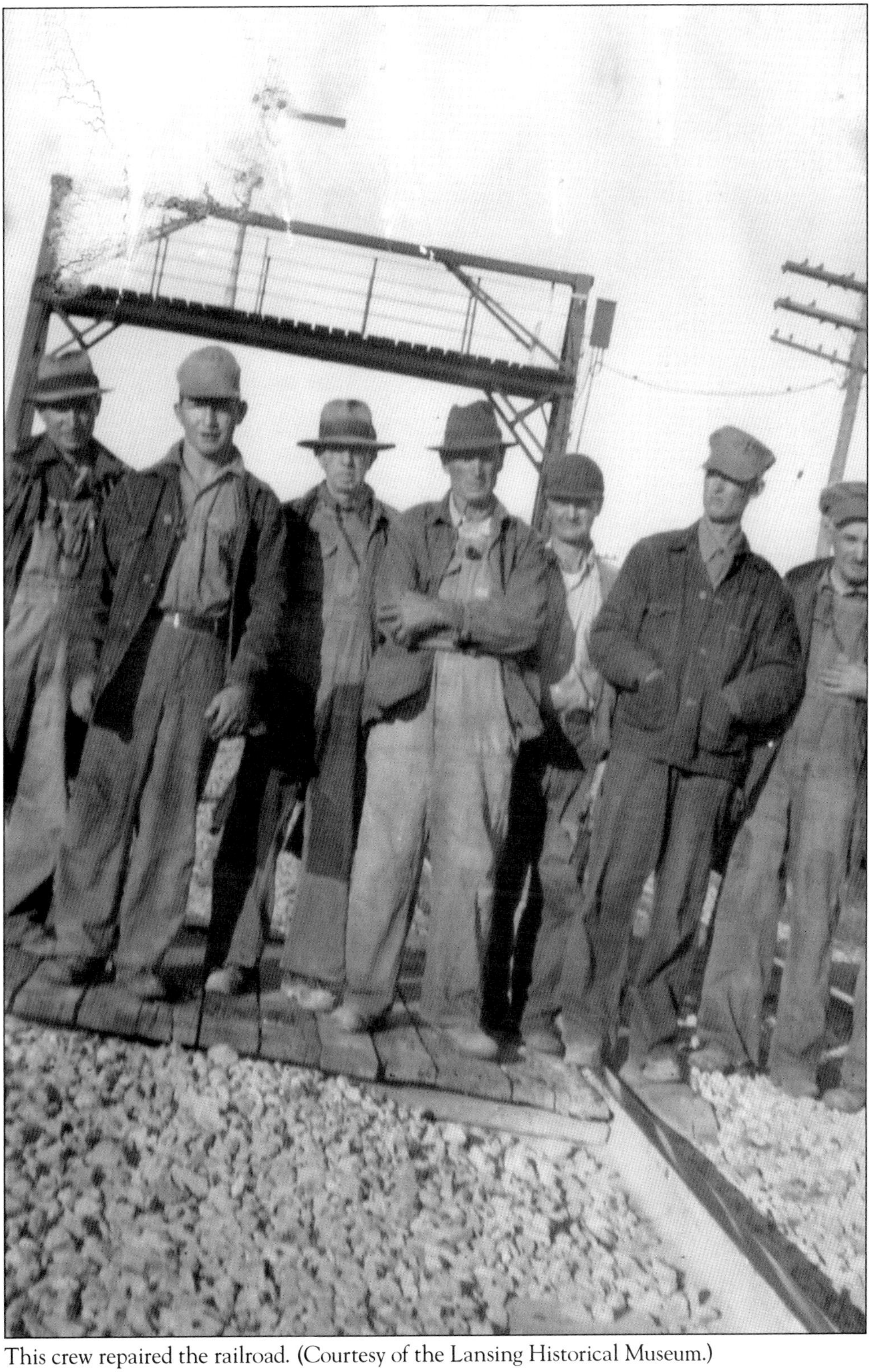

This crew repaired the railroad. (Courtesy of the Lansing Historical Museum.)

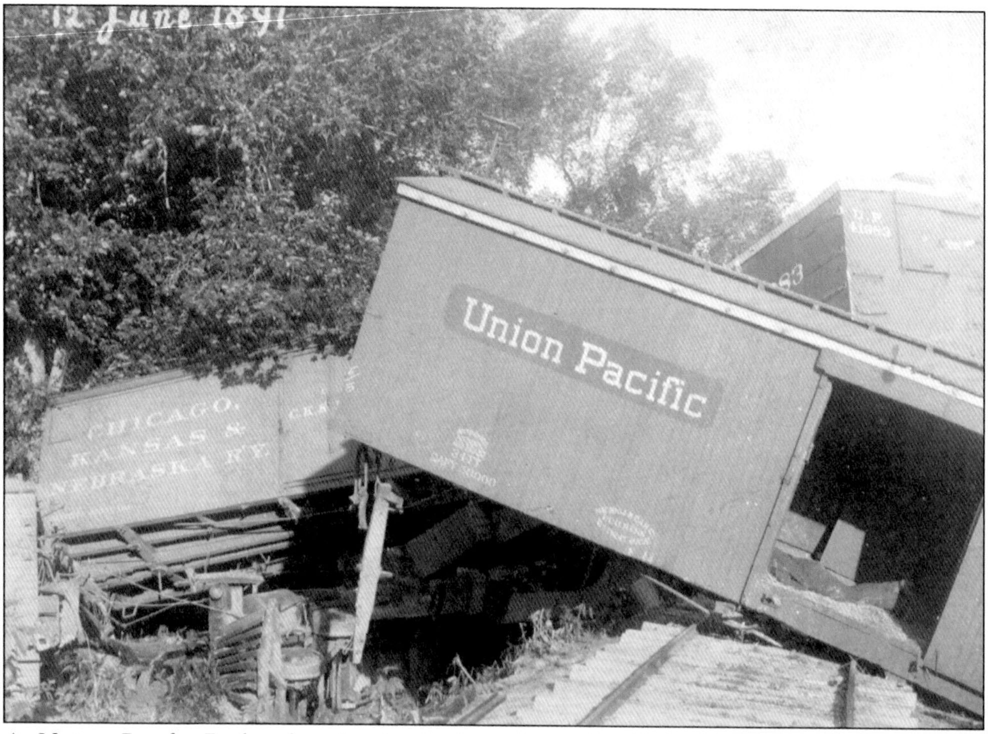

A Union Pacific Railroad train derailed on June 12, 1891. (Courtesy of the Lansing Historical Museum.)

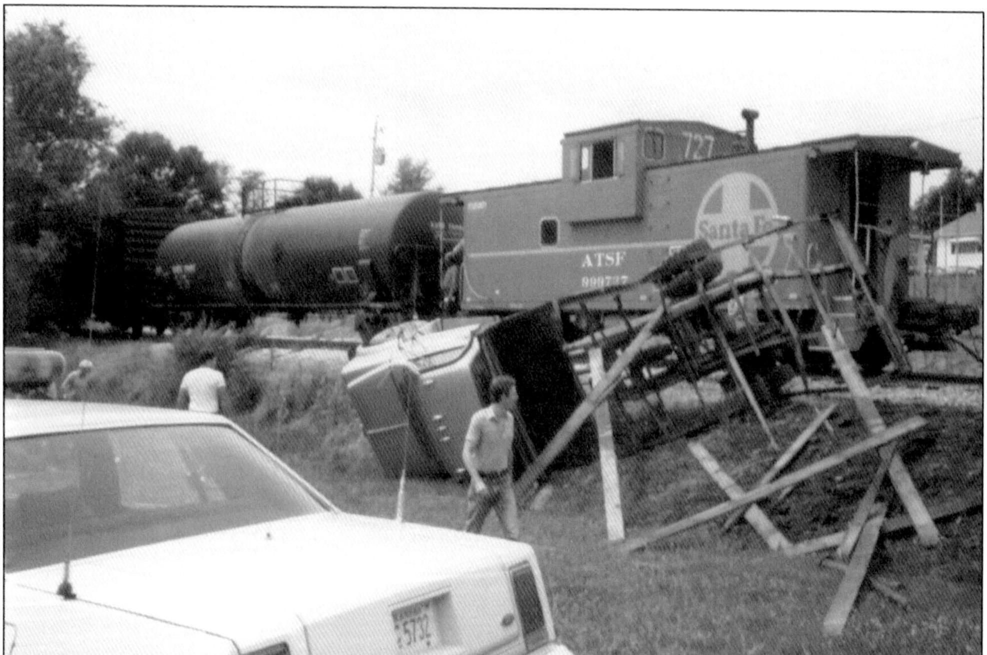

This train wreck occurred in 1983 in Lansing. The railroad tracks in the area of Kansas Avenue and Helen Street were discontinued and removed in the early 1980s. (Courtesy of the Lansing Historical Museum.)

Four

Rural Life

In 1912, Leavenworth County organized one of the first farm bureaus in the United States. The farmers and businessmen joined the bureau to work together for the betterment of agriculture. In the spring of 1912, several prominent farmers from the county went to the first farm bureau meeting in the state. John M. Gilman became the first president of the Leavenworth group, and in 1915, Gilman introduced the farm bureau bill in the Kansas House of Representatives. He also served as a scientific assistant in corn investigation for the United States Department of Agriculture for four years.

Agriculture played an important role in the local economy. The small town of Lansing had the Pulley Dairy Farm, the Zoll Dairy Farm, and the Gable Horse and Dairy Farm. In addition, S. E. Parisa owned a 32-acre orchard and 2 acres for small fruits. An active member of the farm bureau, his wife served as leader of Nine Mile 4-H club in which their children actively participated.

Agriculture has declined in Leavenworth County due to urbanization. However, cattle and hay are still raised on the Gable farm, and in 2005, the value of crops harvested in Leavenworth County totaled $16,107,100. The value of cattle and milk production in the county totaled $9,787,000. Farmers continue to raise wheat, soybeans, corn, hay, sorghum, sunflowers, cattle, hogs, sheep, and poultry.

Despite Lansing's increasing population, the city still has a rural, small-town feel. Members of 11 service organizations dedicate hundreds of hours to making the community a better place. The community supports local groups and the school district through benefit breakfasts and dinners. Dedicated Lansing Lions fans always turn out at sporting events to support the athletes.

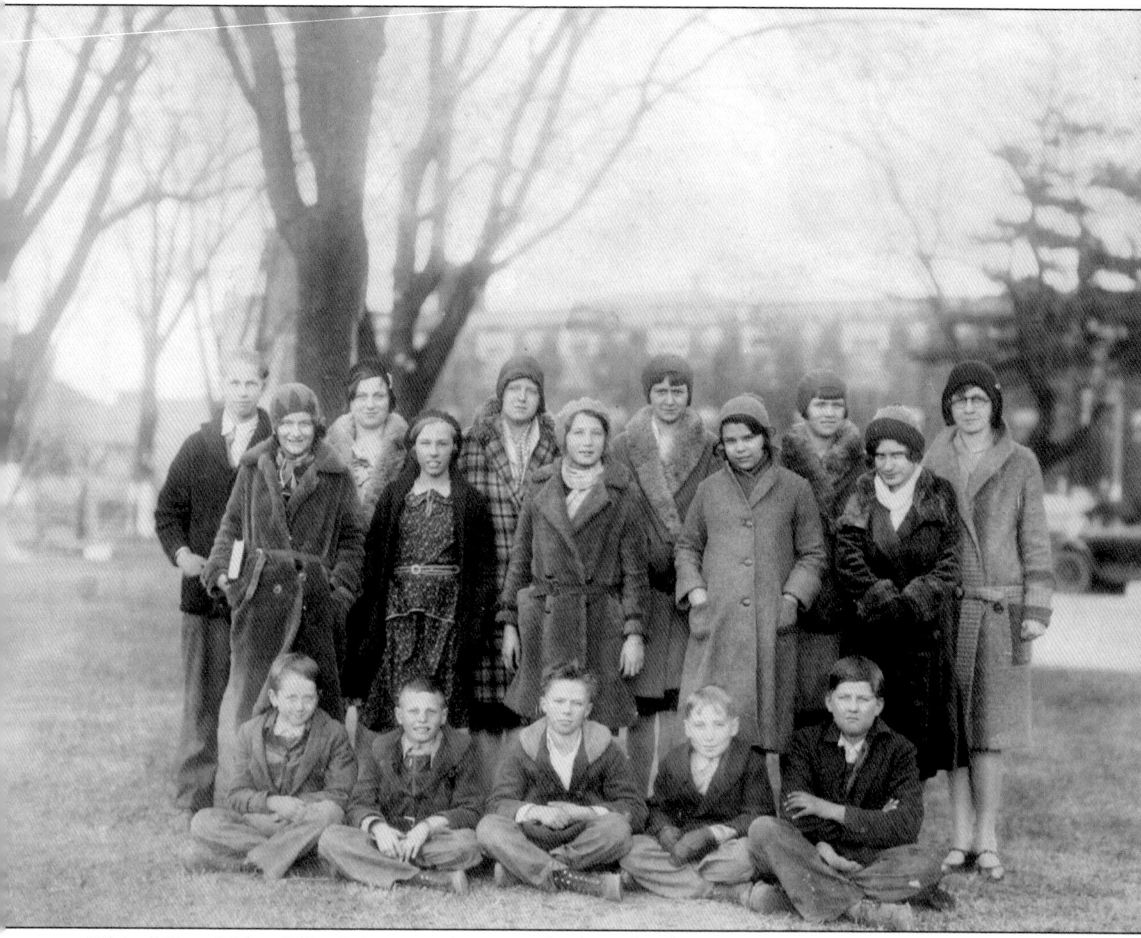

This Nine Mile 4-H club was photographed with the Kansas State Penitentiary in the background. From left to right are (first row) Bob Wilcox, Bob Younghans, Ben Lohman, Victor Parisa, and Ben Wilcox; (second row) unidentified, Maxine Lohman, Rosemary Parisa, unidentified, and Marie Gaiger; (third row) Bob Davis, four unidentified women, and Hulda Parisa. (Courtesy of the Lansing Historical Museum.)

F. Eugene Lallier displays homegrown onions, tomatoes, cantaloupe, and a watermelon in the late 1800s. (Courtesy of the Lansing Historical Museum.)

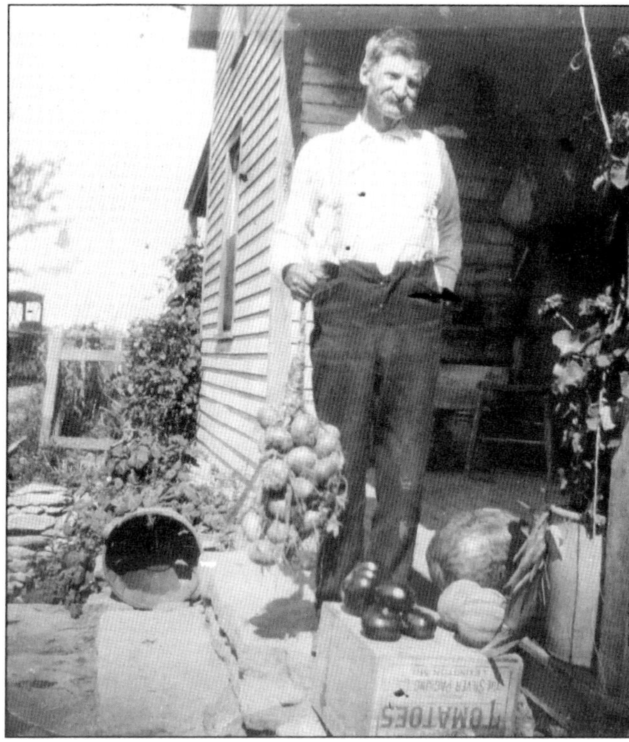

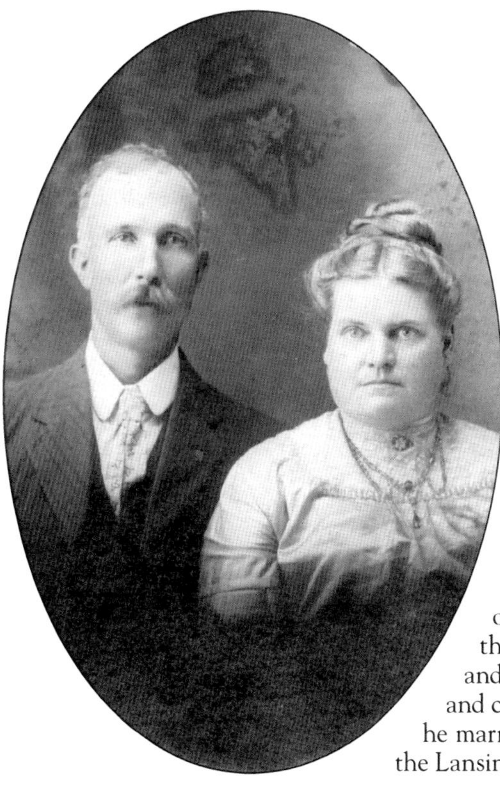

Thomas and Flora Chestnut are pictured here. Thomas's grandfather worked as a trail master on the Santa Fe Trail. Thomas ran a dairy route three days a week through Lansing in the 1920s and 1930s. He sold butter, eggs, milk, chickens, and cottage cheese. After his first wife died in a fire, he married widow Flora Wilcox Watson. (Courtesy of the Lansing Historical Museum.)

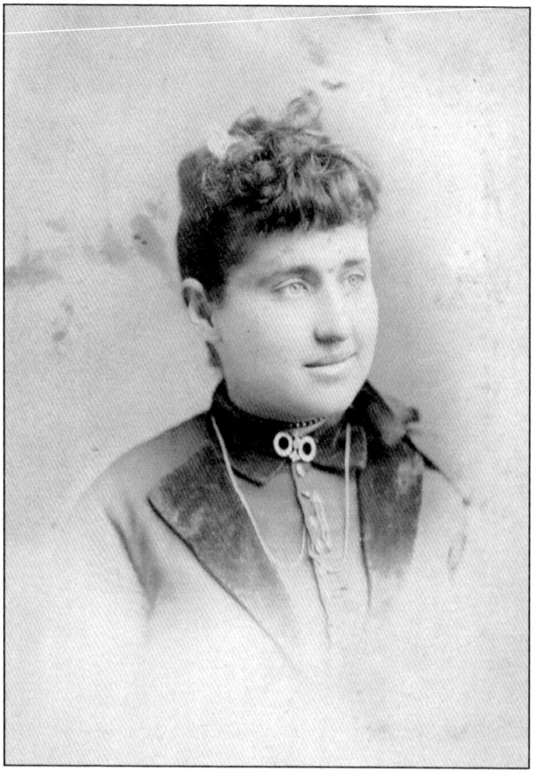

Hattie Jennings Chestnut married Thomas Jefferson Chestnut around 1900. The couple had three children—Mary Ann, Ethel Mae, and Dorothy Pearl. Hattie and Mary Ann died in a house fire in July 1911. The home was across the street from Delaware School. Hattie's cousin William Jennings Bryant ran for president against Abraham Lincoln. (Courtesy of the Lansing Historical Museum.)

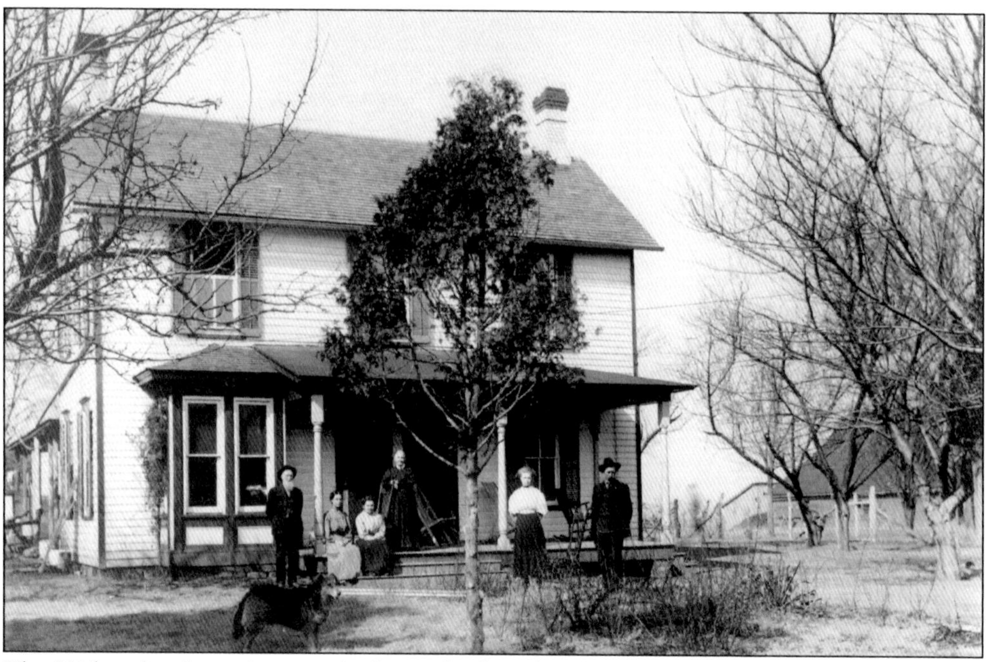

The Dickey family is photographed outside their farmhouse. Jennie Dickey (third from left) taught at Nine Mile School. In 1916, a group of area women founded the Lansing Community Club to hone their homemaking skills. Dickey served as the club's first president and also led the Ever Ready Baking Club. (Courtesy of the Lansing Historical Museum.)

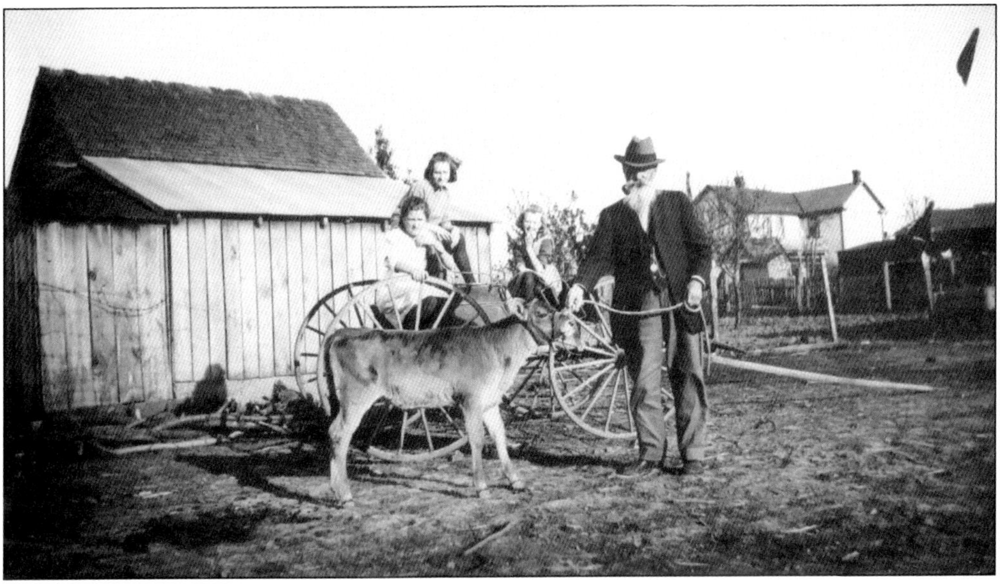

William Hiatt and his family pose for a photograph with their calf. (Courtesy of the Lansing Historical Museum.)

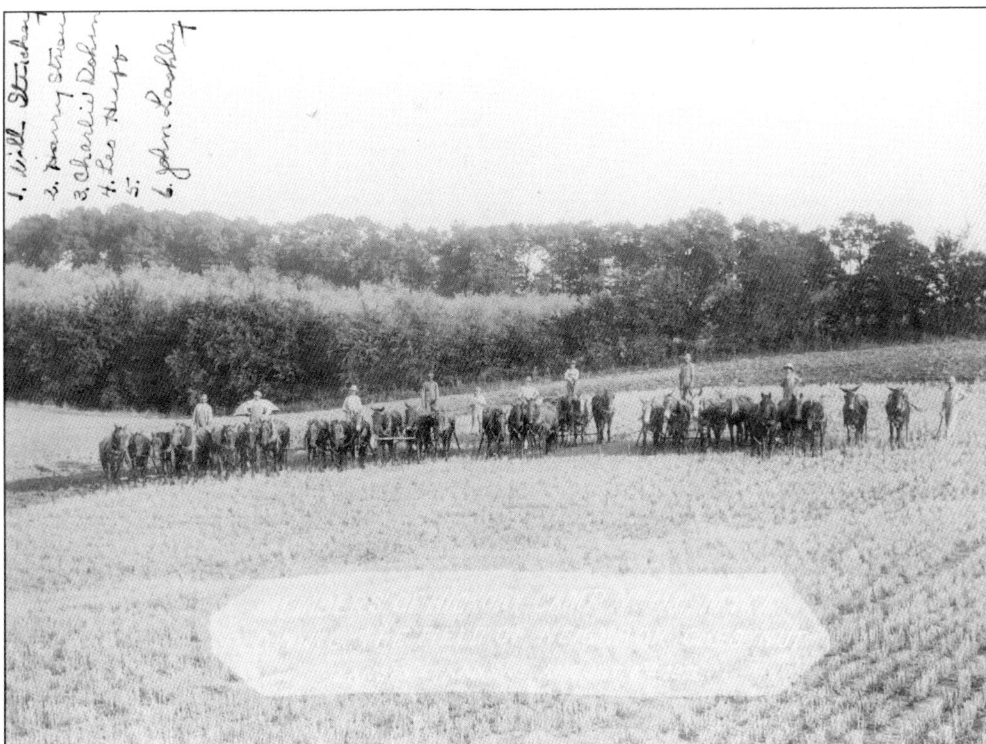

Members of the Hickory Camp No. 1181 MWA plow the field of neighbor Chestnut in Lansing on August 8, 1911. Identified are Will Stuckey, Harry Strouse, Charlie Dohrn, Leo Huff, and John Lashley. John Cassella of Leavenworth took this photograph. (Courtesy of the Lansing Historical Museum.)

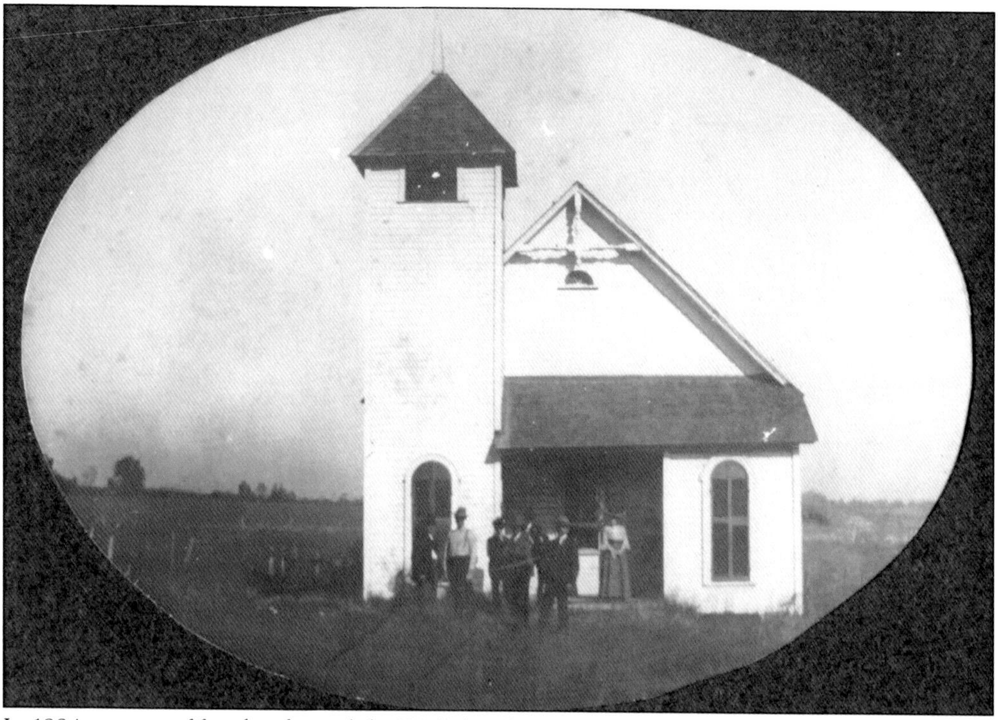

In 1884, a group of families formed the Wallula Christian Church. The church got its name from Wallula School in Wyandotte County, where the congregation met until it raised the funds to build a church on land deeded by Mr. and Mrs. William Ralston. The congregation dedicated the church on June 8, 1890. A second church was built in 1950 on land Nine Mile School teacher Jennie Dickey donated. (Courtesy of the Lansing Historical Museum.)

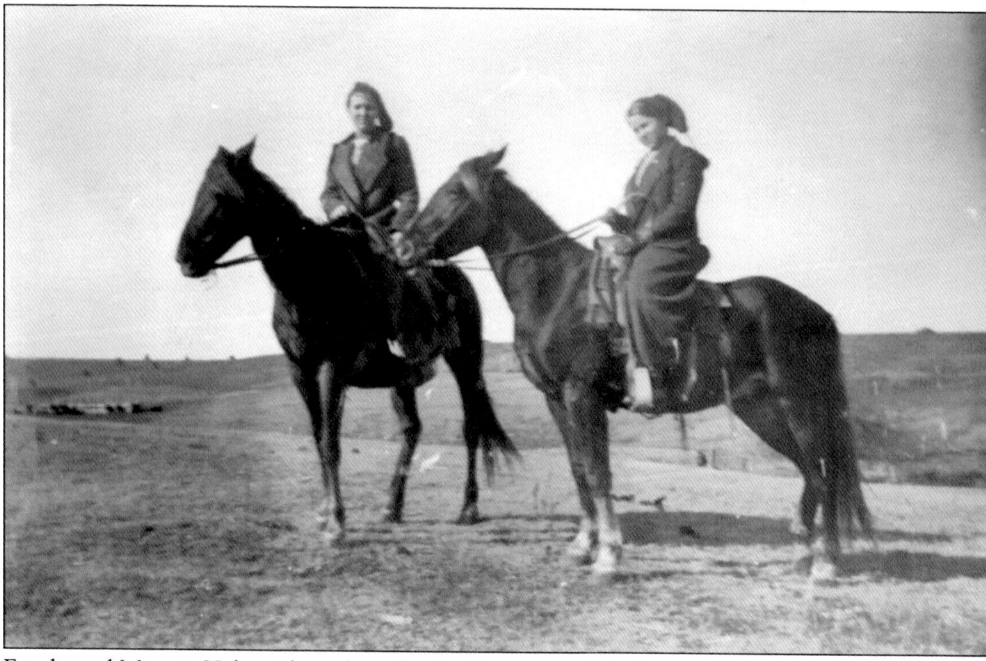

Frieda and Minnie Helm ride on horseback. (Courtesy of the Lansing Historical Museum.)

Glen, Walter, and Carl Linaweaver are pictured with Dorothy Pearl Chestnut. (Courtesy of the Lansing Historical Museum.)

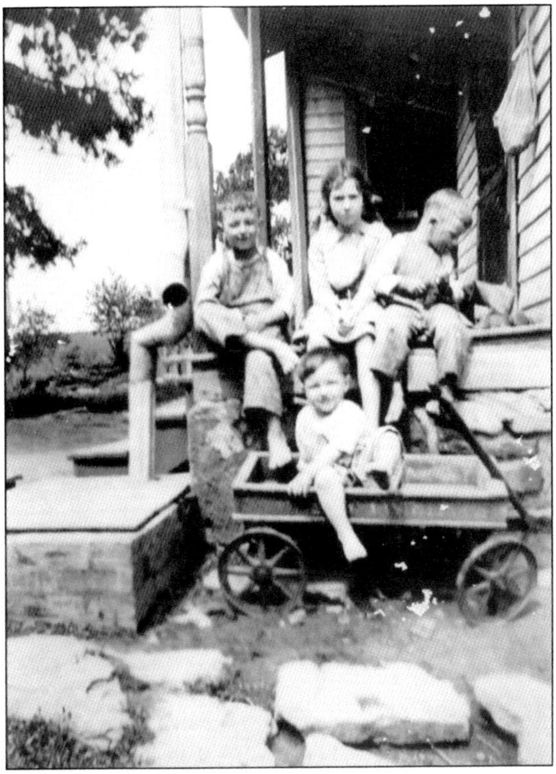

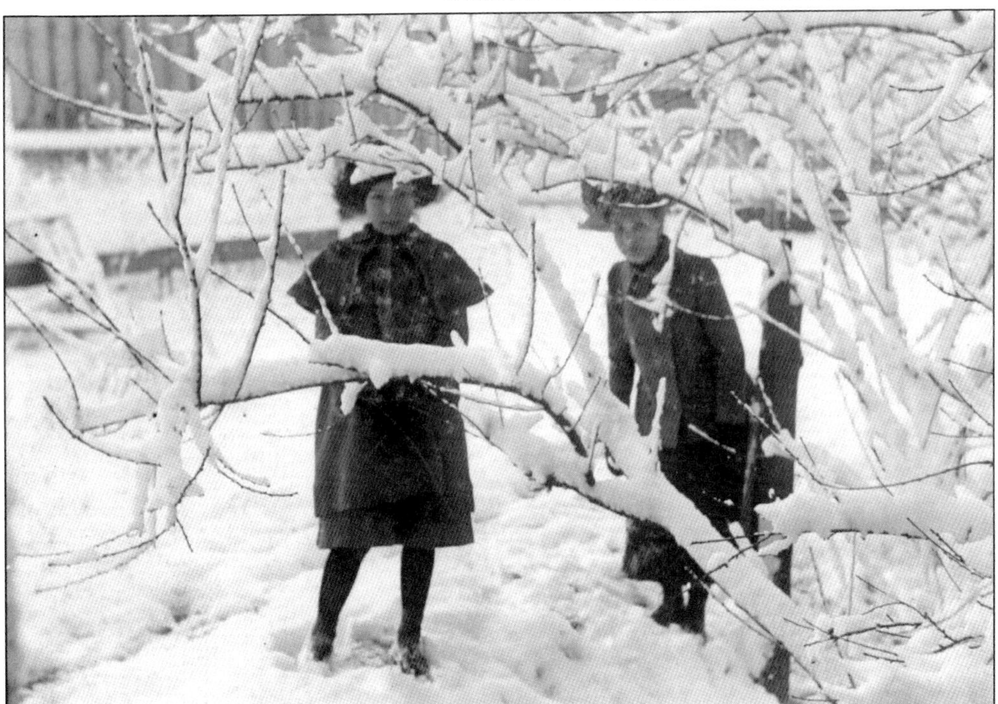

Mary Belle Hansford and a friend enjoy a new snowfall. (Courtesy of the Lansing Historical Museum.)

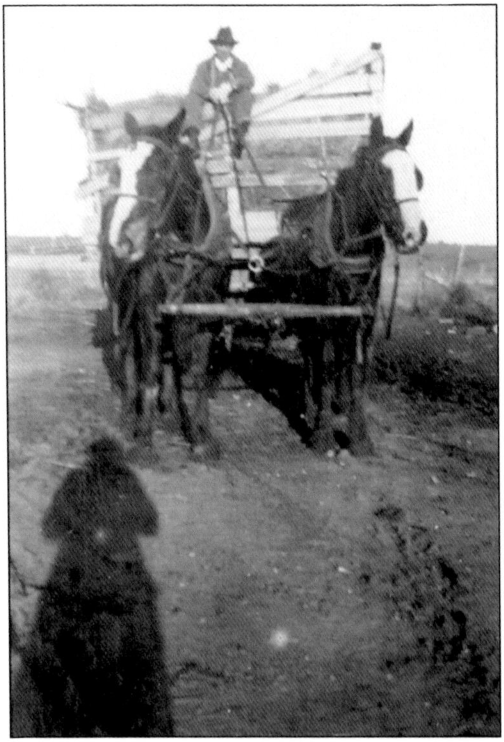

James A. Hiatt drives a team of horses with loose hay in the wagon. (Courtesy of the Lansing Historical Museum.)

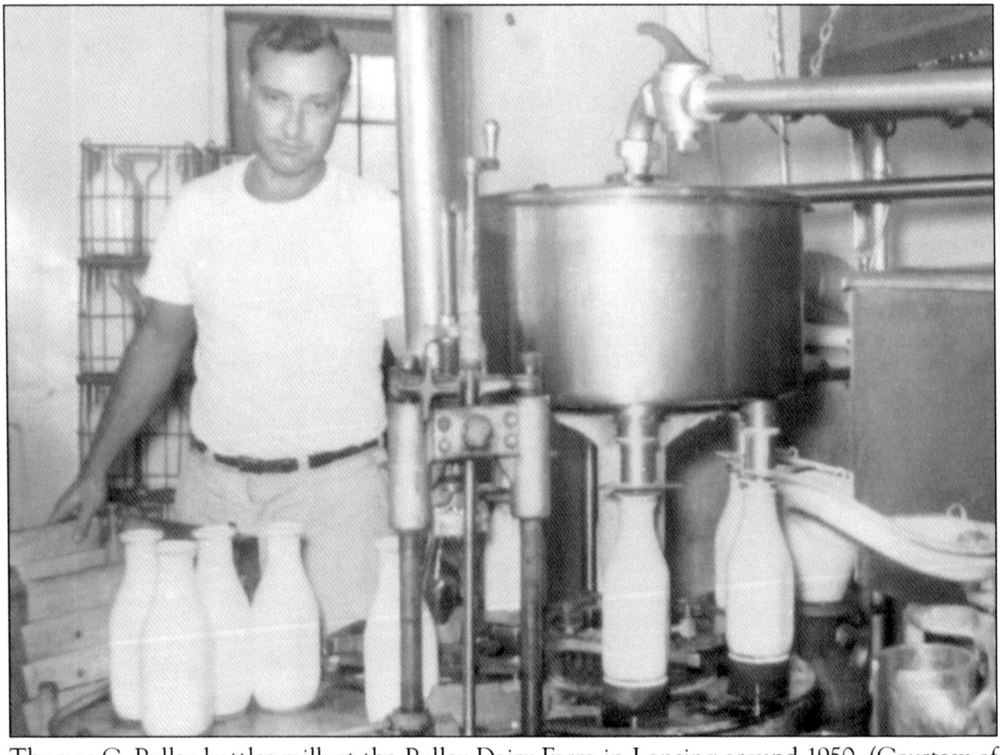

Thomas C. Pulley bottles milk at the Pulley Dairy Farm in Lansing around 1950. (Courtesy of the Lansing Historical Museum.)

Don Wilson, armed with a double-barrel shotgun, and his dog Spike return from a successful duck hunt. (Courtesy of the Lansing Historical Museum.)

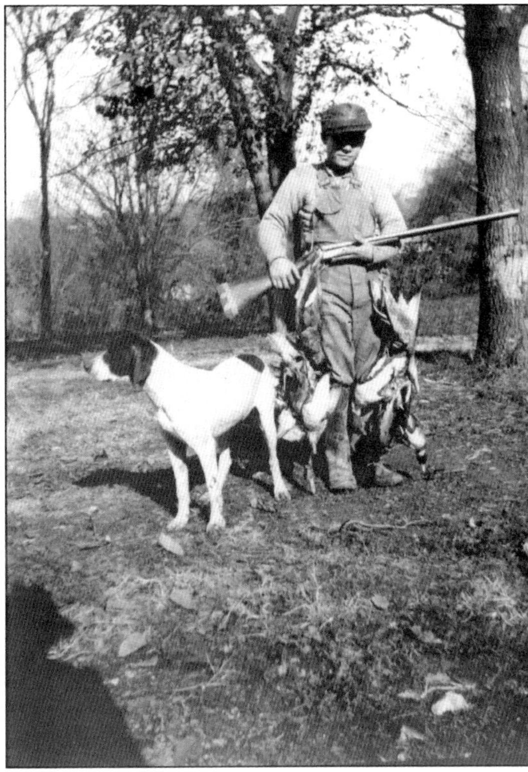

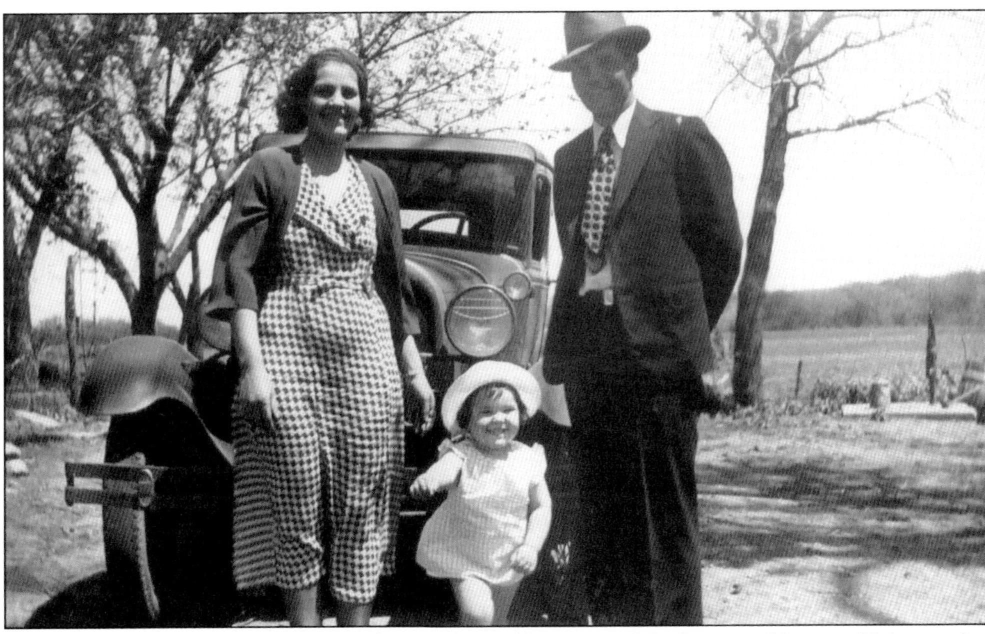

Edith, Barby, and Charles Berry are shown above. (Courtesy of the Lansing Historical Museum.)

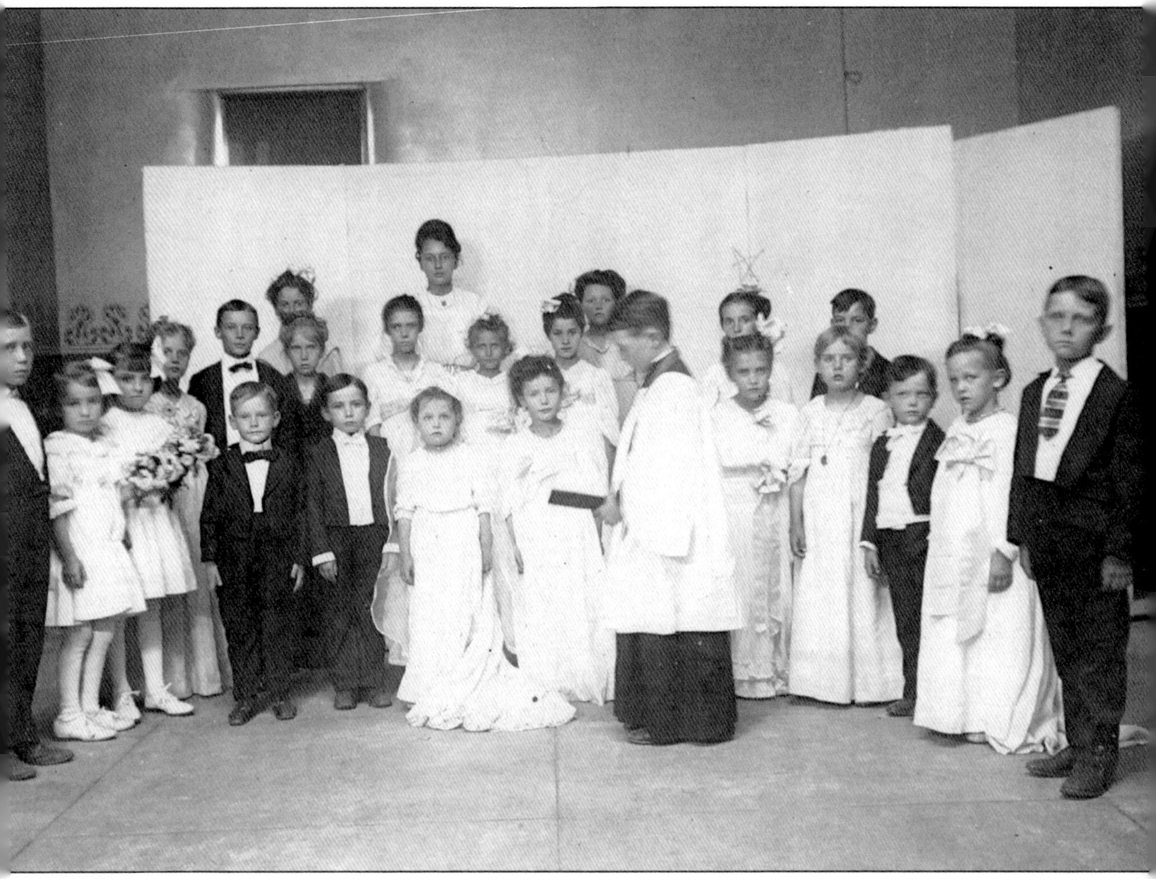

This picture is from a Tom Thumb wedding at the Christian church in the Kansas State Penitentiary prior to 1907. Identified are John Hardman, Esther Meriam, Ted Bird, Maud Campbell, Elsie Scott, Dorcas Hannon, Nellie Blossom, Edith Humphrey, F. Beemer, Gladys Paisl, Luther Shirley, Jimmie Yates, Carl Fulton, Ralph McBrian, Gladys Estep, Roland Estep, Laura Meriam, Homer Walkerausher, and Ethel Humphrey. (Courtesy of the Lansing Historical Museum.)

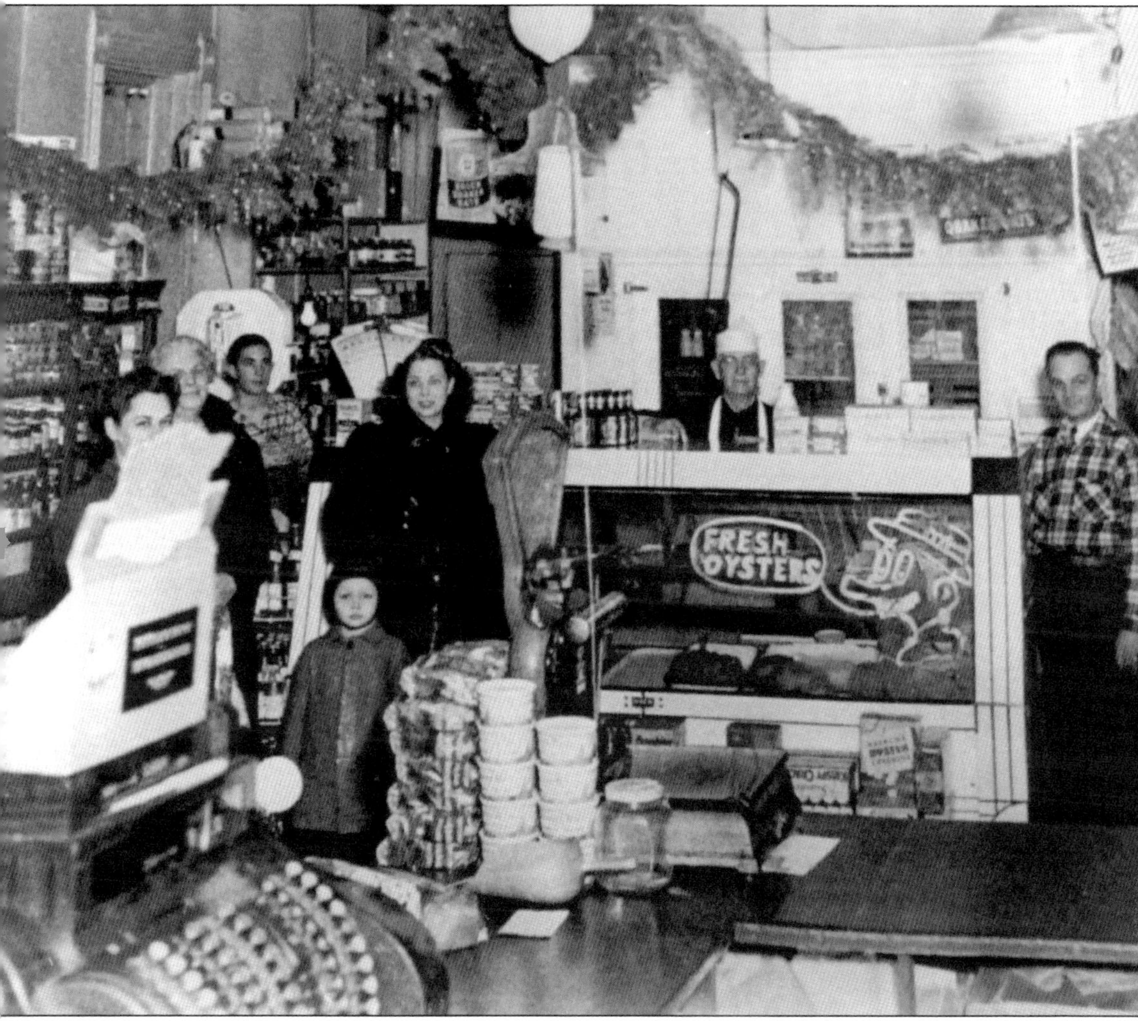

Inside Campbell's Grocery Store are D. W. Woodson, Jack Stewart Jr., Mary R. Stewart, Sam Maxwell, and S. H. Manford. Mable Campbell can also be seen. (Courtesy of the Lansing Historical Museum.)

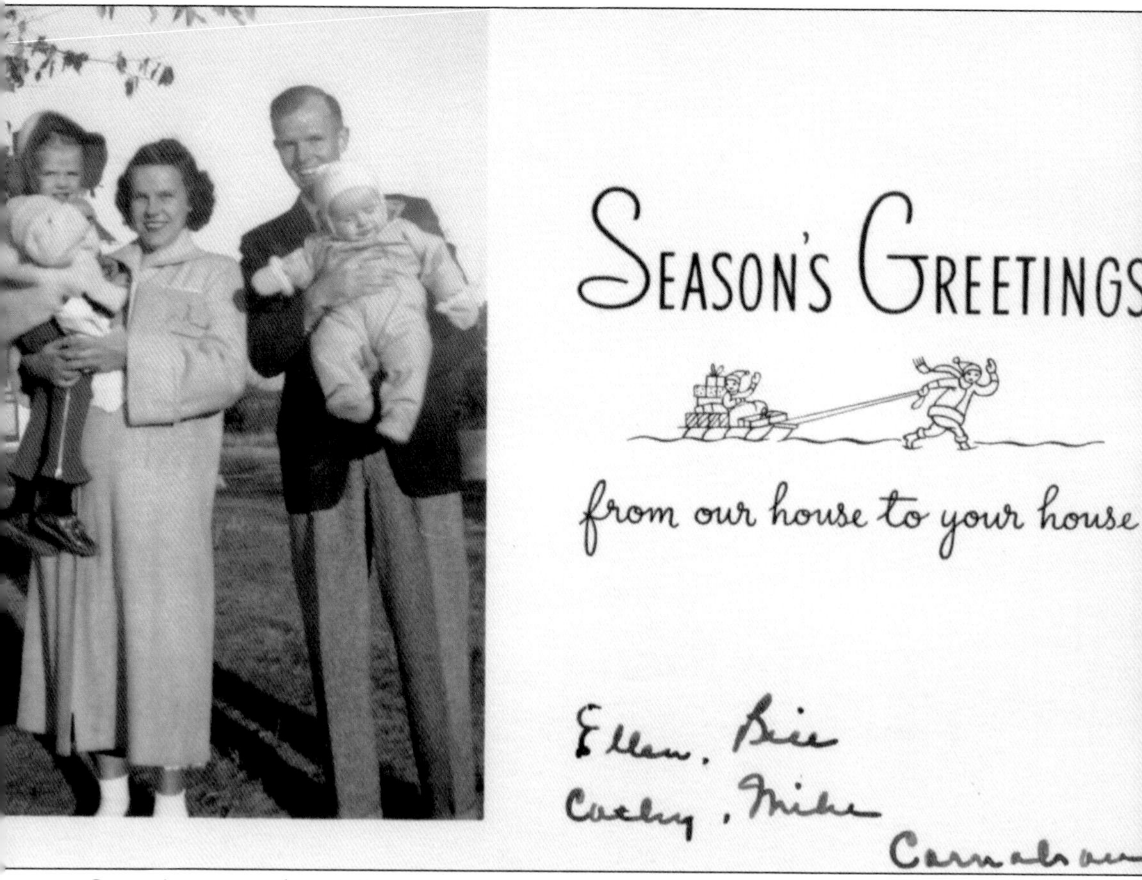

Season's greetings from Bill and Ellen Carnahan and their children Cathy and Mike Carnahan. (Courtesy of the Lansing Historical Museum.)

Five

School Days

The residents of the area now known as Lansing have always promoted the importance of education. The Lansing area had several school districts until unification in 1965. Nine Mile School No. 17 appears to be the oldest with a deed dating back to 1860 on file at the Lansing Historical Museum. Delaware School No. 16 dates back to 1869 and closed in 1985. Other school districts in the Lansing area prior to unification included Richardson School No. 55, Hazel Dell School No. 79, Lansing Rural Grade School No. 75, Lansing Rural High School No. 2, High Prairie School No. 8, Fairmont School No. 35, Mayginnis School No. 38, and Jarbalo Rural High School No. 1.

Founded in 1902, Lansing Rural High School had a student population of two—a boy and a girl. John M. Gilman served as the school's first principal, with James B. Kelsey succeeding him. The student population increased to 70 students by the 1915–1916 academic year. In 1923, the high school moved to a new building on Second Street in Lansing. For the next 40 years, high school students studied in the classrooms, played sports, and staged performances in the gymnasium. The class of 1966 was composed of 55 students and was the last group of seniors to graduate from Lansing Rural High School.

The building on Second Street became an intermediate school until it closed in 1997. The school district leased the building to the City of Lansing to house the parks and recreation department, the public works department, and the Lansing Community Library.

Lansing High School moved to 300 East Olive Street in the early 1960s and had a capacity for 288 students. In 1988, the high school students were moved to a new building at 220 Lion Lane that has a capacity for 750 students. The building on Olive Street became the Lansing Middle School in 1988 and changed to Lansing Intermediate School in 1997. In 2008, the new Lansing Elementary School opened on West Mary Street, combining the elementary and intermediate schools into one building for kindergarten through fifth grade.

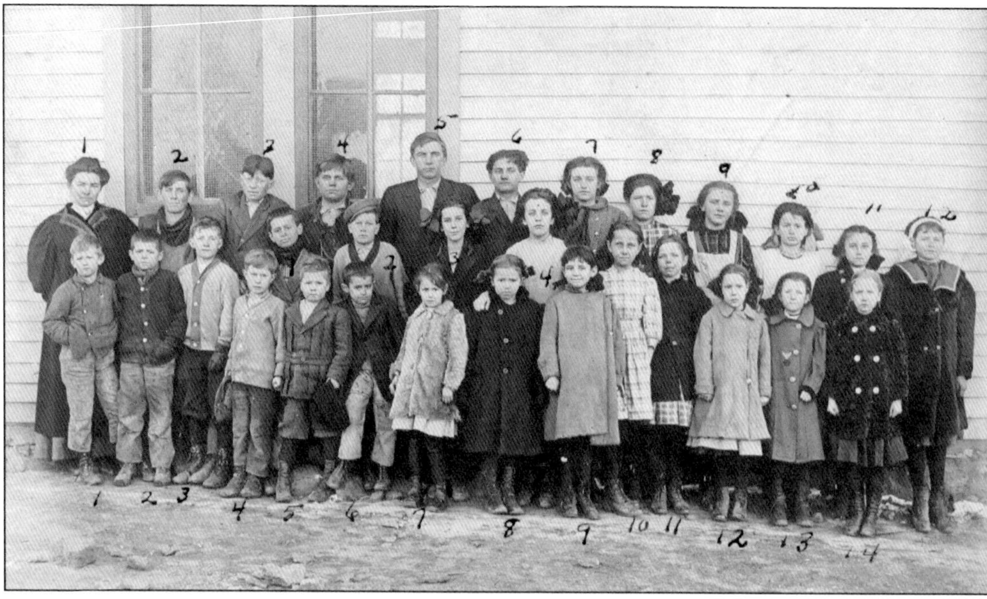

This Nine Mile School class photograph was taken in 1912 with, (first row) Earl Lashley, Paul Jamison, Clay Young, Lee Owens, Francis Gast, Gerty Gladder, Marie Gast, Esther Currey, Buelah Jordan, Margaret Jordan, Helen Stiler, Ruth Young, and Gertrude Gauger; (second row) John Jamison, Raymond Owens, Florence Currey, and Grace Young; (third row) Jennie Dickey, Frank Currey, Patrice Kirby, Cecil Jordan, Maylin Young, Floyd Morris, Pauline Linaweaver, Alia Kirby, Edna Gieser, Ruby Jamison, Geneva Linaweaver, and Florence Jamison. (Courtesy of the Lansing Historical Museum.)

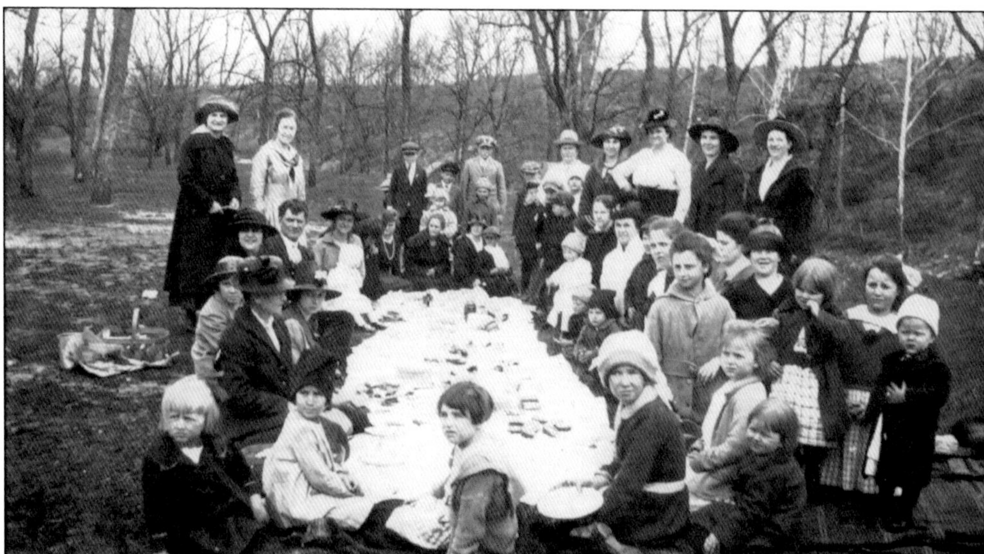

Every year, Nine Mile School had a picnic. Identified are Dorothy Gaiser Marxen, Louise Gaiser, Edwin Borchardt, Feney Gaiser, teacher Helen Bader, Mrs. Mel Brooks, Mrs. Charles Wilcox, Ruth Wilcox, Louise Jamison, Mrs. Frank Brooks, Zelma Brooks, Jacob Gaiser, Mabel Gaiser, Anna Gaiser Borchardt, Anna Krohne, Effie Jamison, Edna Helm, Pansy Brooks, Frieda Helm, Velma Meyer, Mary Emge, Ben Wilcox, May Wilcox, Pearl Chestnut, and Opal Curry. (Courtesy of the Lansing Historical Museum.)

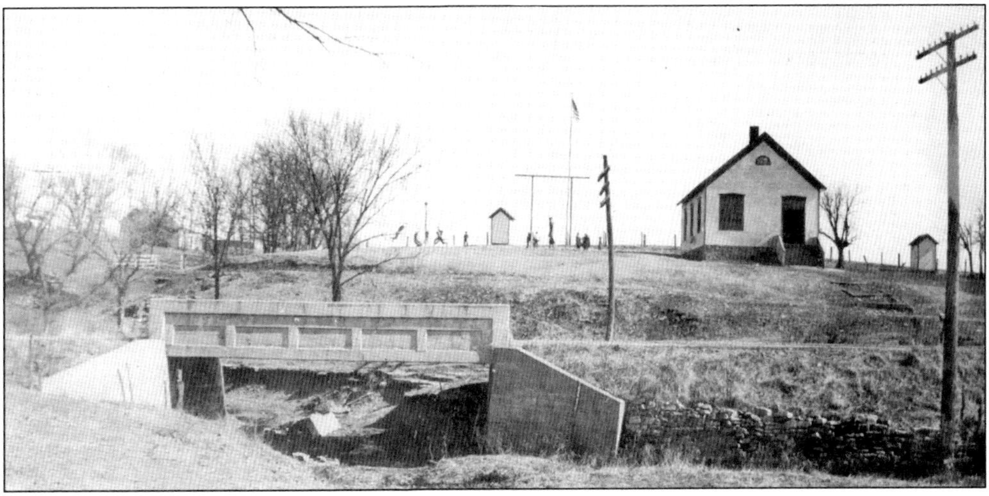

Nine Mile School, built around 1860, educated children in Delaware Township. In 1874, 69 students attended the school to learn reading, writing, and arithmetic from Mrs. A. A. Lombly. Other classes included history, grammar, geography, and penmanship. Students only attended Nine Mile School eight months a year in order to assist their parents on the farm. Through the years, the school added maps and a library to aid in the students' education. (Courtesy of the Lansing Historical Museum.)

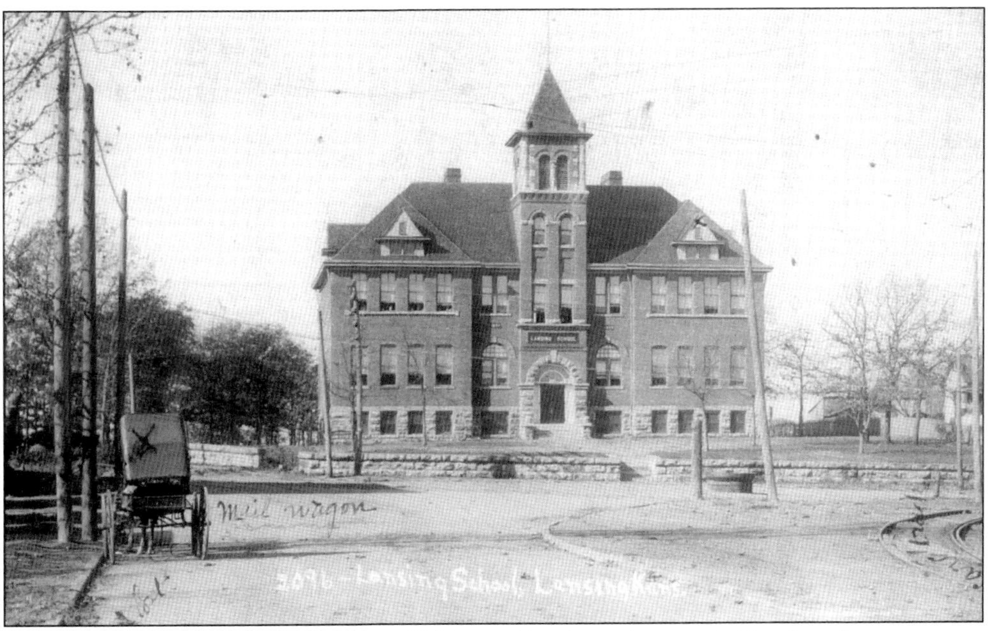

Lansing School stood next to Highway 73/Kansas 7 and was destroyed either by a fire or a storm. A horse-drawn mail carriage is on the left side of Kansas Avenue, and a well and interurban rail tracks are on the right side. A grade school was later built on the site. After the school closed, the building became apartments. (Courtesy of the Lansing Historical Museum.)

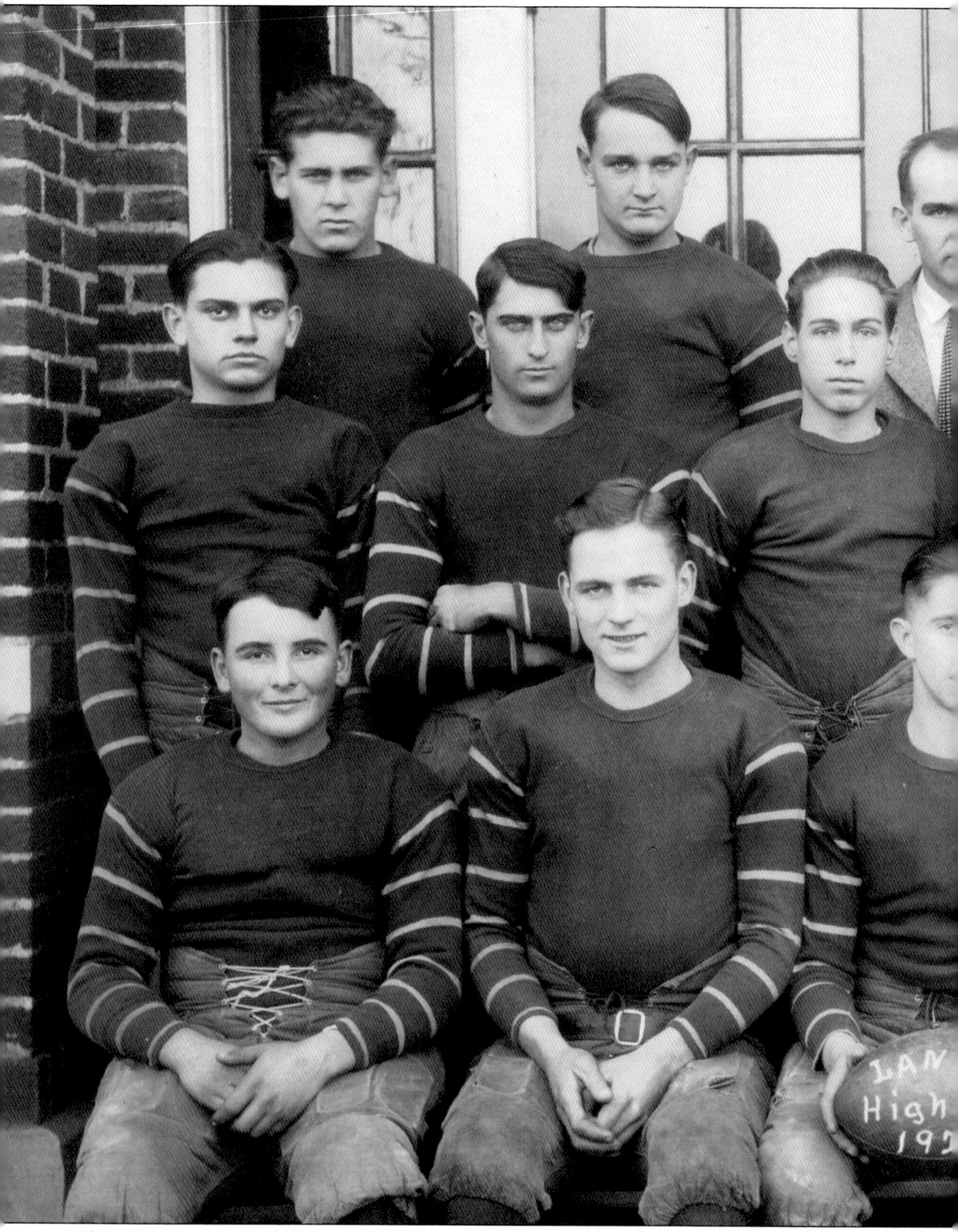

The 1927 Lansing High School football team poses here. Identified are Lester Mills (first row, fourth from left), Merle Jamison (first row, far right), Carl Hatfield (second row, first on the left), Ralph Bouchard (back row, second from left), Coach Starbuck (back row, center), ? Morrison

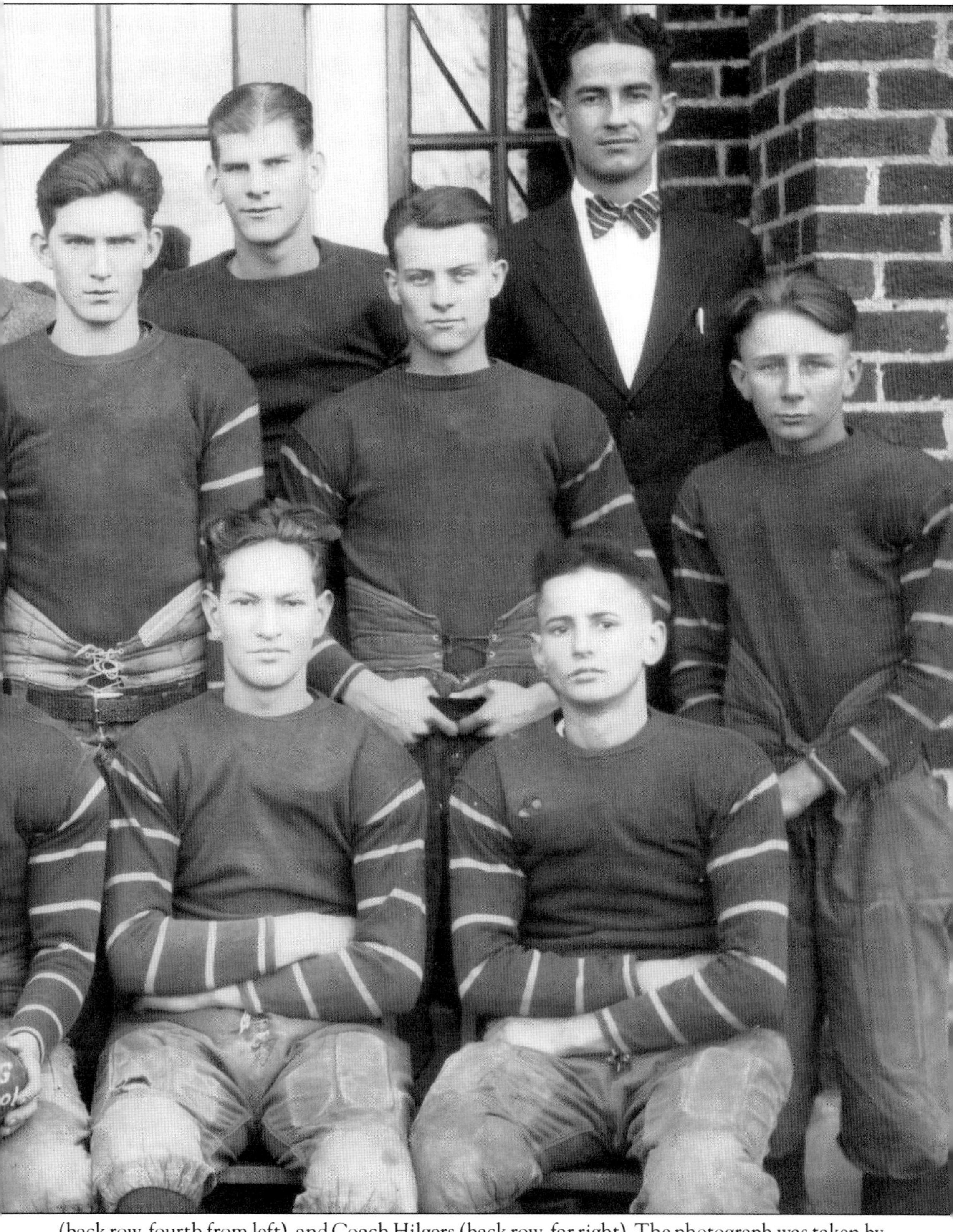

(back row, fourth from left), and Coach Hilgers (back row, far right). The photograph was taken by Stevenson Photography Studio in Leavenworth. (Courtesy of the Lansing Historical Museum.)

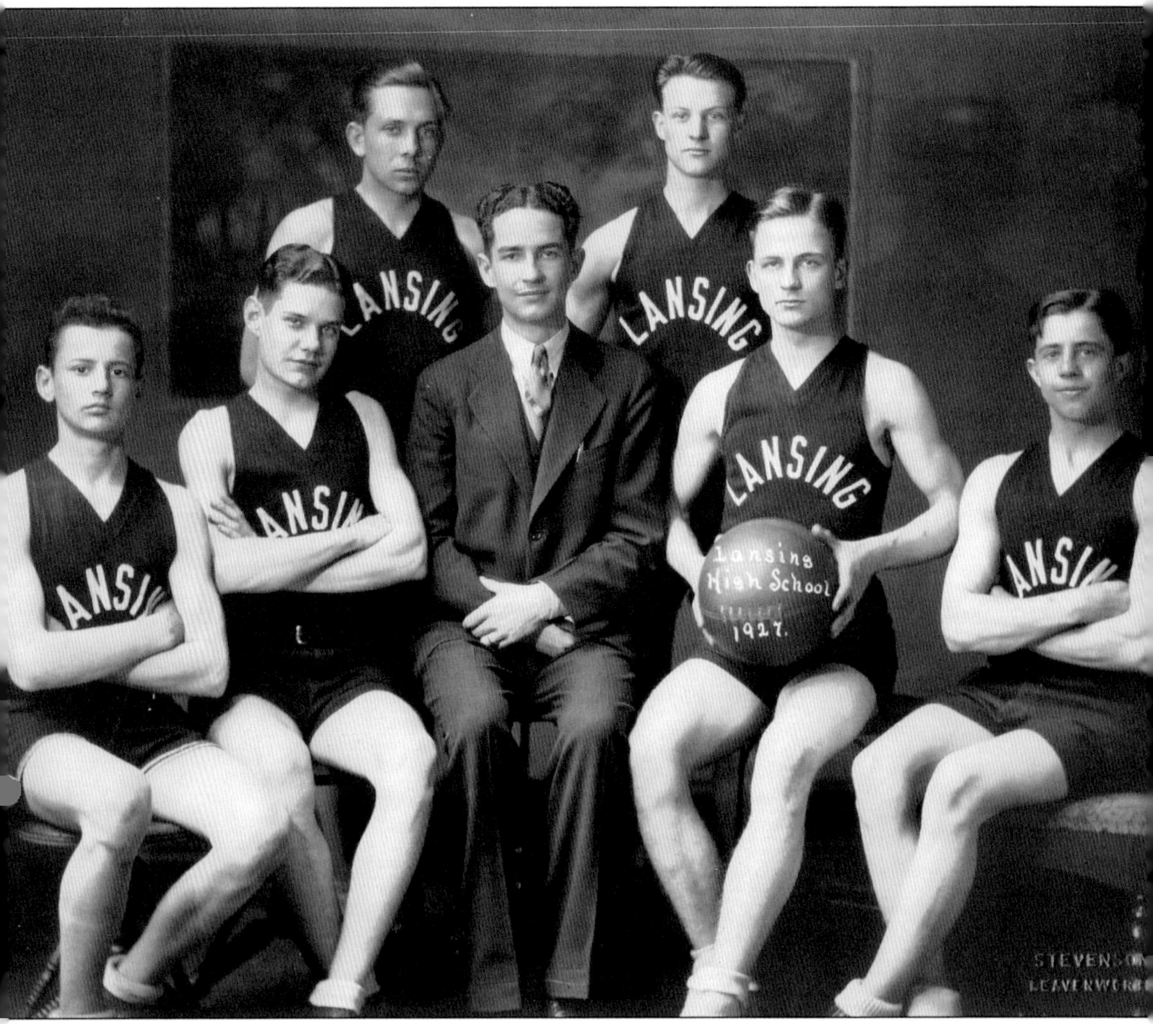

The 1927 Lansing High School basketball team lines up for a shot. From left to right are (first row) Merle Jamison, John Brown, coach Hilgers, Charles Lambert, and Andrew Erhart; (second row) George Walker and unidentified. The photograph was taken by Stevenson Photography Studio in Leavenworth. (Courtesy of the Lansing Historical Museum.)

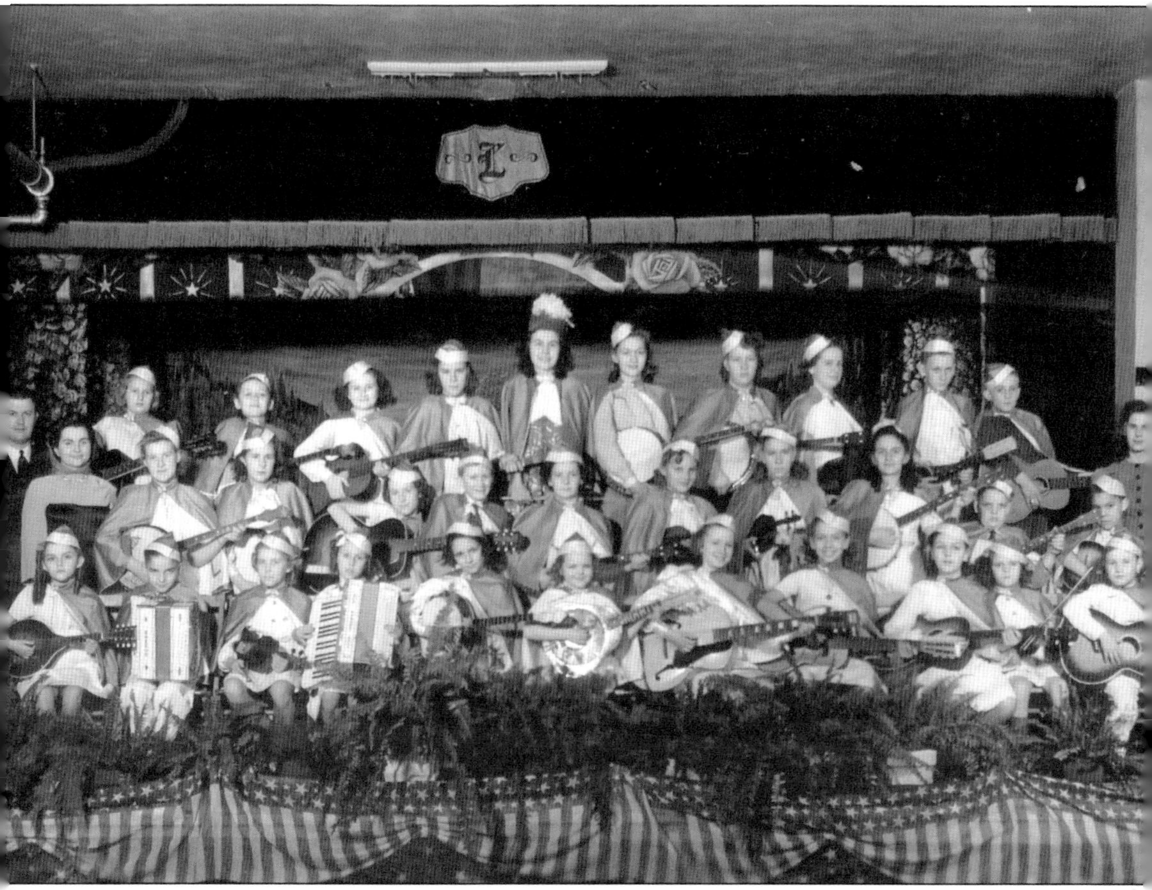

On November 14, 1941, the Lansing Grade School string band gave a performance. From left to right are (first row) Earlene Peters, Richard Farley, Anita Borchardt, Rosemary Simoncic, Margaret Zoll, Peggy Zoll, Betty Zoll, Shirley Maxwell, Dorothy Mae Ray, Jacquie Farley, and Lonnie Rush; (second row) the director Mrs. Painter, Mary Alice Perry, Rita Lippert, Bertha Mae Concannon, Ross Perkins, Charlotte Camp, Geraldine McCormick, Willa Deanne Mills, Mary Linaweaver, Everett Kirby, and Joseph Blake; (third row) Ted Painter, Ada Mondero, Shirley Bullard, Peggy McQuillian, Vivianne Eastwood, Norma Courtney, student director, Billie Marie Bullard, Emma Jean Mills, Beverly Stewart, Thomas Welt, and Junior Asbury. The band teacher on the far right is Thelma Frederick. (Courtesy of the Lansing Historical Museum.)

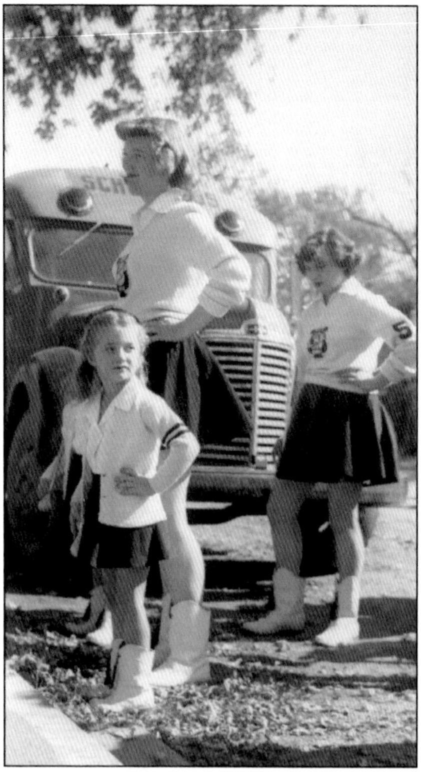

Mary Lee Lohman, an elementary school student here, joined the Lansing Rural High School Majorettes. Tommie Louise Studdard (middle) graduated in 1956, and Maryellen Gould (right) graduated in 1955. (Courtesy of the Lansing Historical Museum.)

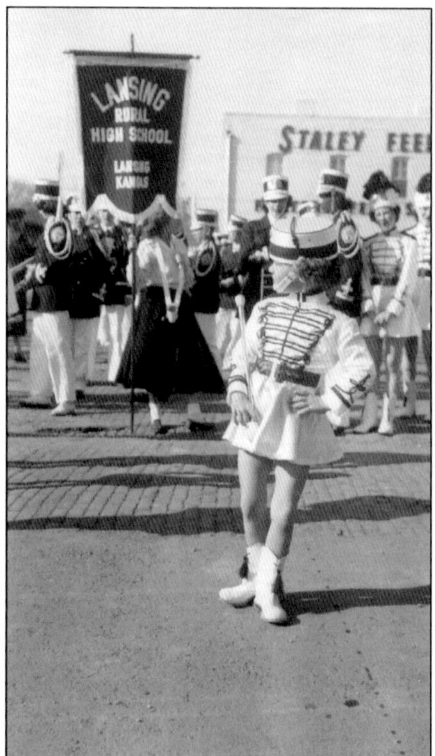

Lohman, in the foreground, marches with the Lansing Rural High School marching band. (Courtesy of the Lansing Historical Museum.)

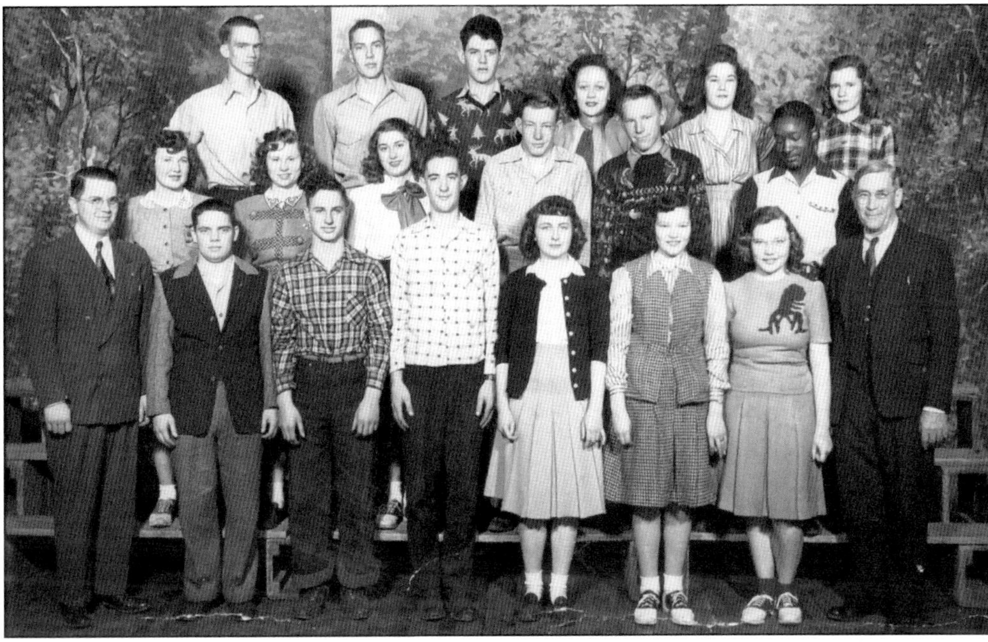

This Lansing Rural High School 10th-grade class photograph was taken during the 1947–1948 school year. From left to right are (first row) class sponsor Mr. Fleming, Everett Kirby, John Jamison, D. W. Woodson, Mary Ellen O'Connor, Mary Collins, Alta Marxen, and principal H. O. Aldman; (second row) Dorothy Trimble, Billie Jean Wade, Doris Mervin, Lambert Mills, Charles Bagwell, and John Tolbert; (third row) Bill Young, Raymond Hencheck, Donald McQuillan, Shirley Collier, Janice Stafford, and Dorothy Bieri. (Courtesy of the Lansing Historical Museum.)

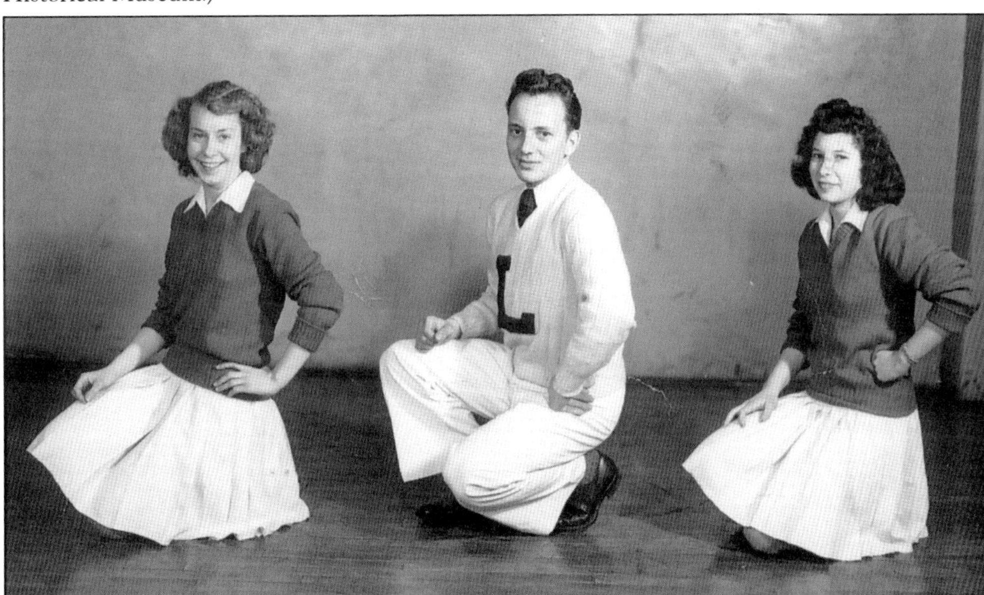

Cheerleader Willa Deanne Mills (left), yell leader Bernard Gemmell, and cheerleader Virginia Powell show their Lansing Rural High School spirit. (Courtesy of the Lansing Historical Museum.)

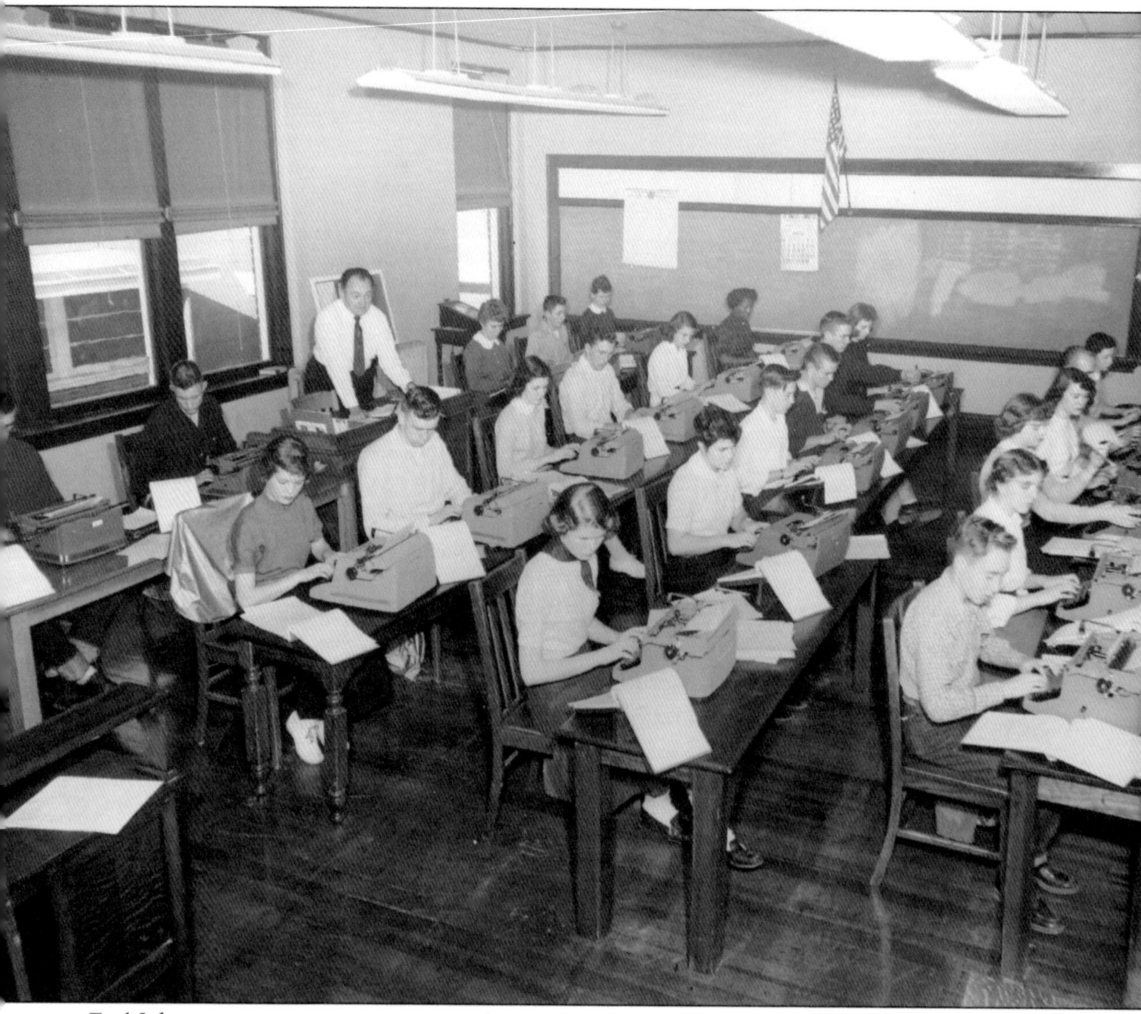

Earl Johnsmeyer supervises seniors in his typing class in 1957. From left to right are (first row) Glenn Linaweaver, Ed Skerko, Earl Johnsmeyer, Sally Butler, Charlie Emge, and Connie Krumm; (second row) Juanita Russell, Jim Kimber, Lorretta Zoll, Joseph Jauerning, Roberta Cummins, and Grace Tolbert; (third row) Phyllis Curtis, JoAnn Perry, Alan Ronnebaum, Charles Rand, Lon Trulove, and Jeanie Rogers; (fourth row) James Hintz, Pat Chambers, Mary Hall, Janet Harrod, Roger Olsen, and Marguerite McCarthy. (Courtesy of the Lansing Historical Museum.)

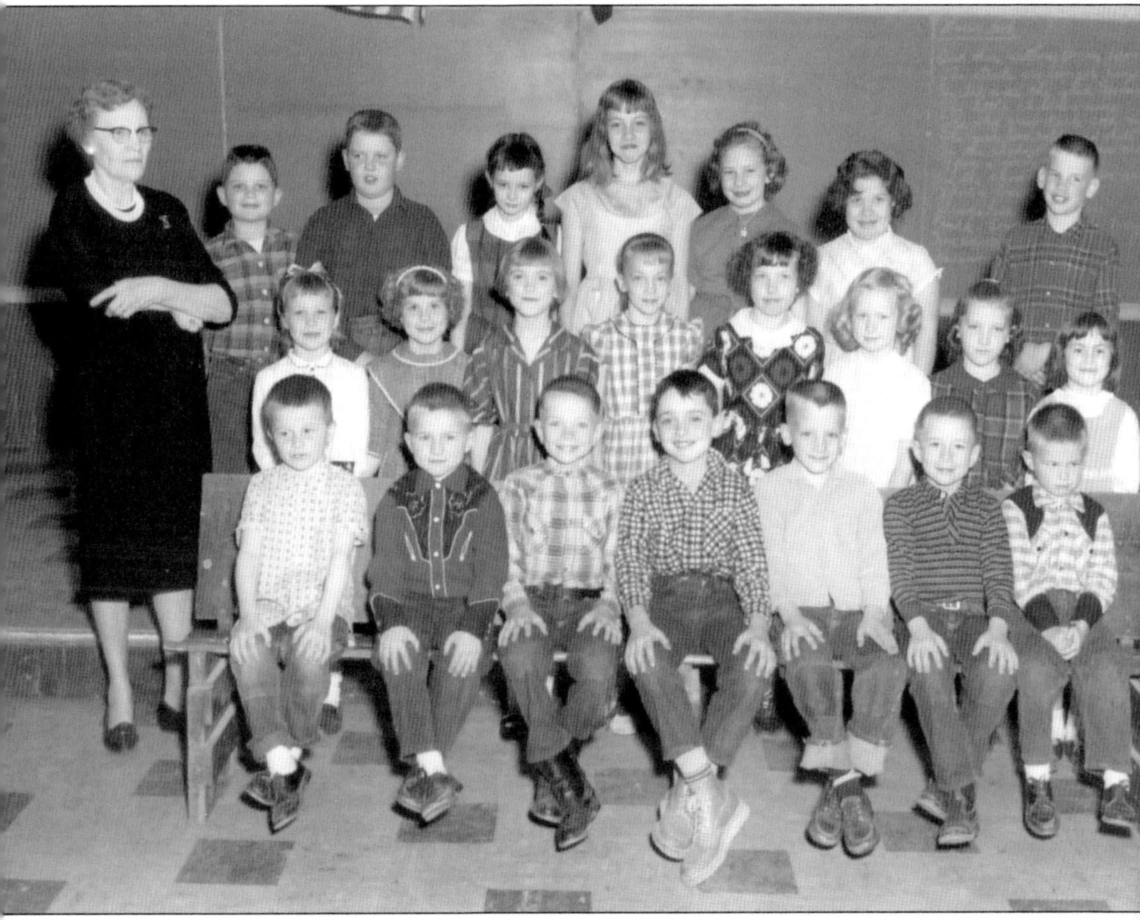

Above is a Delaware School class photograph. (Courtesy of the Lansing Historical Museum.)

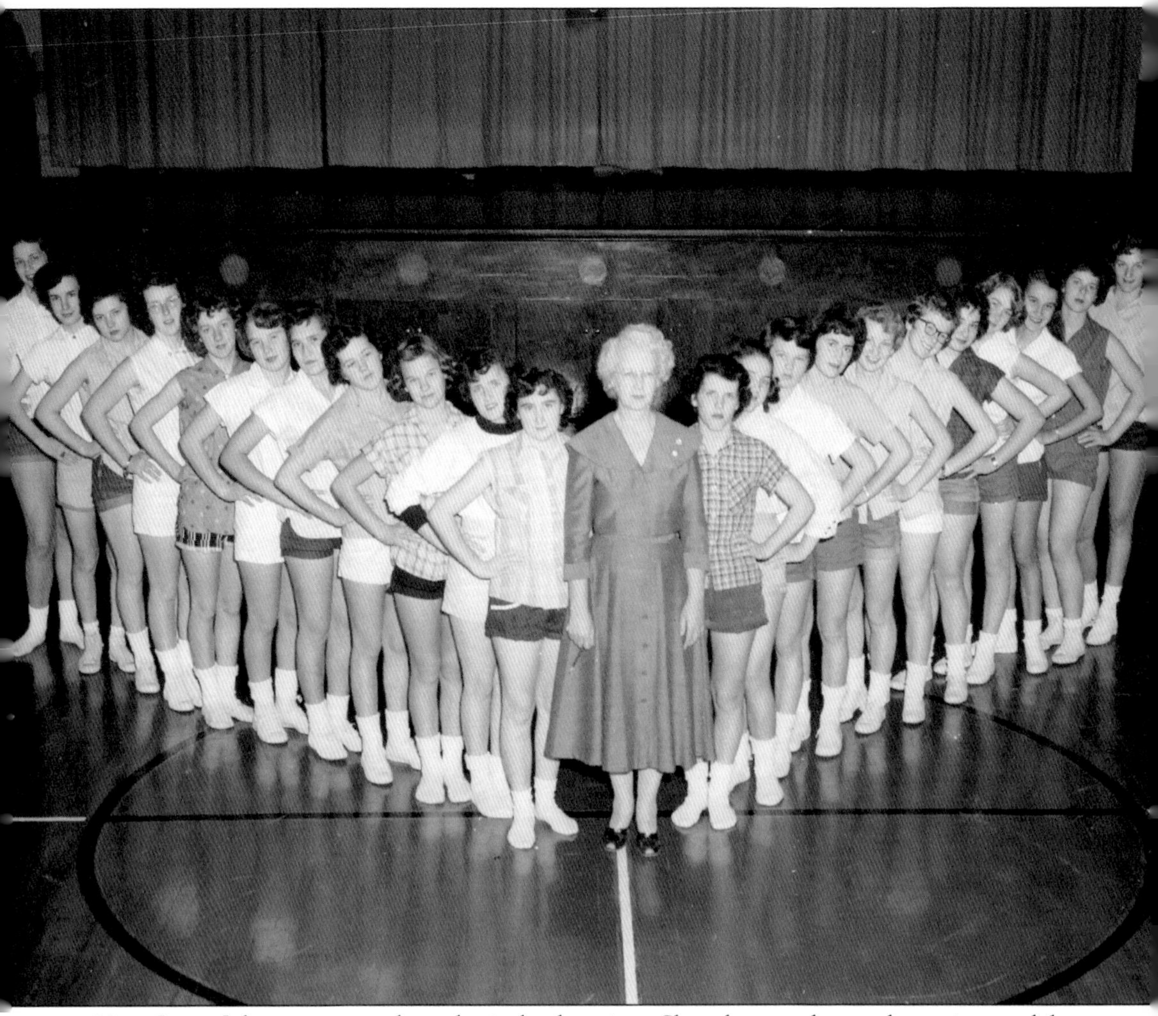

Here Irene Johnsmeyer teaches physical education. She also taught mathematics, and her husband, Earl, taught and coached at Lansing Rural High School. (Courtesy of the Lansing Historical Museum.)

Six

Mount Muncie Cemetery

In 1882, cemetery president George A. Eddy stated, "May we, while living, and those who shall take our places when we are resting within its quiet walls, kept faithful watch and care over this sacred city of the dead." For over 140 years, Mount Muncie Cemetery has guarded the final resting places of many of Leavenworth County's residents. The cemetery has several famous and infamous people, from a governor to murderers. In the early history of the county, individuals were laid to rest at the summit of Pilot Knob. The exact location of Pilot Knob is lost to history; however, it is somewhere near the current Leavenworth High School.

Some residents objected to using the Greenwood Cemetery because of its size and the fact that it resided on private property. In December 1865, a meeting occurred to form an organization to create a new cemetery. The newly appointed trustees chose a place south of Leavenworth, known as Muncie Lands, for the cemetery. The name Muncie Lands came from the Native Americans who once lived there. Dr. Madison Mills offered a tract of 173 acres to the Mount Muncie Cemetery Association for $12,000, and it accepted the proposition.

On June 21, 1866, Leah Jacobs became the first person to be buried at Mount Muncie Cemetery. In 1966, the cemetery board purchased a marker for Jacobs's unmarked grave. Today the cemetery is located on 190 acres and has over 28,300 burials. There are over 25 types of trees in the cemetery, including tulip poplar and Norway spruce. In the autumn, the tree leaves turn to reds and gold, creating a beautiful and serene resting place for loved ones.

In the early days, carvers used limestone to create monuments. Then tombstone art transitioned to marble and granite markers until the late 1940s, when garden cemeteries became popular with flat bronze markers. The latest innovation in cemetery art is the use of lasers to etch inscriptions and symbols into the marker. Visitors can see the different tombstone periods in the cemetery.

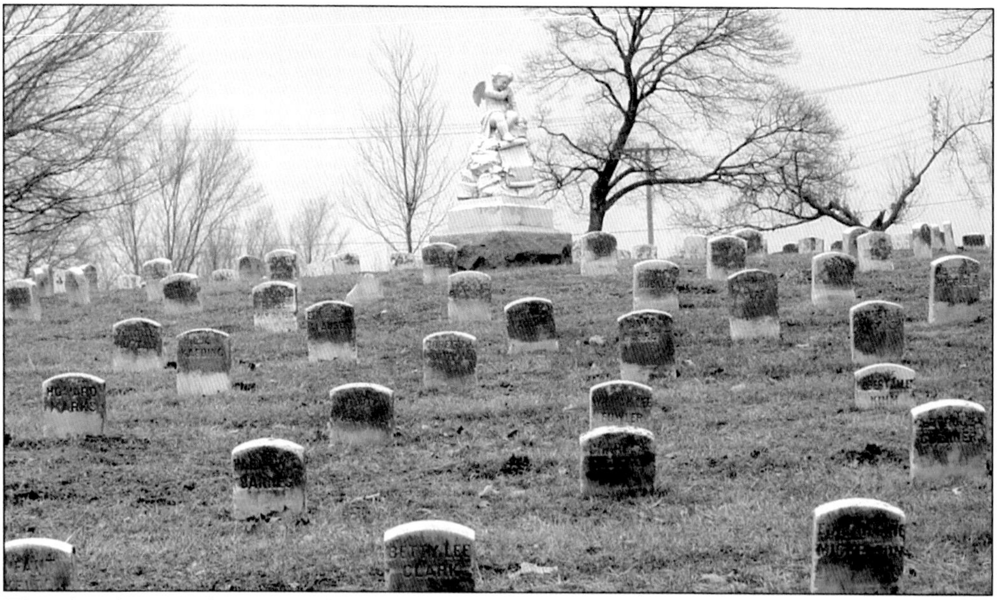

This cherub is watching over children's graves at Mount Muncie Cemetery in section 13. Due to malnutrition, disease, accidents, and lack of medical care, the mortality rate of children was high in the Victorian age. Between the years 1866 and 1876, 732 children were laid to rest at the cemetery. From 1980 to 1990, only 37 children were buried here. The decline in the mortality rate is due to advancements in medicine, such as the introduction of antibiotics in the 1930s. (Photograph by Laura Phillippi.)

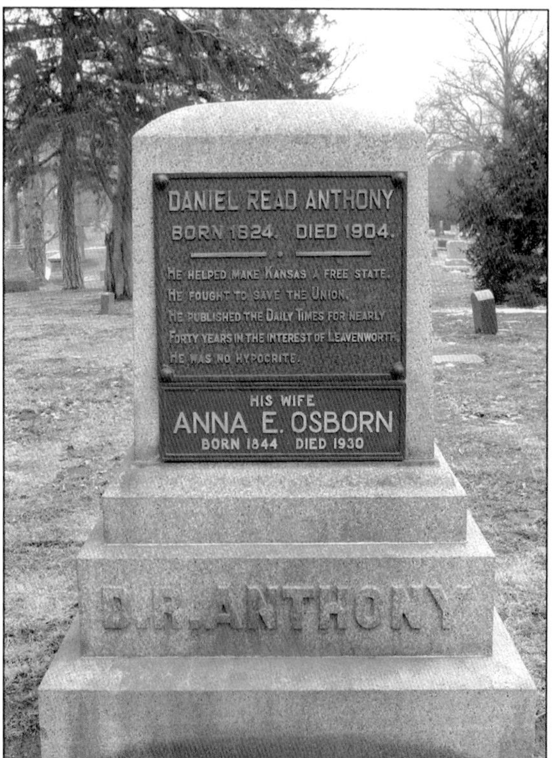

Daniel Read Anthony first visited Kansas in 1854 with the New England Emigrant Aid Society. He permanently relocated to Leavenworth in 1857. During the Civil War, Anthony became a lieutenant colonel in the First Kansas Cavalry. On January 21, 1864, he married Annie Osborn. During his career, Anthony served as Leavenworth's mayor and postmaster and published the *Leavenworth Times*. In 1875, he survived being shot in the face at the Leavenworth Opera House. (Photograph by Laura Phillippi.)

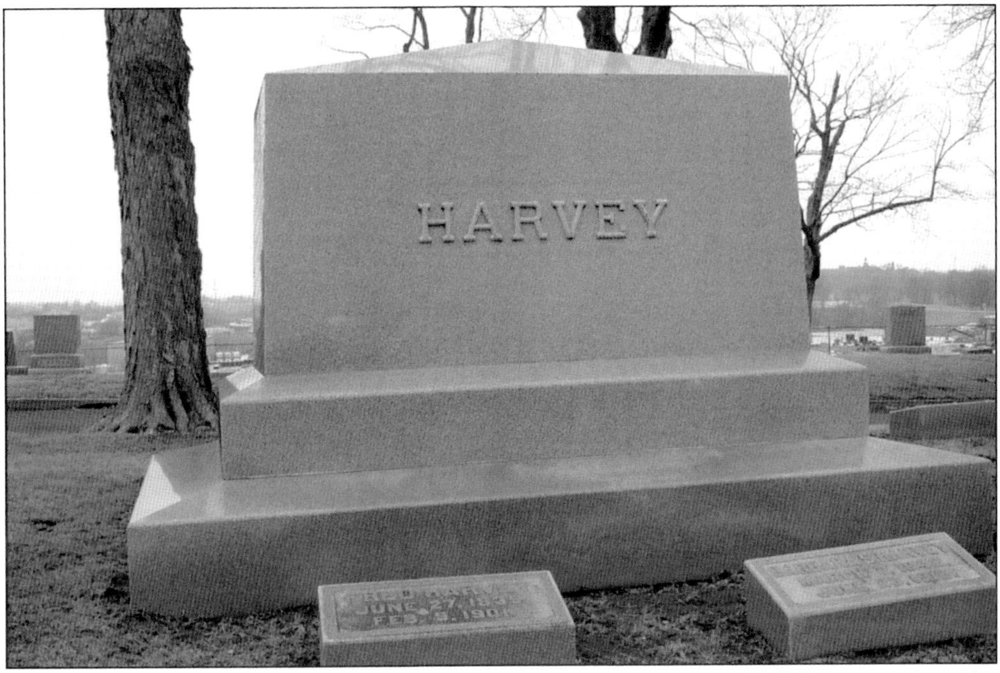

A native of London, Fred Harvey immigrated to the United States in 1850. Fifteen years later, he moved to Leavenworth and worked for the Chicago, Burlington, and Quincy Railroad. Appalled by the quality of food and lodging for railroad travelers, Harvey opened the first Harvey House restaurant at Topeka's Santa Fe depot in 1876. The venture proved to be an instant success. When Harvey died in 1901, there were 47 Harvey House restaurants, 15 hotels, and 30 dining cars on the Atchison, Topeka, and Santa Fe Railway. (Photographs by Laura Phillippi.)

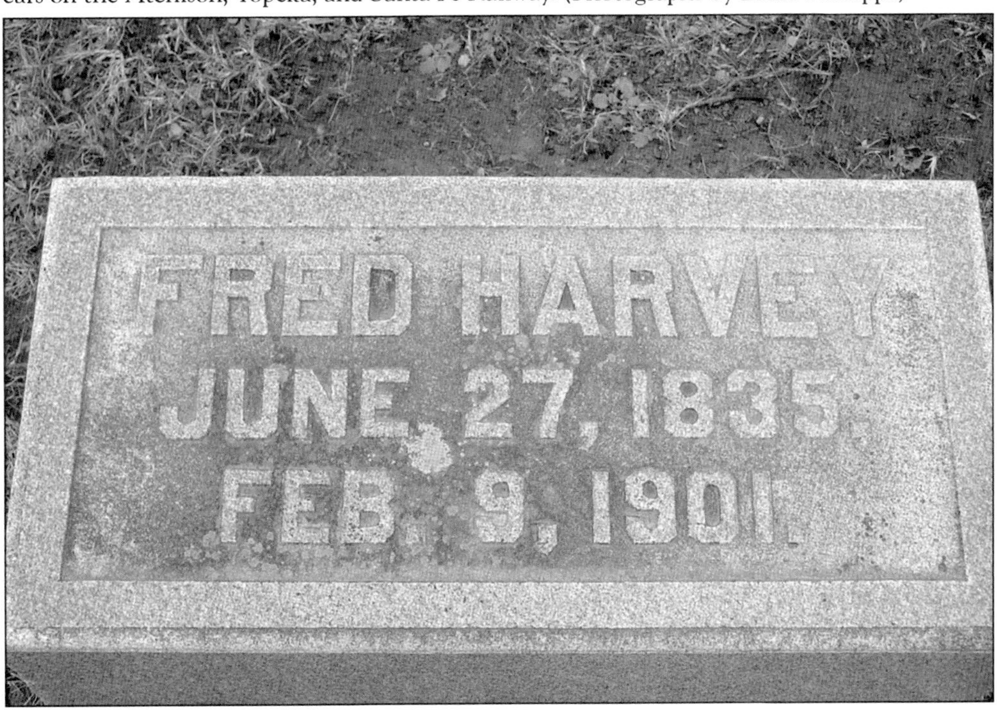

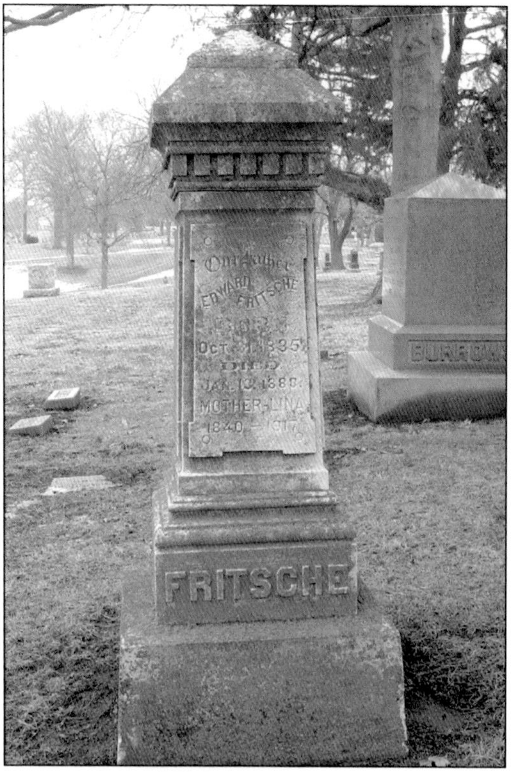

Businessman Edward Fritsche owned part of the Continental Hotel in Leavenworth. He was the great-grandfather of famous news anchor Walter Cronkite. Cronkite's grandfather Edward C. Fritsche, a druggist, and his mother, Helen Fritsche Cronkite, are also buried at Mount Muncie Cemetery. (Photograph by Laura Phillippi)

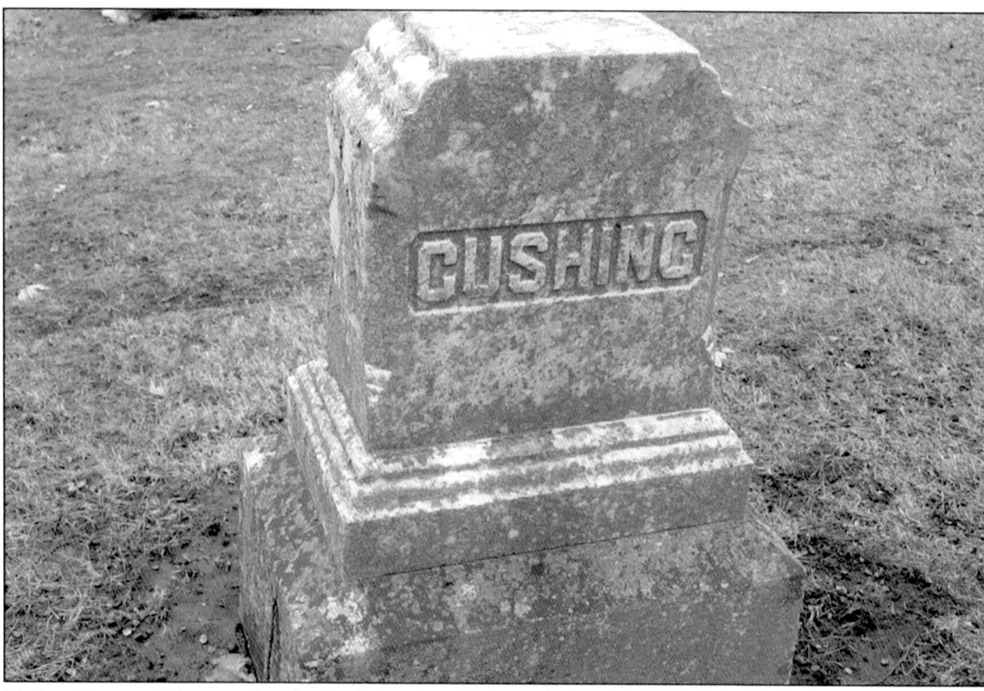

Philanthropist Harriet Smith Cushing founded Cushing Hospital in 1894. For over a century, Cushing Hospital has cared for the area's sick and injured. The faith-based not-for-profit hospital has 74 beds. (Photograph by Laura Phillippi.)

There are numerous cemeteries on the Great Plains that contain wrought iron grave markers. Most examples can be found in the Dakotas, Kansas, Montana, Texas, and the Alberta, Manitoba, and Saskatchewan provinces in Canada. Immigrants of German Russian heritage settled in these areas with some talented blacksmiths. Blacksmiths provided essential services to settlements. They made tools, repaired wagon wheels, cauterized wounds, and pulled infected teeth. They also made intricate iron crosses to mark the graves of community members. (Photograph by Laura Phillippi.)

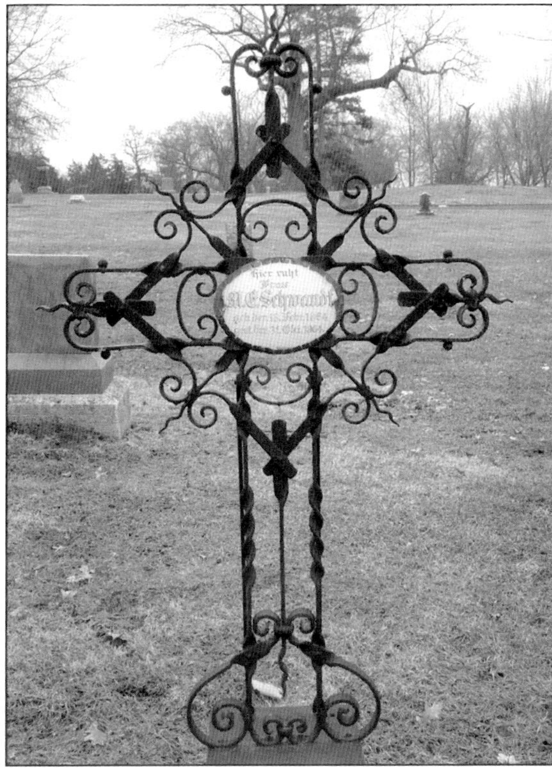

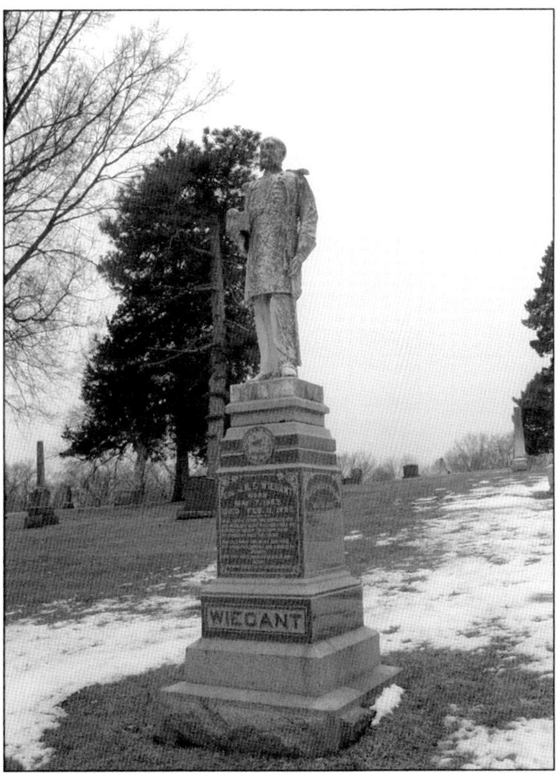

Things are not always what they appear to be in the cemetery. One might think J. H. E. Wiegant served as a colonel in the military with the uniform the statue is wearing and the title etched into the stone. In actuality, the statue is wearing a secret society uniform. Wiegant belonged to a number of secret societies, including the Knights of Pythias. A native German, Wiegant was a businessman and active in politics. (Photograph by Laura Phillippi.)

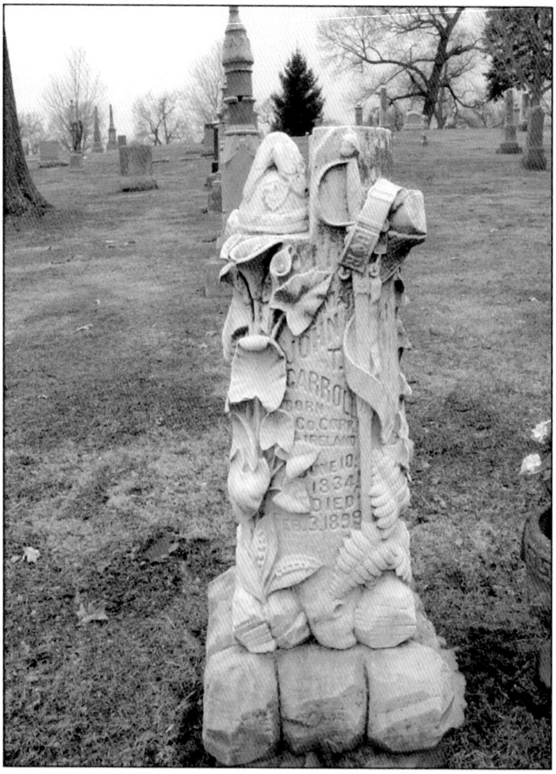

The immigration of the Irish to the United States greatly influenced the development of cities across the country. In 1880, approximately 16,546 Irish immigrants lived and worked in nearby Leavenworth. Many Irishmen served in the military at Fort Leavenworth. John T. Carroll immigrated from County Cork, located in southern Ireland. (Photograph by Laura Phillippi.)

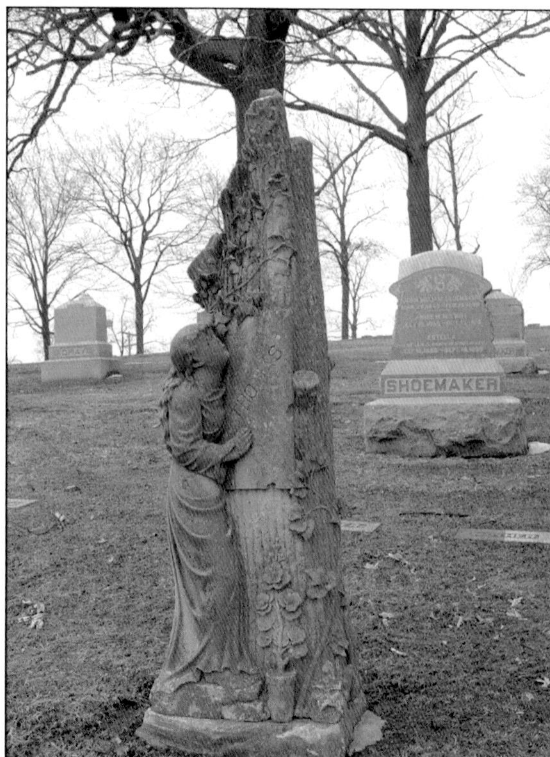

Interpretation of cemetery iconography and symbolism can give insight to the life of the deceased. For example, this tombstone has ivy at the top. Due to ivy's eternal green despite harsh conditions, it is associated with immortality and fidelity. Since ivy clings to objects for support, it can symbolize attachment, friendship, and affection. The three points on the leaf can also represent the Trinity. (Photograph by Laura Phillippi.)

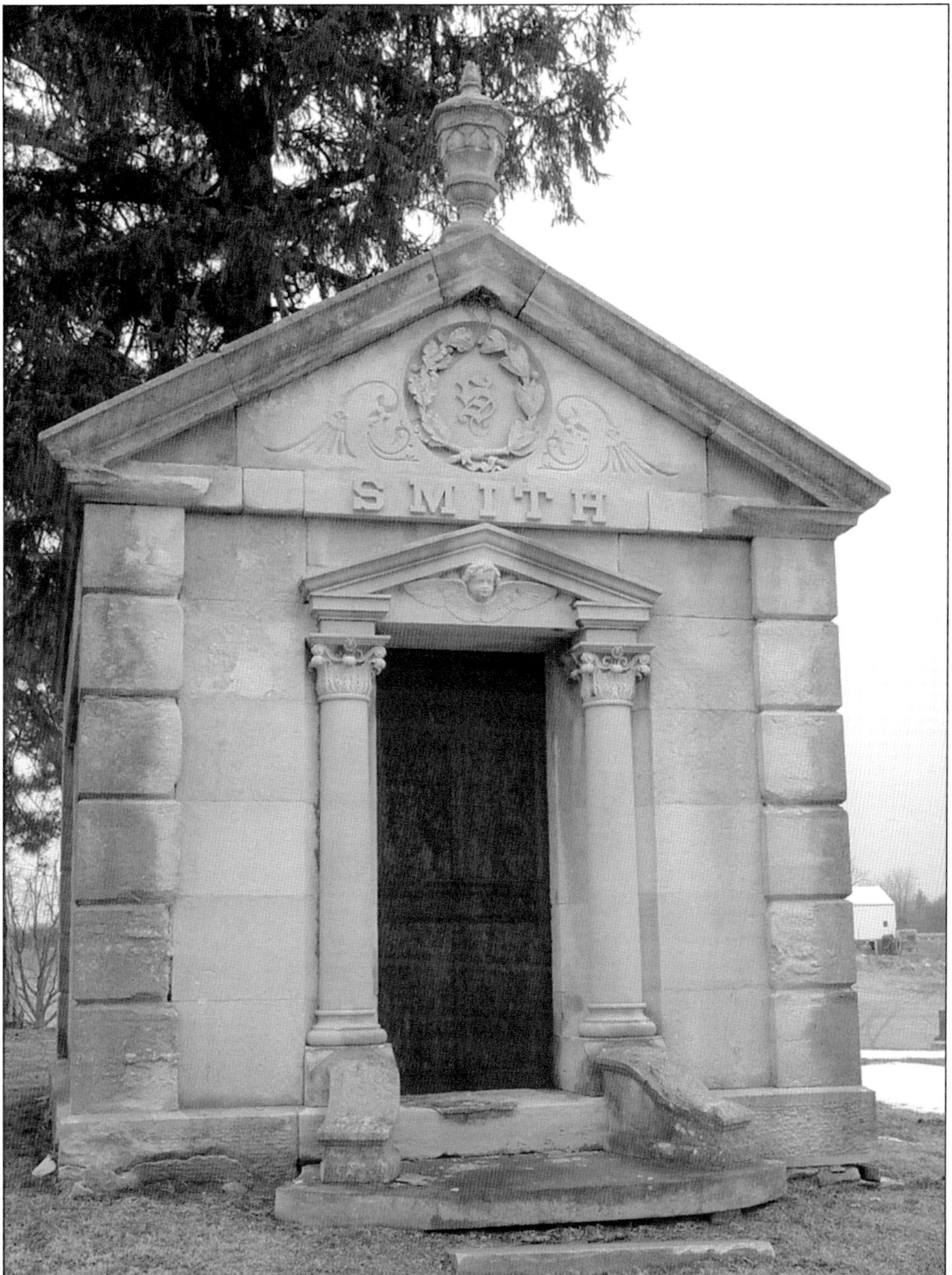

Before the Reformation, cemeteries consisted of unorganized tombstones. Wealthy patrons bought the right to be buried in the church. Reformation edicts and fewer church constructions led to the end of burials inside the church. The wealthy commissioned memorials, statues, and mausoleums for themselves and loves ones in cemeteries. This mausoleum is the resting place for 11 members of the Smith family. Daniel R. Smith was laid to rest in 1879, and in 1945, the last internment took place with Carlotta R. Hewitt. (Photograph by Laura Phillippi.)

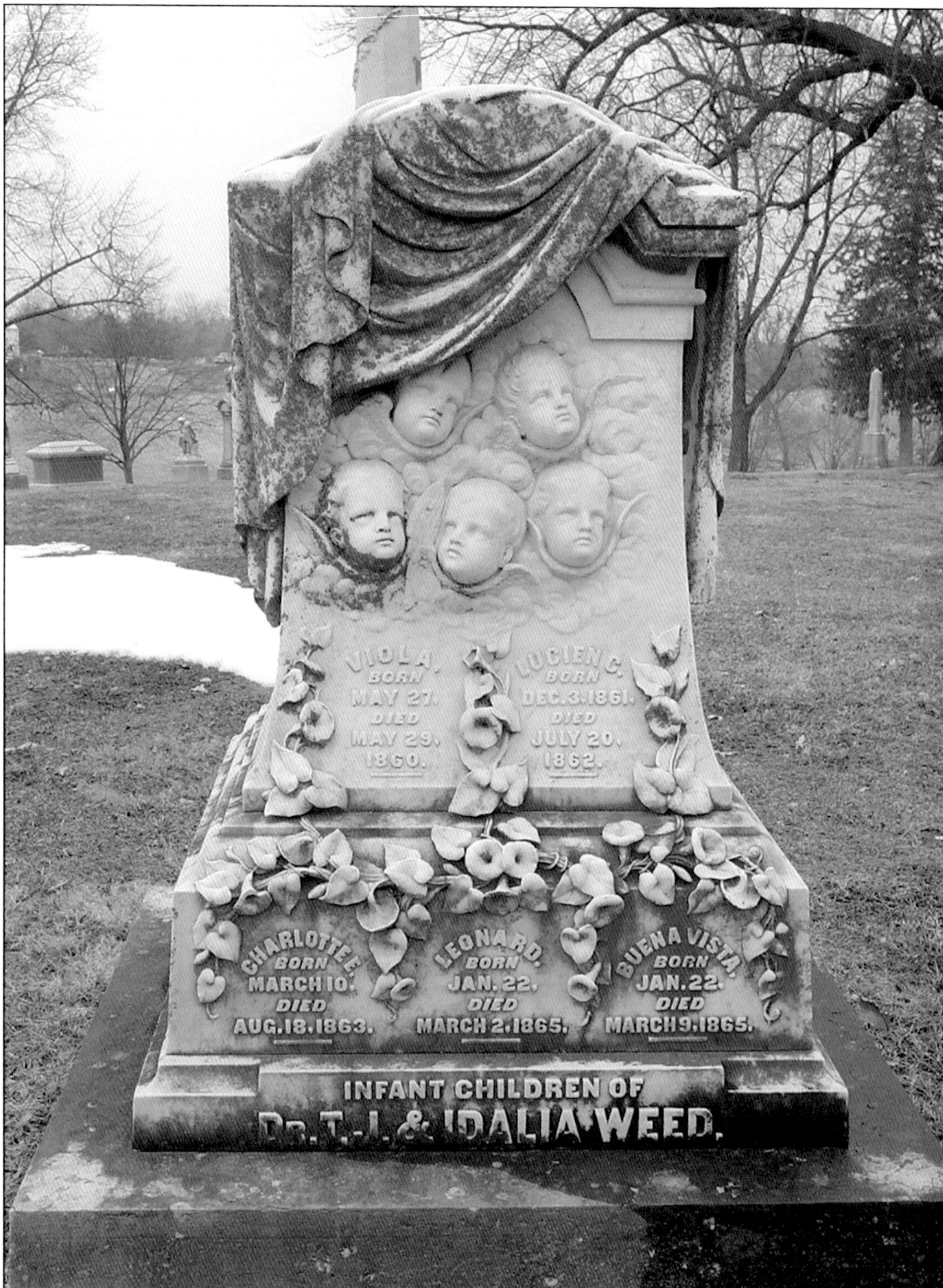

Dr. T. J. Weed and his wife, Idalia, lost five small children, Viola, Lucien, Charlotte, and twins Leonard and Buena Vista, in a five-year period. The drape on top of the tombstone can be interpreted as a reverential accessory or as a symbol of the veil between earth and heaven. (Photograph by Laura Phillippi.)

Seven

Military Heritage

For generations, men and women from Lansing have answered the call to serve their country in the military. Some Lansing residents are stationed or work at nearby Fort Leavenworth. Founded in 1827, Fort Leavenworth is the oldest continuously running army facility west of the Mississippi River. Throughout the years, thousands of troops have served at Fort Leavenworth, including some that rose through the ranks, like Gen. Dwight D. Eisenhower, Gen. George C. Marshall, and Gen. Colin Powell.

Americans celebrate when the troops come home from serving tours overseas by cutting down yellow ribbons tied to trees. For those who paid the ultimate price while protecting freedom, they are remembered, and Americans pay tribute to these fallen servicemen and servicewomen on Veterans Day. Lansing lost three of its own during World War II. Petty Officer 2nd Class Robert E. Potter served as an aviation radioman and died in a plane crash near Astoria, Oregon. Lt. Charles Yunghans served in the Army Air Corps and flew 100 missions out of Africa and Italy. He perished in a plane crash in the Indian Ocean, and the plane was never found. Pfc. Thomas Young served in Company I, 515th Infantry, 79th Division of Gen. George S. Patton's Third Army. He died in the battle of Foret de Parroy near Luneville, France.

Lansing's veterans play a major role in the community. Of the current nine Lansing City Council members, four are veterans, and two are married to veterans. Nine Lansing Police Department officers are veterans, and four veterans serve as firefighters for Leavenworth County Fire District No. 1. The following is a sampling of the local veterans who served their country. Lansing thanks those brave men and women who have protected freedom and the country.

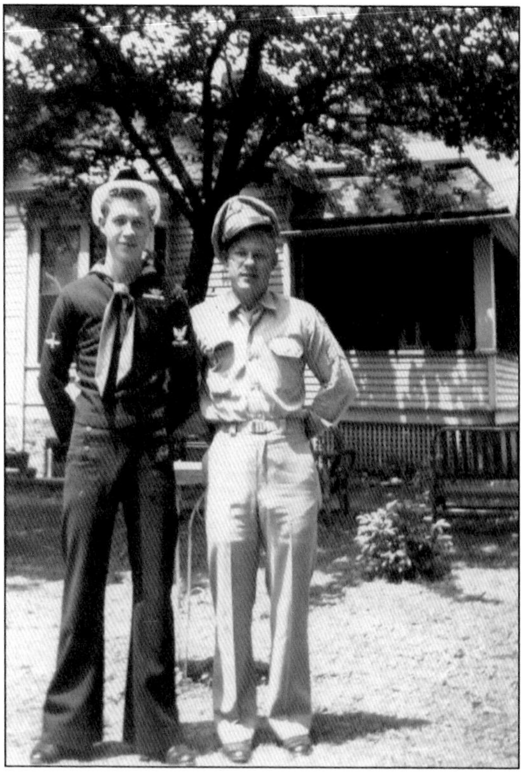

Petty Officer 2nd Class Robert Potter (left) graduated from Lansing Rural High School in 1942 and joined the naval reserve. He served as a radioman and died in a plane crash near Astoria, Oregon, on June 24, 1944. He is buried at Fort Leavenworth National Cemetery. (Courtesy of the Lansing Historical Museum.)

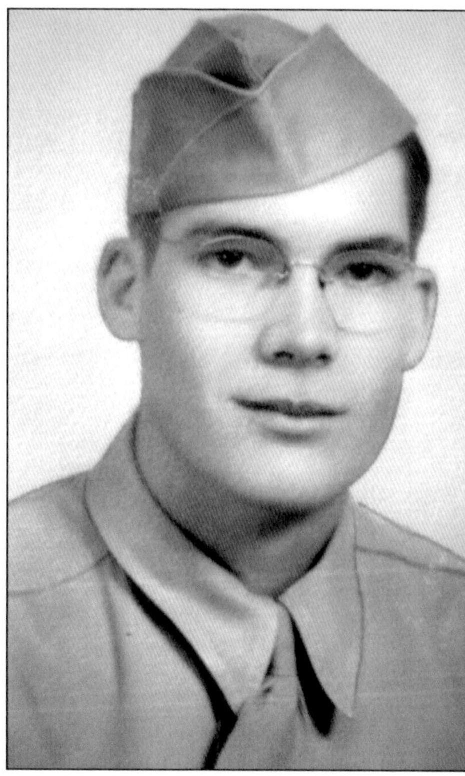

Pfc. Thomas Young graduated from Lansing Rural High School in 1940. He worked for the Farm Credit Administration in Kansas City before being inducted into the army at Fort Leavenworth in 1943. On July 19, 1944, he was permanently assigned to Company I, 515th Infantry, 79th Division of Gen. George S. Patton's Third Army. He died from wounds sustained from artillery fire near Luneville, France. He received the Purple Heart posthumously. (Courtesy of Gene Young.)

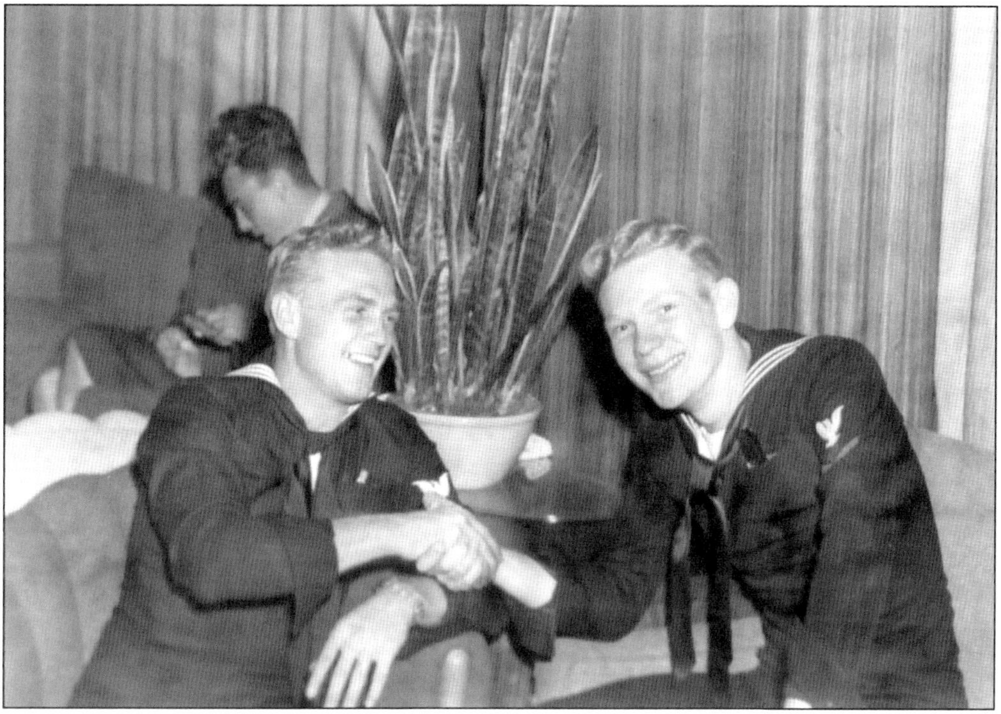

J. T. Brown and Don Clark celebrate V-J Day (Victory over Japan Day) in San Francisco, California. (Courtesy of the Lansing Historical Museum.)

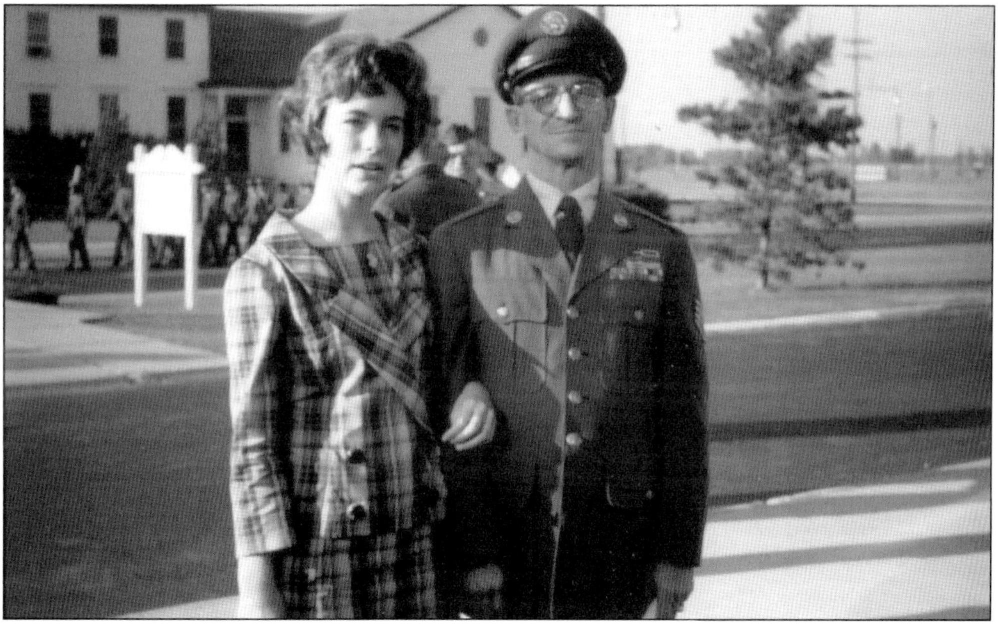

Born in December 1906 in Wamego, S.Sgt. Wilbur Charles Bressler grew up in Lansing. He served in the Marine Corps, navy, and air force. During World War II, he served on the USS *San Jacinto* and was stationed in the Pacific, including in Iwo Jima, the Marianas, the Philippines, Palau Island, and Okinawa. He retired from the air force on October 8, 1964, and passed away a week later. (Courtesy of Karen Piper.)

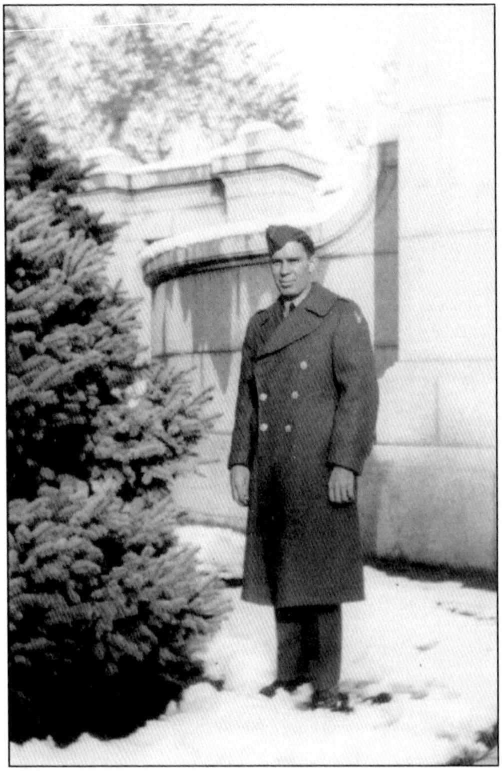

Born in 1918, Wallace Wiehe graduated from Lansing Rural High School and attended Kansas State College in Manhattan. He joined the Army Air Corps, and while stationed at Fort Logan, Colorado, he learned bombsight mechanics and autopilot repair. During World War II, he served with the 20th Air Force in the Marianas. After the war, he farmed for 37 years and was instrumental in organizing Wyandotte Rural Water District No. 2 in 1960. (Courtesy of Karen Piper.)

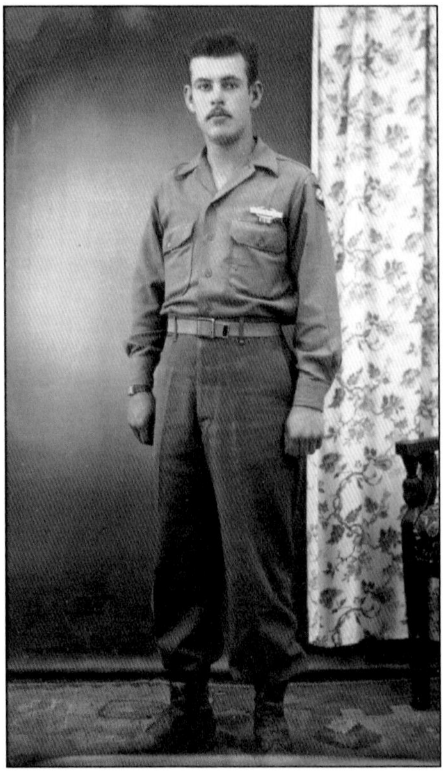

Pfc. Verlin Tompkins enlisted in the army in the autumn of 1942. As part of the 99th Infantry Division, he saw action in Europe. He earned the Bronze Star, Victory Medal, and Belgian Fourragere, among others. He taught math and science at the Haskell Institute in Lawrence. He also worked as a civilian for the army. He is an active member of the Lansing Historical Society, Veterans of Foreign Wars, and Convention and Visitors Bureau committee. (Courtesy of Verlin Tompkins.)

Petty Officer 2nd Class Charles Hall joined the navy in 1952 and served as part of the Seabees in Korea. During his service, a man set himself on fire in a mechanical accident, and Hall tackled the man and smothered the flames. He also played in a band on Armed Forces Radio while stationed in Alaska. He served on the Lansing City Council for 12 years and designed and built Immanuel Church in Lansing. (Courtesy of Verlin Tompkins.)

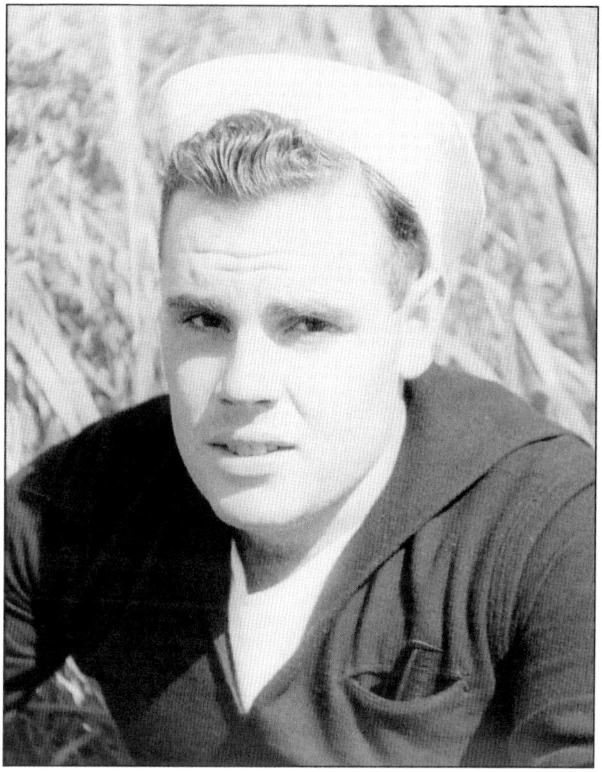

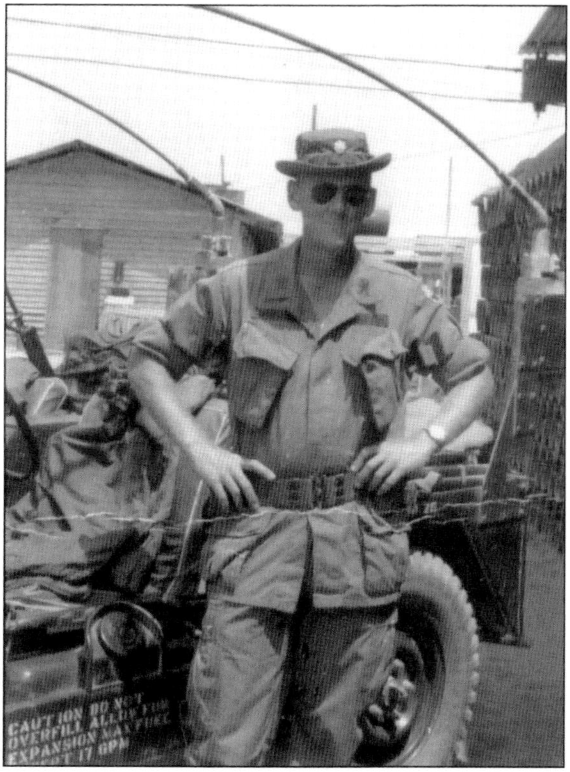

Lt. Col. Clyde Huffman entered the army in 1956 and served in Korea, Vietnam, and Germany. He later became a faculty member at the Command and General Staff College at Fort Leavenworth. He earned an Air Medal, Purple Heart, and two Bronze Stars, among others. Huffman is an active member of several organizations and serves on the Lansing Planning Commission, Lansing Historical Society board, and Mount Calvary Cemetery board. (Courtesy of Sarah Huffman.)

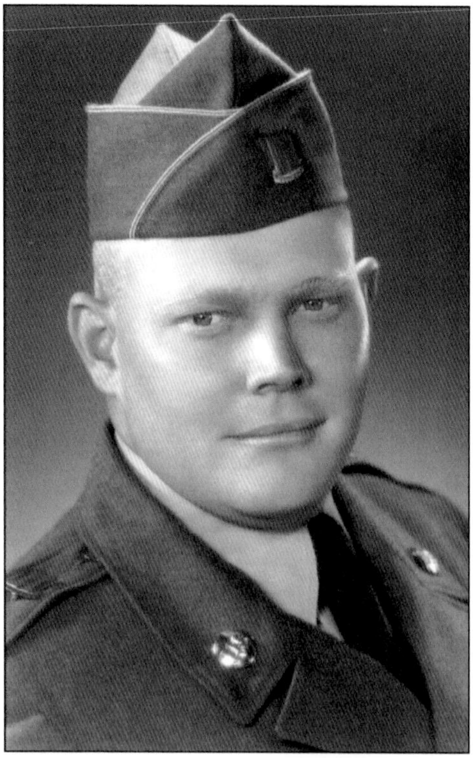

Pfc. Francis Wayman entered basic training and graduated from Signal Corps Replacement Training Center at Fort Gordon, Georgia. He served with the 432nd Engineer Construction Battalion, 311th Group in Germany during the Korean War. He operated heavy equipment to build sports fields, warehouses, railroads, and so on. Wayman is an elder of the First Christian Church, a Lansing Historical Society board member, and a member of the Masonic lodge No. 45 and the Scottish Rite. (Courtesy of Eva Wayman.)

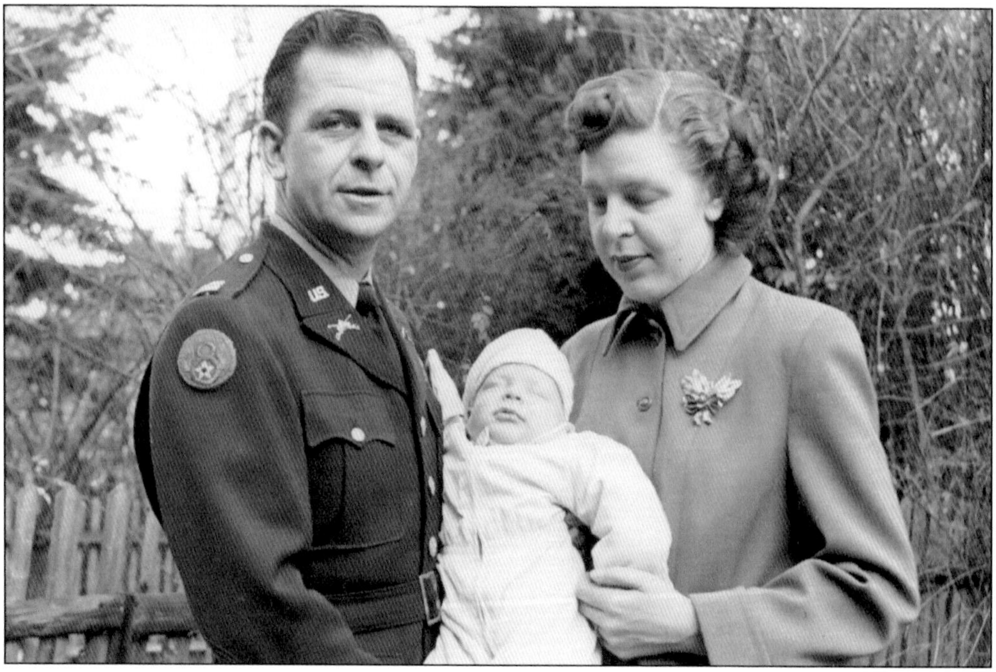

Born on October 24, 1918, in Wichita, Capt. Raymond D. Martin retired from the army in February 1958. A graduate of St. Mary College, Martin taught history and economics at Lansing High School for 15 years. He also served as a class sponsor. Here his wife, Kathleen, and son Arthur pose for a photograph in Munich, Germany. (Courtesy of Karen Piper.)

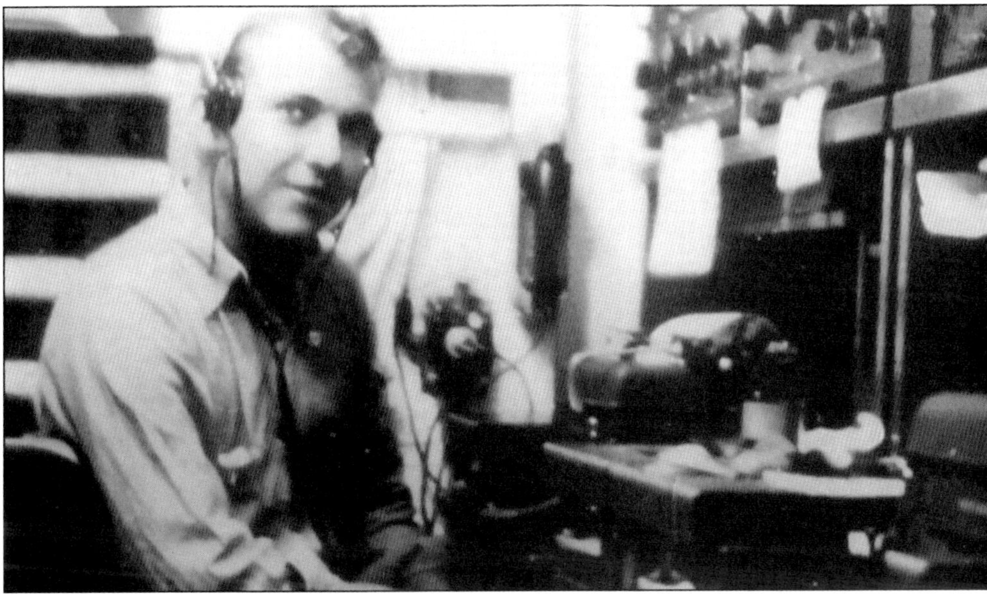

William Powell Jr. enlisted with the U.S. Navy in December 1942. The navy sent him to Port Moresby, New Guinea, where he joined Adm. Thomas Cassin Kinkaid's 7th Fleet radio station headquarters. He served on the USS *Wasatch*. After a 30-day leave in 1945, Powell served as a radioman on a minesweeper. He left the military on January 15, 1946, and became a telegraph operator for the Atchison, Topeka, and Santa Fe Railroad in Lansing. (Courtesy of William Powell Jr.)

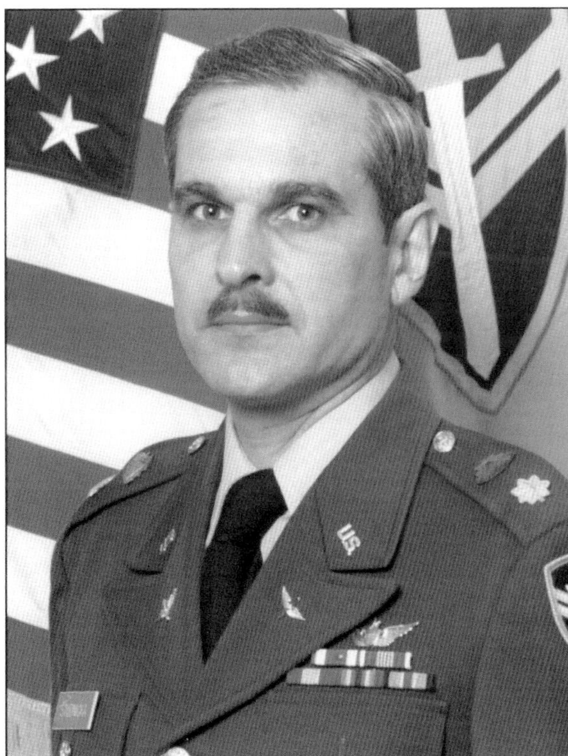

Lt. Col. Donald Studnicka received his commission in the army in 1971. He immediately went on active duty as an armor/cavalry officer. He later attended flight school and became a helicopter pilot. He served in many places, including Korea and Germany. He is currently a defense contractor at Fort Leavenworth. He has served as a Lansing City Council member since 1997 and is assistant scoutmaster to Boy Scout Troop 165. (Courtesy of Donald Studnicka.)

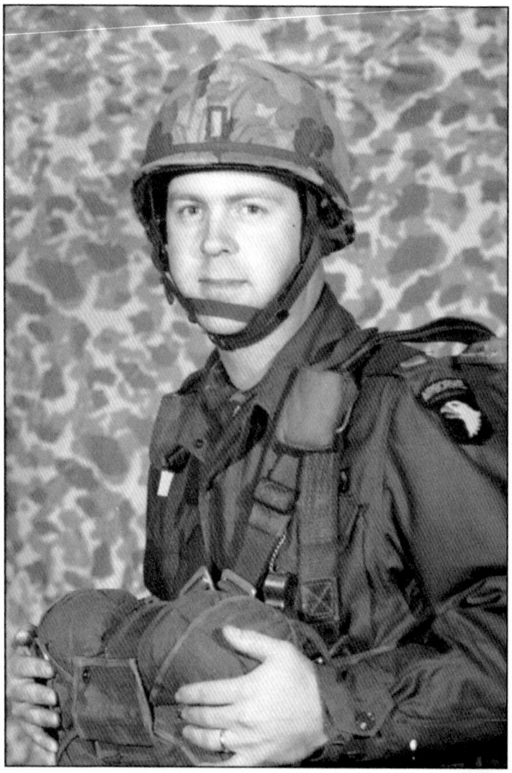

Lt. Col. John Bennett participated in the ROTC program, and after graduation from the University of Missouri, he was assigned to the army's 101st Airborne Division in 1961. He served in Korea, Vietnam, and Germany. From 1968 to 1974, he served as an assistant professor of military science at Colorado College. Bennett served on the Lansing City Council and is an active member of Lansing Lions, Lansing PRIDE, and the Kansas City Barbeque Society. He also teaches computer classes to senior citizens. (Courtesy of John Bennett.)

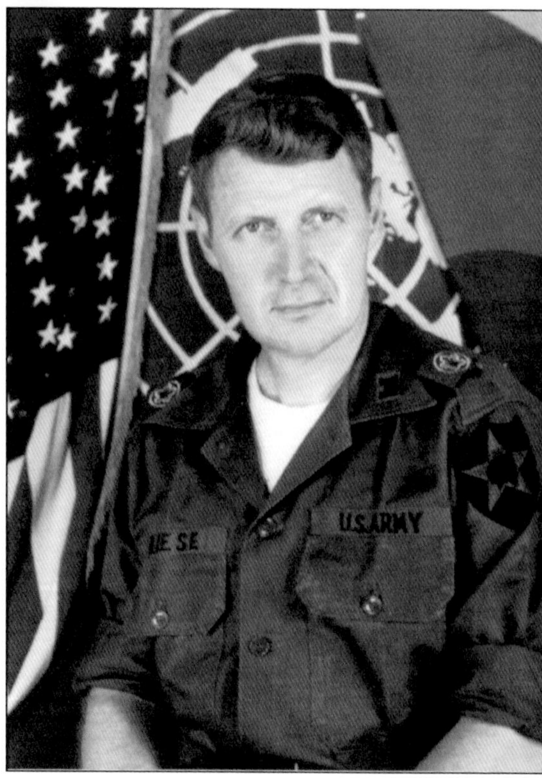

Lt. Col. Robert Riese began his military career as a platoon leader and company commander for B Company, 13th Engineer Battalion, 7th Infantry Division in Korea. He also served in Germany, Taiwan, and Vietnam. He received several awards, including the Bronze Star and Air Medal. Riese also served in the United States, including at Fort Leavenworth, where he was an instructor. He serves on the St. Francis de Sales steering committee and the Lansing Historical Society board. (Courtesy of Robert Riese.)

Born to Irish immigrants in New York, Lt. Col. Michael Keohane enlisted in the army in 1967. He served in Korea, Vietnam, and Greece before becoming an instructor at Fort Leavenworth. Since 1995, he has worked as a nurse at Cushing Hospital. He is a member of the Rotary Club, president of the Kansas City Regional Chapter of the American Association of Diabetic Educators, and a Lay Eucharistic Minister at St. Francis de Sales Church. (Courtesy of Michael Keohane.)

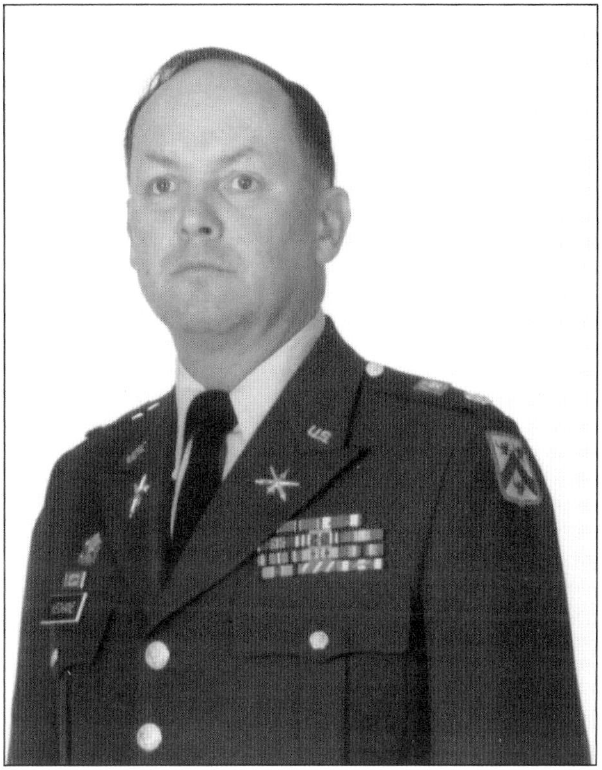

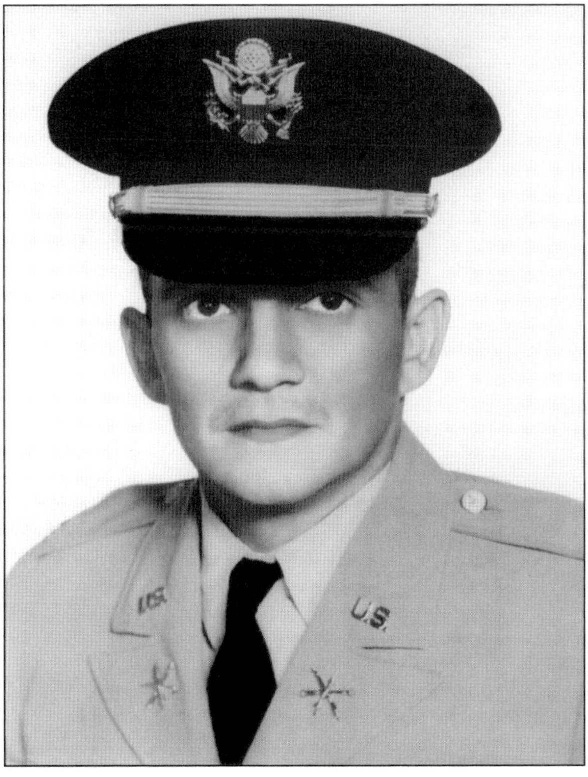

A native of North Dakota, Maj. Kenneth Bernard entered the army in 1958 and served for more than 20 years in various artillery and staff assignments. He received several awards, including the Silver Star, Bronze Star, and Purple Heart. Bernard has served as mayor of Lansing from 1983 to 1991 and from 1993 to the present. (Courtesy of Kenneth Bernard.)

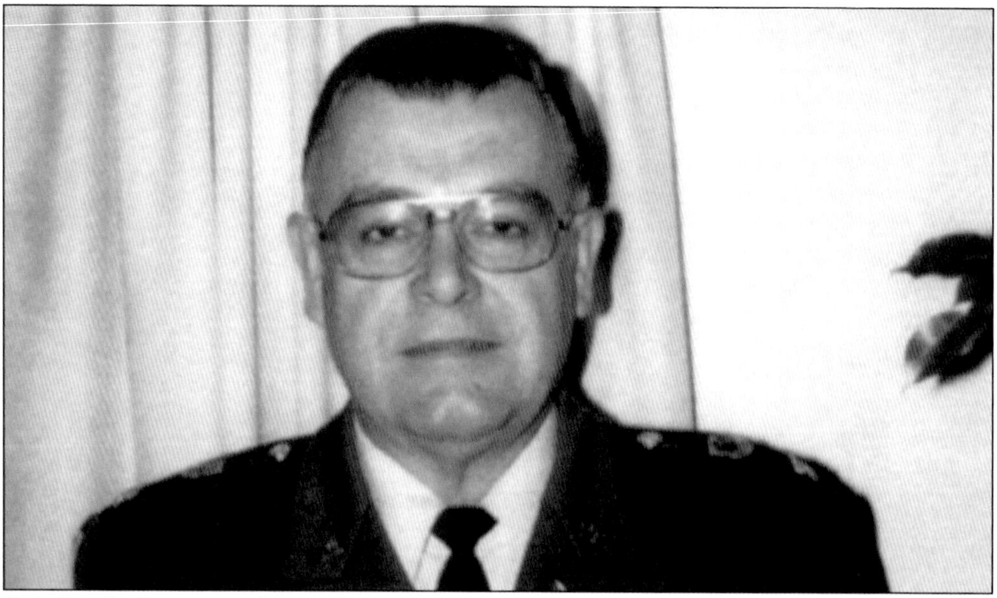

Col. Orville Butts started his military career as a platoon leader with the 208th Military Police at Fort Ritchie, Maryland. He served in Germany, Thailand, Vietnam, Korea, and in the United States. He later became assistant deputy commandant at Fort Leavenworth's Command and General Staff College. He earned several awards, including the Bronze Star, Meritorious Service Medal, and Army Commendation Medal with five oak leaf clusters. (Courtesy of Orville Butts.)

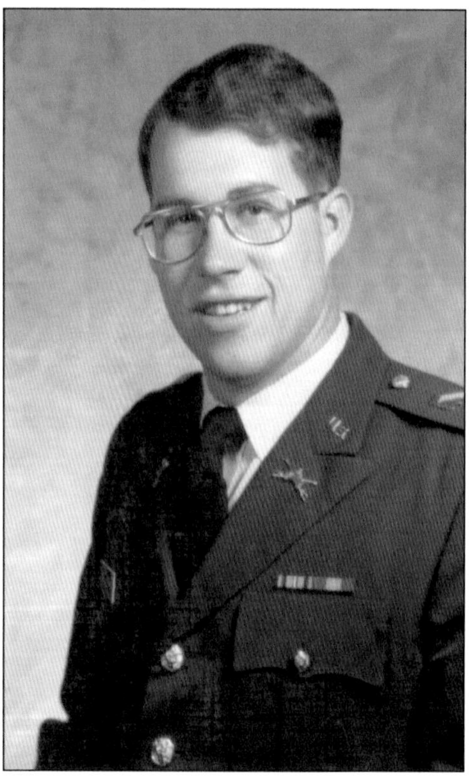

Lt. Col. Tom Smith was commissioned into the army in 1970. He served in Germany and Korea in addition to several stateside posts. At Fort Leavenworth, he taught students and wrote doctrine. He has served on the Lansing Planning Commission and is currently a Ward 4 city council member. (Courtesy of Tom Smith.)

Petty Officer 1st Class Forrest Holdeman served in the navy from 1960 to 1964. He also served in the Kansas National Guard and the naval air reserve. Holdeman served in the Persian Gulf War on the USS *America*. He received a number of medals, including the Navy Good Conduct Medal and Naval Reserve Meritorious Service Medal. He is a member of several organizations, including the Veterans of Foreign Wars, American Legion, Lansing Lions, and Lansing Historical Society. (Courtesy of Forrest Holdeman.)

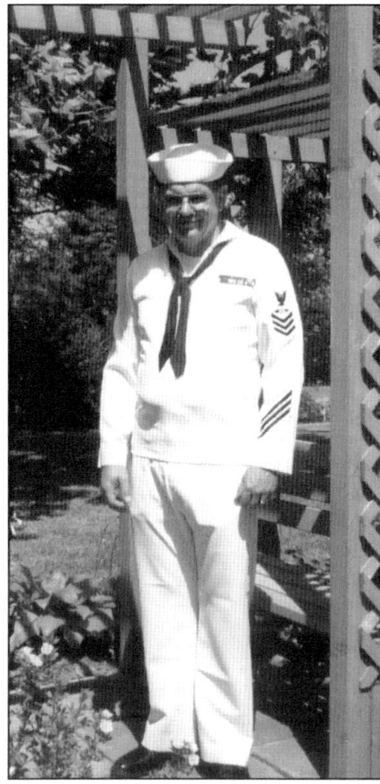

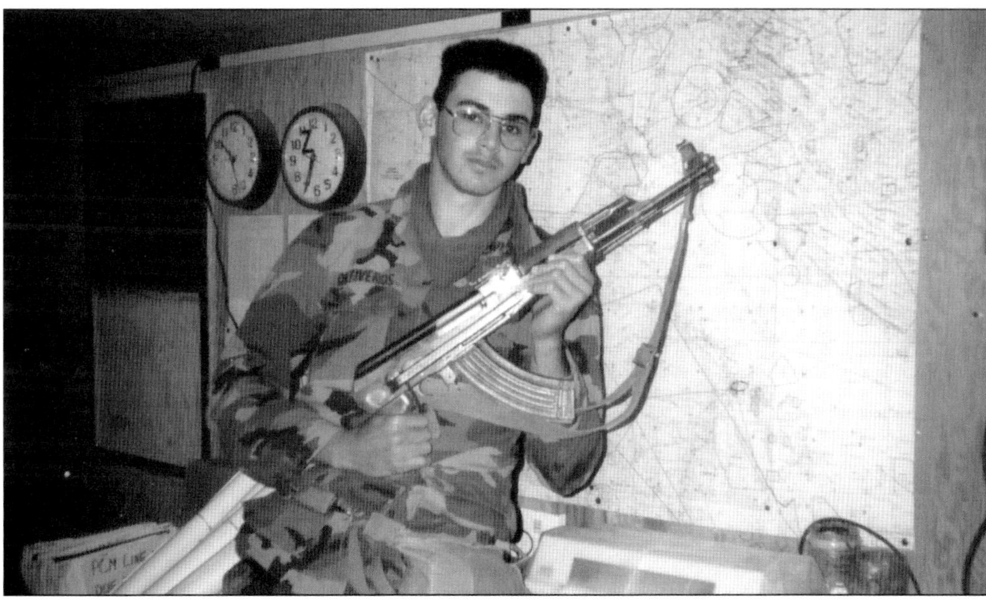

Sgt. Benjamin Ontiveros joined the army in 1989. He served in operations Desert Shield and Desert Storm. As an intelligence analyst, he received raw intelligence data and forwarded pertinent information on to commanders. He also served as a physical security specialist. He received the Army Commendation Award and the Liberation of Kuwait Medal. He left the military in 1996 and is now a captain in the Lansing Police Department. (Courtesy of Benjamin Ontiveros.)

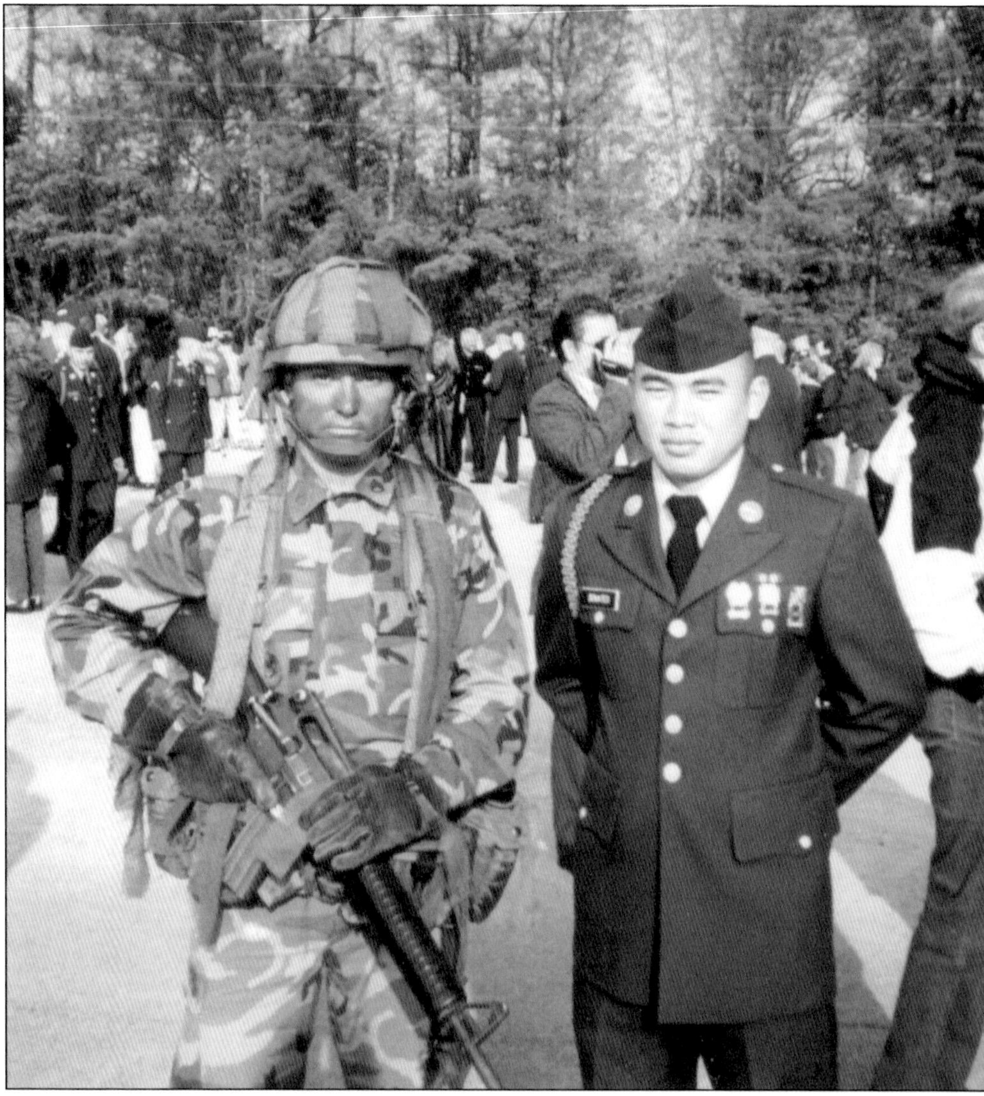

Born in the Philippines, Specialist E4 Richard DeMateo (right) served in the 25th Infantry Division from 1997 to 2000. He served in Hawaii, Georgia, Louisiana, and Japan. He received the Expert Infantry Badge, Army Commendation Medal, Overseas Medal, Service Ribbon, and two Army Achievement Medals. DeMateo is currently a patrol officer with the Lansing Police Department. He coaches fourth-, fifth-, and sixth-grade basketball. (Courtesy of Richard DeMateo.)

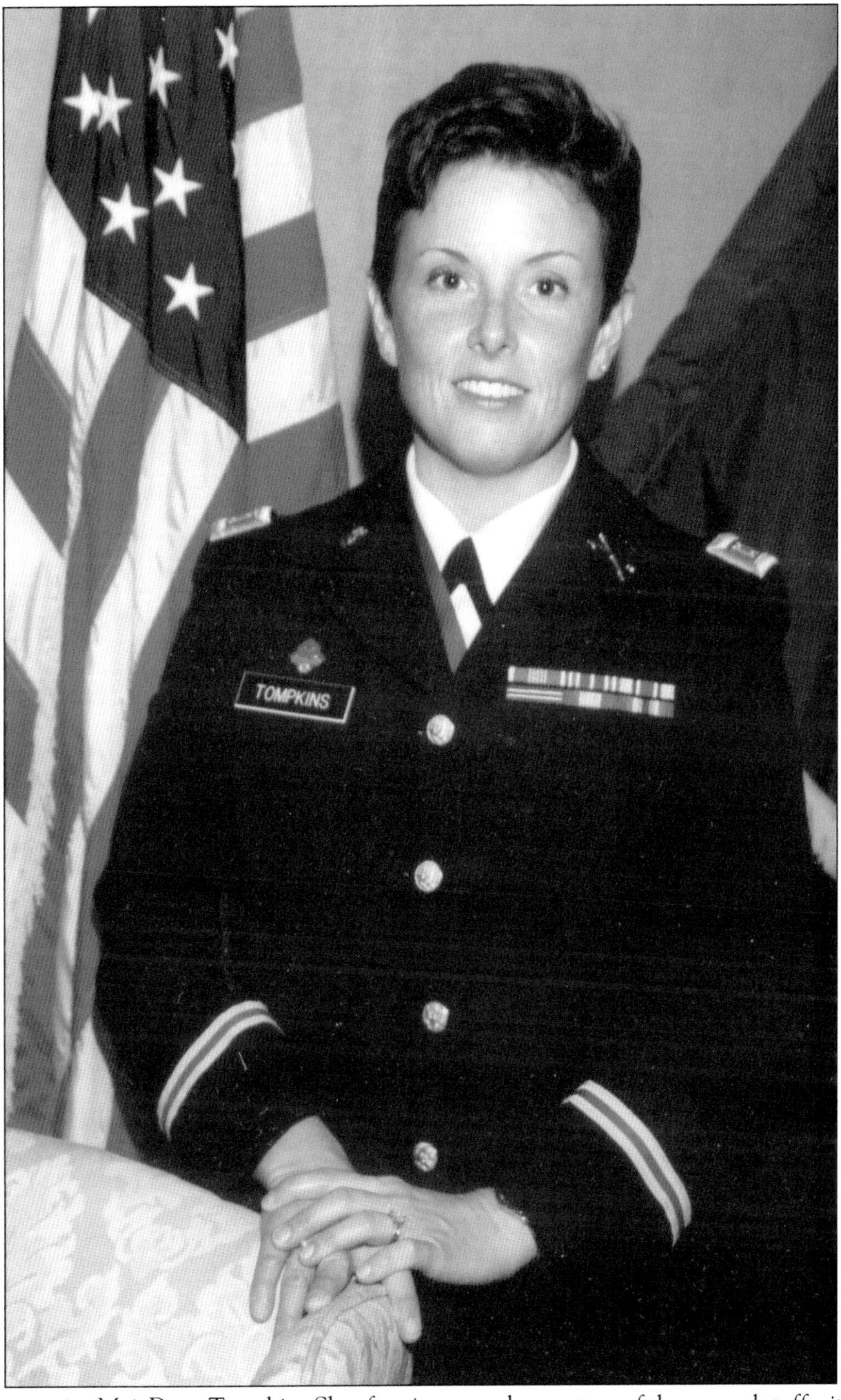

Lansing native Maj. Dana Tompkins Shopfner is currently secretary of the general staff with the 35th Infantry Division headquarters company in Kosovo. Shopfner became the first female field artillery commander in the Kansas Army National Guard. She has previously served in Bosnia, in part of the former Yugoslavia, and in the Balkans. (Courtesy of Verlin Tompkins.)

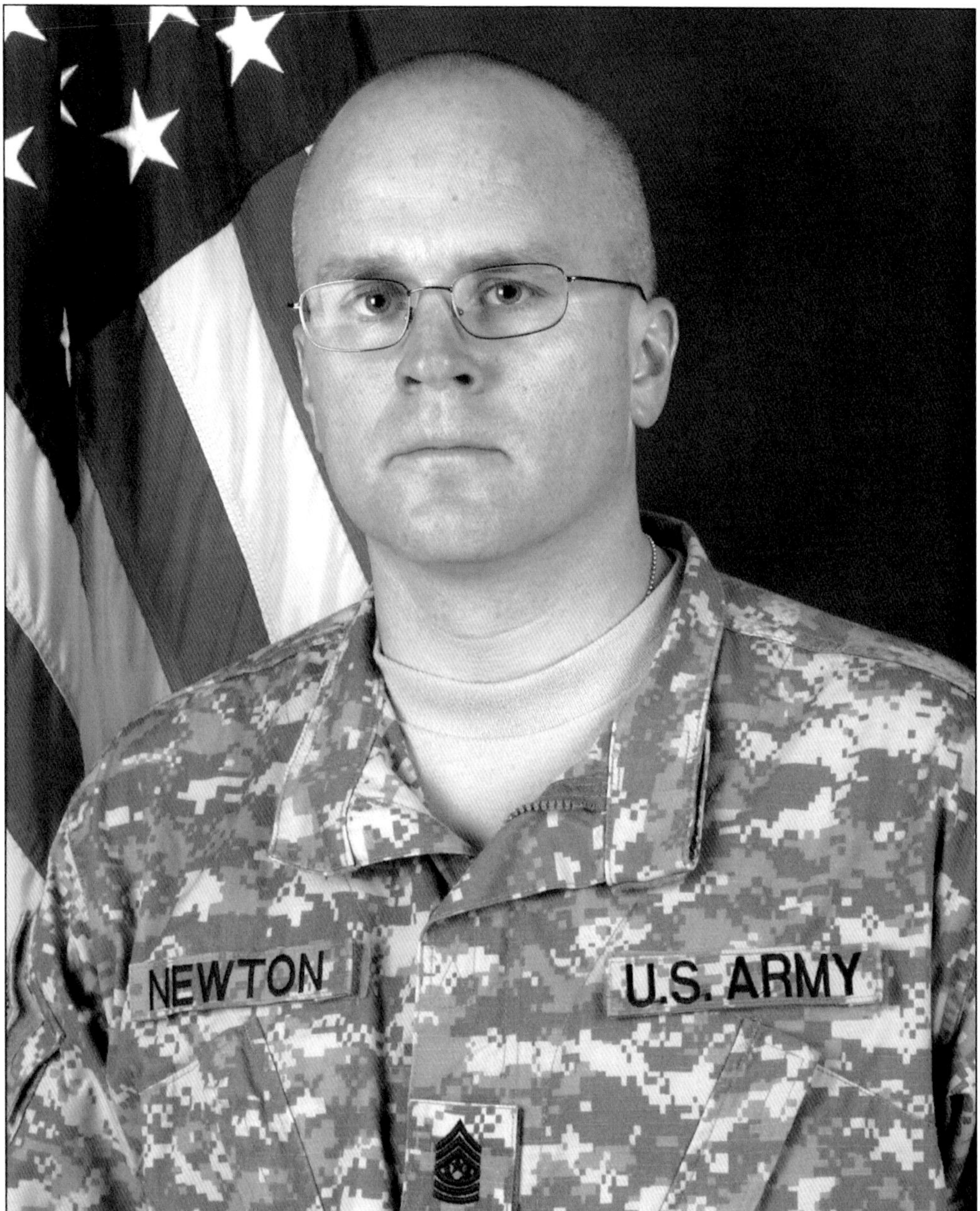

Command Sgt. Maj. Timothy Newton served in the Persian Gulf War and is currently stationed with the 287th Sustainment Brigade at Wichita. He received several awards, including the Bronze Star, Kuwait Liberation Medals, and Kansas National Guard Service Medal. Since 2002, he has served as principal at Lansing Elementary School. He is a member of several organizations, including Kiwanis Club, United School Administrators, and Veterans of Foreign Wars. (Courtesy of Timothy Newton.)

Eight

Incorporation and Expansion

In the fall of 1899, the Leavenworth County commissioners received a petition for the incorporation of Lansing. The commissioners denied the request because the petition only named Lansing when the town consisted of two entities—Lansing and Progress. On February 5, 1900, another attempt to incorporate Lansing as a city of the third class was made. Attorneys from the Atchison, Topeka, and Santa Fe Railroad company appeared at the meeting and requested the commissioners table the petition until they could present an argument against the incorporation of Lansing. Other opponents of the incorporation petition included H. T. Green, who owned a large farm east of Lansing, and other railroad companies that would be inside the city limits as described by the petition.

The *Leavenworth Times* reported the petition itself spanned 15 feet in length and contained 260 names from Lansing and 255 names from Progress. The petitioners claimed the signatures represented the majority of the electors of the two towns, which entitled them to incorporation. The railroads fought the petition because they believed their taxes would increase. The motion failed because the petitioners did not properly publish the notices of the proposed action. The law required the petition be published in the limits of the town or towns requesting incorporation. A local paper published the petition; however, the distribution of the paper was within Progress only.

Decades passed before residents succeeded in incorporating Lansing. The first Lansing government election took place on July 14, 1959. George K. Caraway won the race for mayor with 219 votes out of 228 cast. The electorate voted Robert Hatfield as police judge, and the five council members were Edward G. Hamler, Jacob M. Henchek, John C. Kendall, Oscar G. Lichte, and Eugene F. Young. Caraway called for a special meeting on July 28, 1959, at Lansing High School. The council adopted rules of order and voted to join the League of Kansas Municipalities. The council appointed John Murray as city attorney, Melvin Parson as city clerk, and Helen McCarthy as city treasurer.

Through the city government, improvements were made to Lansing's infrastructure, resulting in an increase in population and businesses. Today the city council includes a mayor and eight council members.

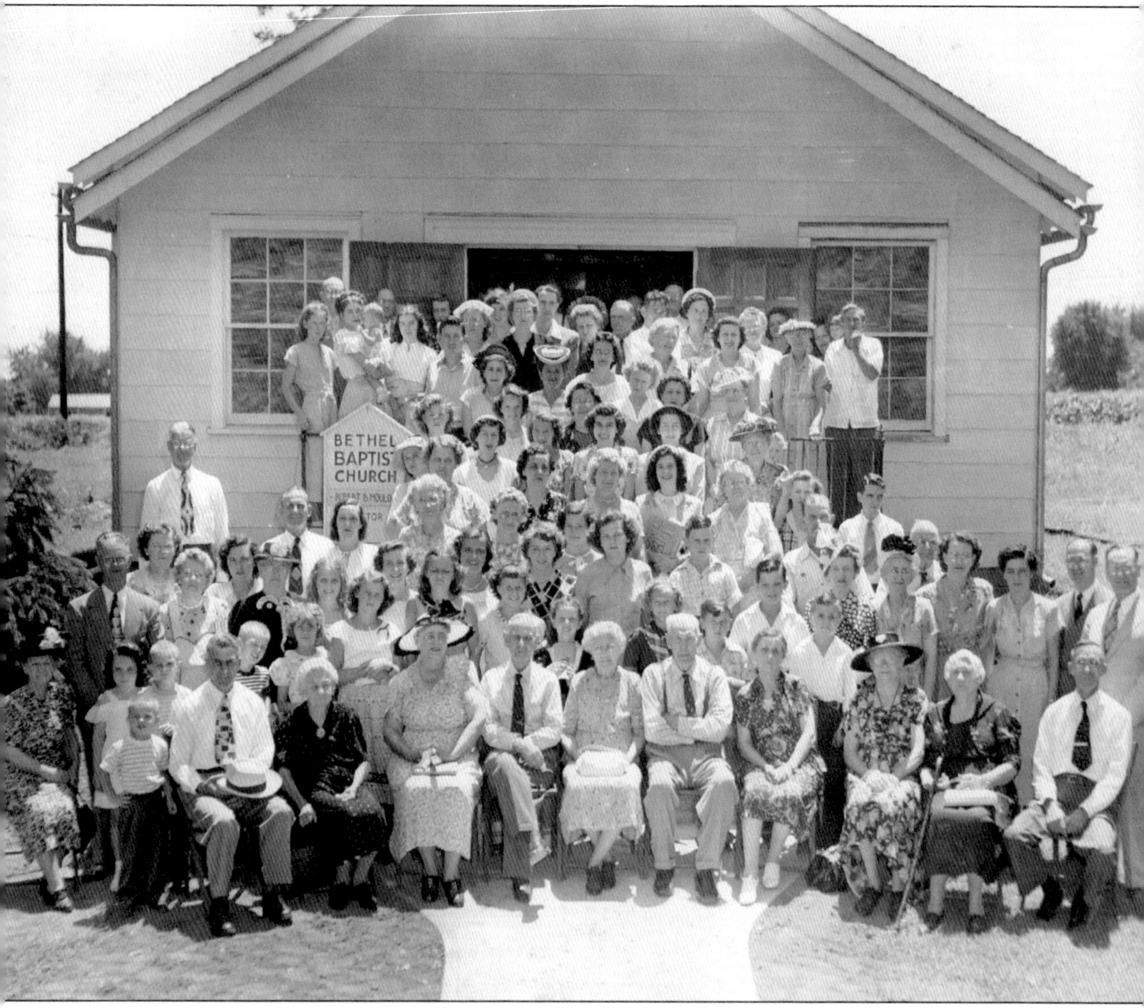

This Bethel Baptist Church congregation photograph includes (1st row) Rupert Edmonds (2nd), Mrs. Patterson (3rd), Mrs. Lashley (4th), Mr. Lashley (5th), Mrs. Cook (6th), Mr. Courtney (7th), and Mrs. Courtney (8th); (2nd row) Juanita Russell (4th), Carol Eagles (5th), Barbara Rogers (6th), Twyla Walker (9th), Karen Linaweaver (10th), Jerry Linaweaver (11th), Lester Russell (12th), Pauline Lyens (14th), and Irene Edmonds (15th); (3rd row) Mrs. Schafer (2nd), Jeanie Rogers (4th), Nadine Swink (5th), Judy Rogers (6th), Carolyn Hobbs (7th), Joann Camp (8th), and Paul O'Brien (9th); (4th row) Carol Meeker (2nd), Ralph Rogers (3rd), Mrs. Julia Rogers (4th), Dorothy Dean (6th), Ralph Spain (7th), Martha Swink (9th), Mary Schafer (10th), and Reverend Mould (11th); (5th row) Alma Spain (2nd), Frances Courtney (3rd), Billie Jean Wade (4th), and Bernice Swink (5th); (6th row) Janice Edmonds (2nd), Jeanie Hobbs (3rd), and Patricia Edmonds (5th); (7th row) Margaret Fisher (1st), Ethel Russell (2nd), Geraldine McCormick (4th), and Louise Eagles (6th); (8th row) Joann Wendel (1st), Mary Linaweaver (3rd), Buelah Camp (4th), and Shirley Bullard (5th); (9th row) Marilyn Walker (1st), Mrs. Bill Potter and baby (2nd), Betty Potter (3rd), and Leroy Walker (4th); (10th row) Mrs. Potter (6th), Jack Potter (7th), Pete Kley (8th), Irene Kley (9th), and Mrs. VanMeter (10th). Opal Hobbs is next to the right door. (Courtesy of the Lansing Historical Museum.)

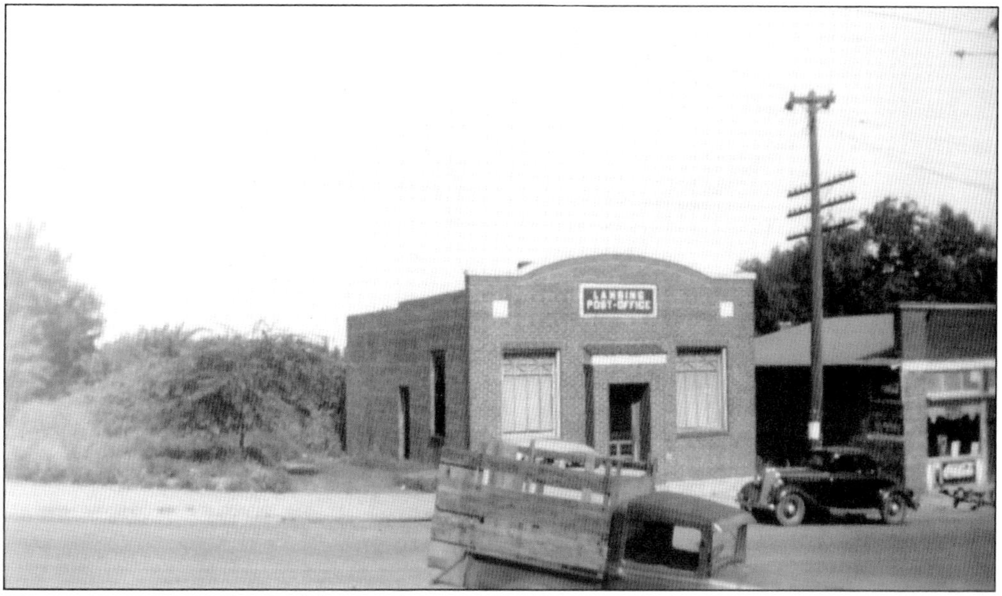

The Lansing Post Office building is photographed here around 1930. Lansing residents had to pick up their mail at the post office since the houses did not have numbers. In order to get mail delivery, the Lions Club formed a committee to number the houses. Members sold numbers to residents, and those funds purchased street signs in 1960. The building also served as a bank and Lansing City Hall and is currently Kern Real Estate Appraisal. (Courtesy of the Lansing Historical Museum.)

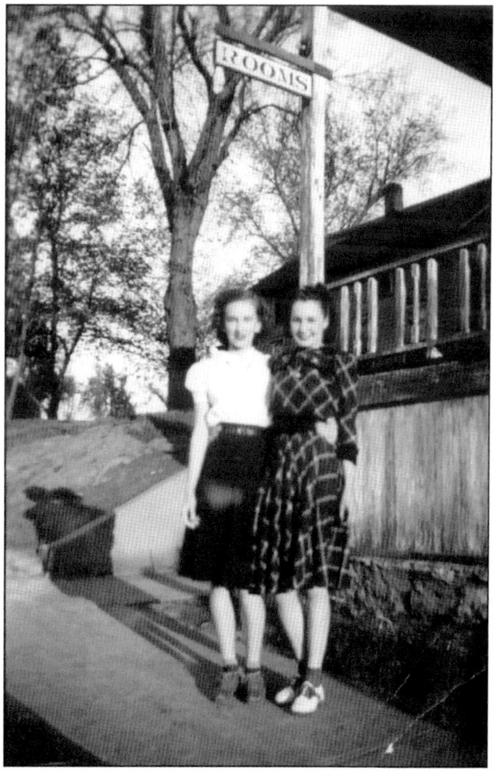

Frances Sanders and Sybil Brown are pictured in front of the Lansing Hotel that used to stand at 132 East Kay Street. The building had three floors and a basement and was the tallest building in Lansing. Many political rallies were held on the hotel's porch in the 1930s. (Courtesy of the Lansing Historical Museum.)

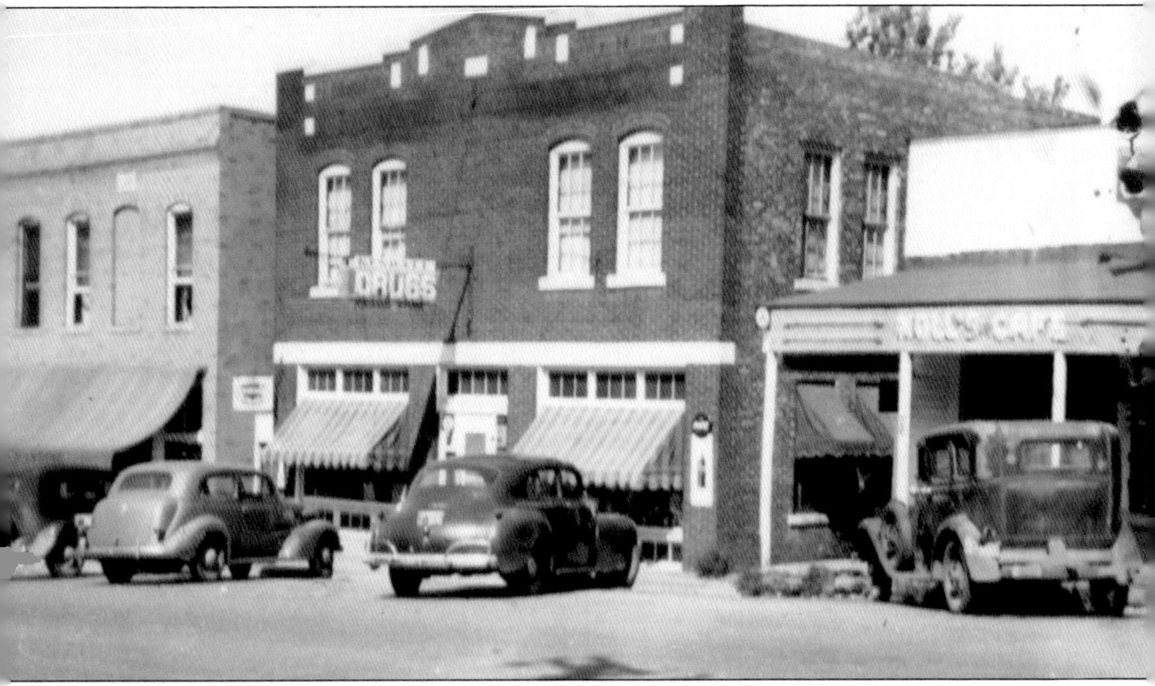

These buildings were destroyed when Highway 73/Kansas 7 expanded to four lanes in the 1960s, including Campbell's Grocery (left), Kendall Drug Store (center), and Noll's Café (right). (Courtesy of the Lansing Historical Museum.)

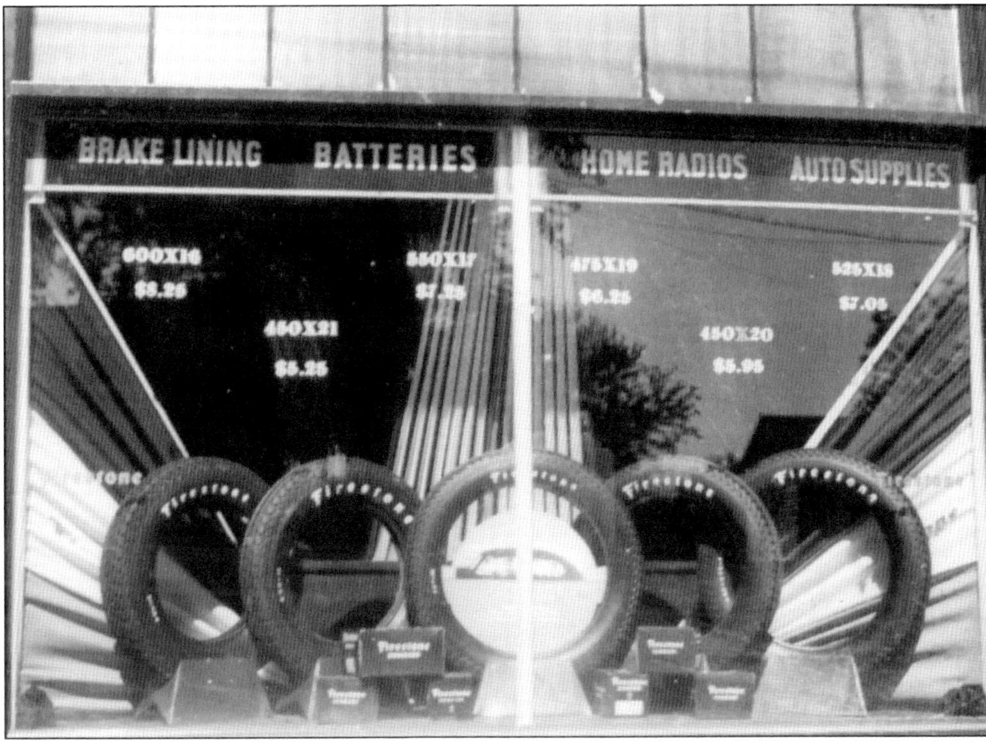

Hazel and Ernie Wendell owned this store on the west side of Main Street. The garage did many car repairs, including bodywork by Arnold Wendell. In addition, they fixed small appliances, sold gasoline, and had the fire alarm phone. Hazel also scheduled the school bus routes for Lansing. Ernie served as a charter member of the Lions Club. (Courtesy of the Lansing Historical Museum.)

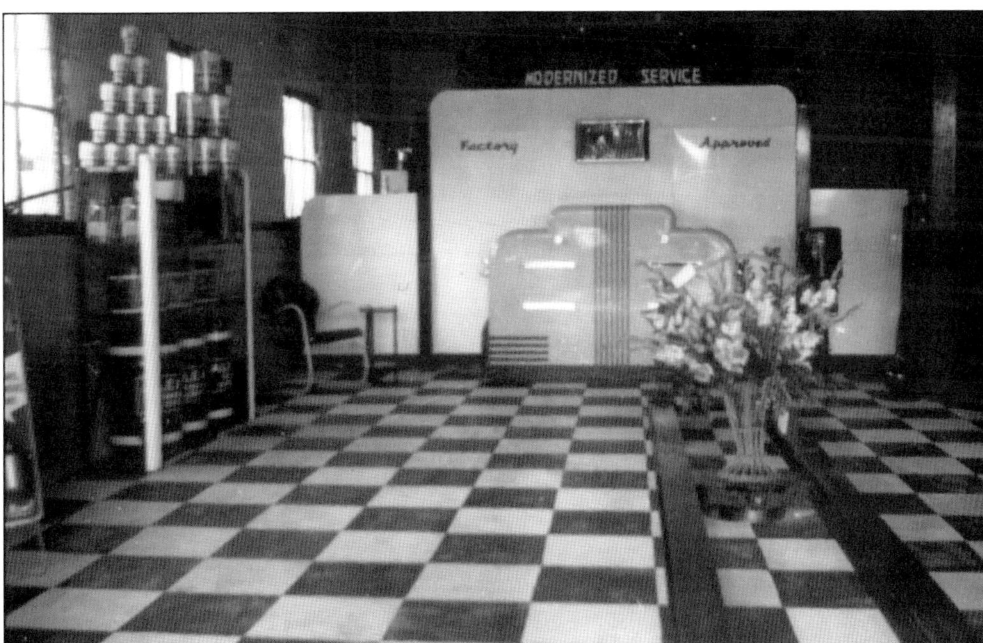

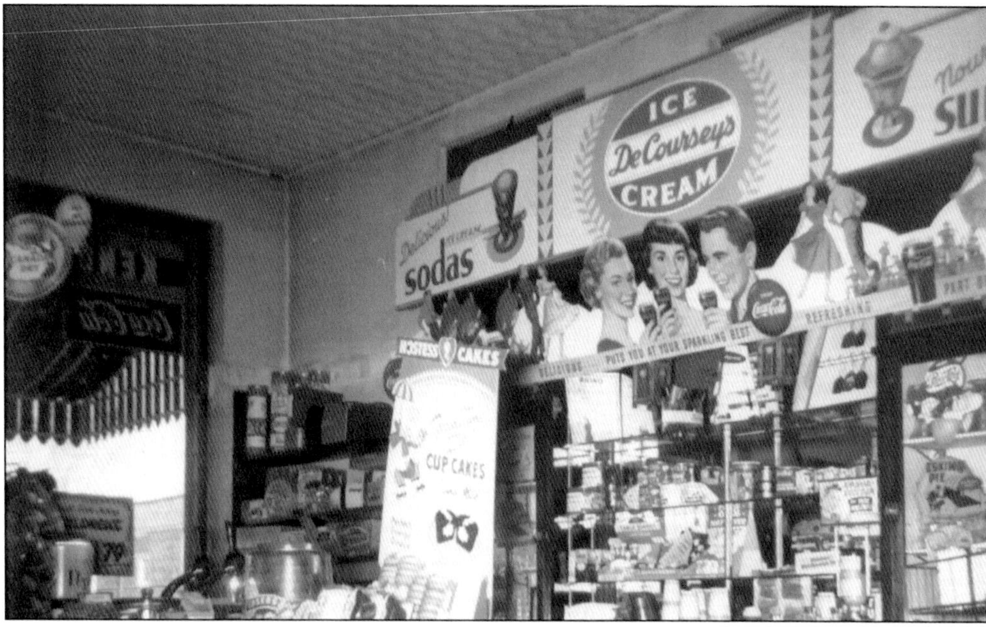

John Kendall purchased the drugstore from Audry Purcell in 1946. In addition to pharmaceuticals, one could purchase nickel ice-cream cones and drinks, such as a Green River, at the store. Families also purchased schoolbooks from Kendall's. This picture depicts the soda fountain inside the store. The building also had Dr. Robert Moore's office and Woodman Hall on the top floor. In the 1930s, a telephone office and apartments could be found in the building. (Courtesy of the Lansing Historical Museum.)

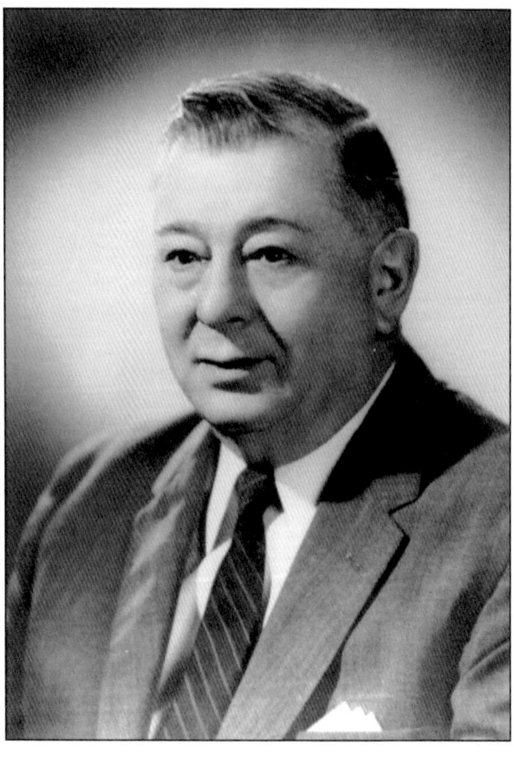

Moore practiced medicine in Lansing until April 1967. He served as clerk for the Lansing Rural High School and president of the Leavenworth Saddle Club in the 1950s. (Courtesy of the Lansing Historical Museum.)

In 1960, Gene Young placed the first "Welcome to Lansing" sign at the city limits. A second sign replaced the first 20 years later. However, it was destroyed by fire. In 2007, Young installed a third welcome sign that features the logos of local service groups. The origins of the city's motto are unknown; however, the motto has rung true throughout the years. This is the first of the three signs. (Courtesy of the Lansing Historical Museum.)

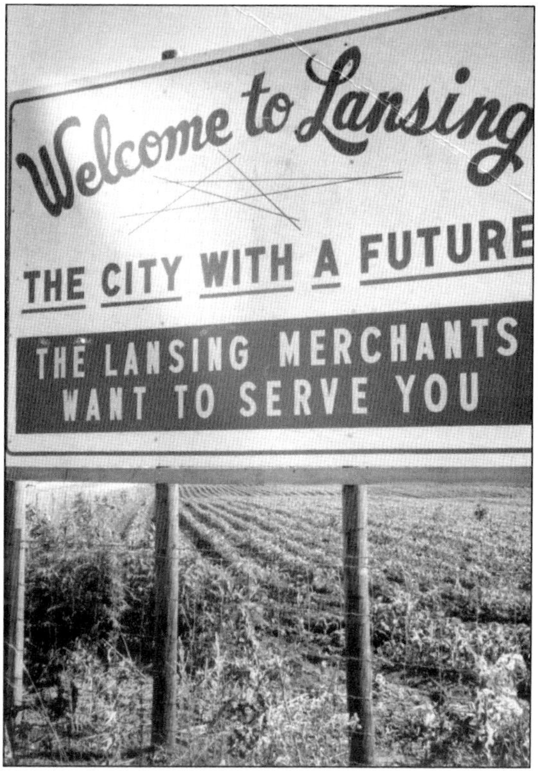

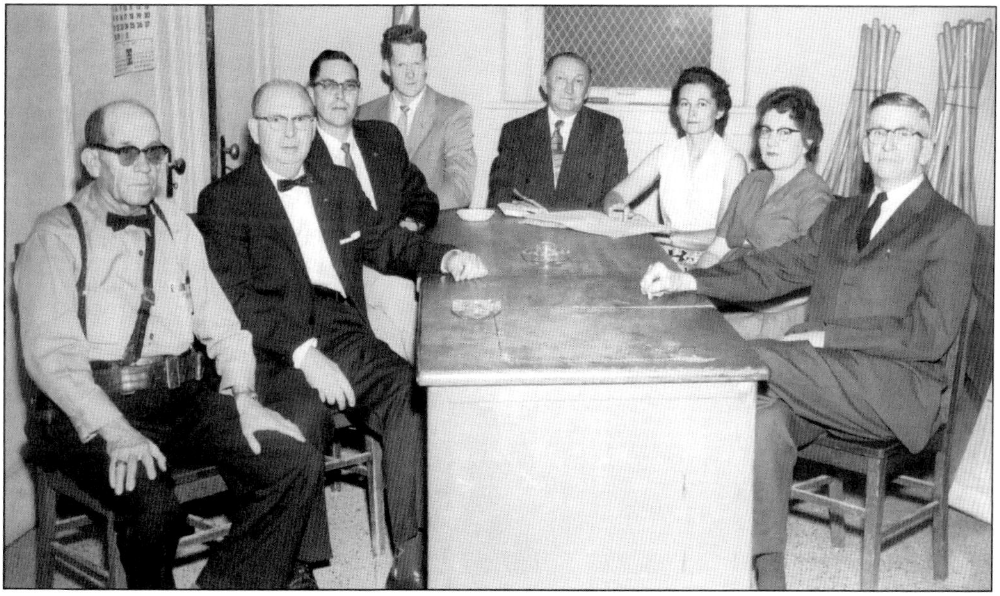

City officers meet at a 1961 Lansing City Council meeting. From left to right are police officer Jack Potter, Kendall, council member Jacob Henchek, Gene Young, Mayor George Caraway, city clerk Francis Graham, city treasurer Helen McCarthy, and council member Oscar Litchte. Caraway served as mayor of Lansing from July 15, 1959, to April 13, 1965. The original council consisted of a mayor and five council members. Today the city council has a mayor and eight council members representing four wards. (Courtesy of the Lansing Historical Museum.)

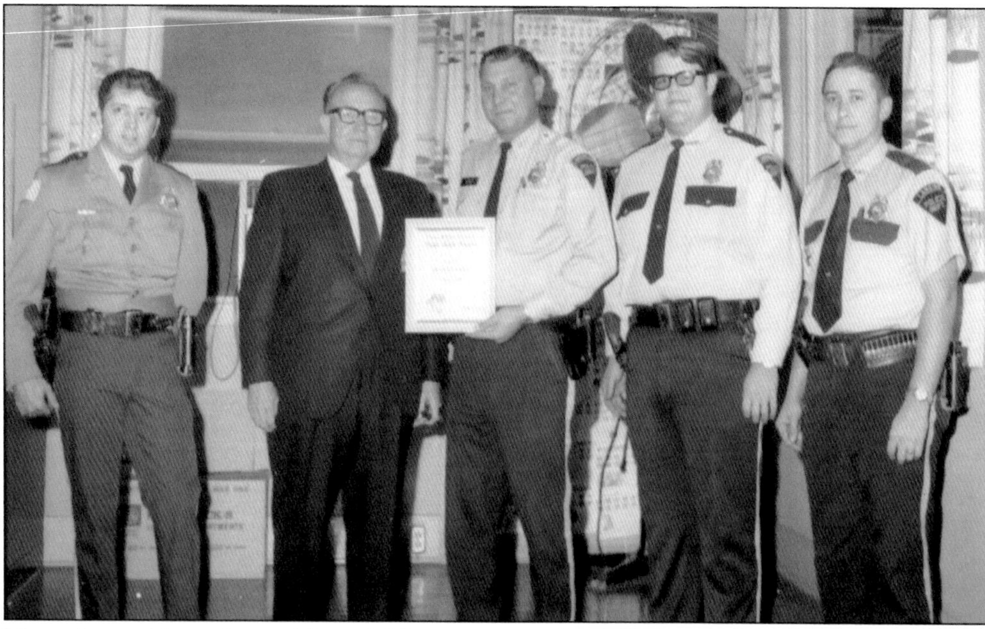

Mayor James Hayes (second from left) gives police chief Arthur Graf a certificate, and Rory Pierce and Gary Kenton stand to the right. The photograph was taken between 1971 and 1973. The city's police department started out small with Robert Hatfield as the first police judge and officers using their own cars for transportation. Today the Lansing Police Department has 17 full-time officers and four reserve officers. (Courtesy of the Lansing Historical Museum.)

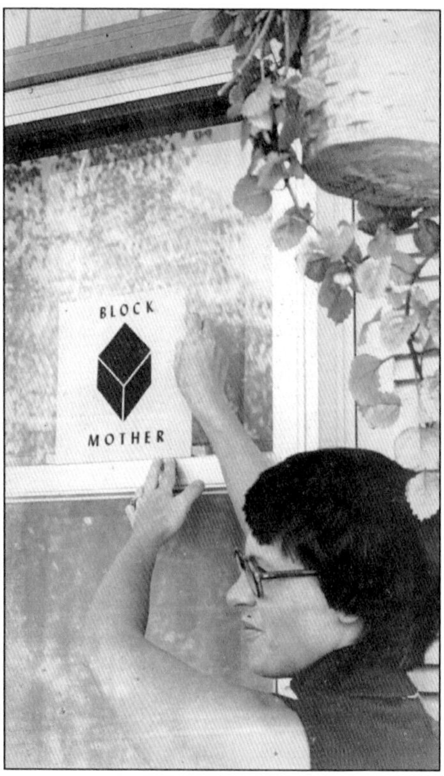

In 1976, Pat Schimke prepared for the school year by placing a "Block Mother" sign in her window on Nina Street. Schimke and several mothers volunteered to help children walking to and from area schools. Nancy Sneed, president of the Lansing Educational Trio, and Bev Williamson established the program. (Courtesy of the Lansing Historical Museum.)

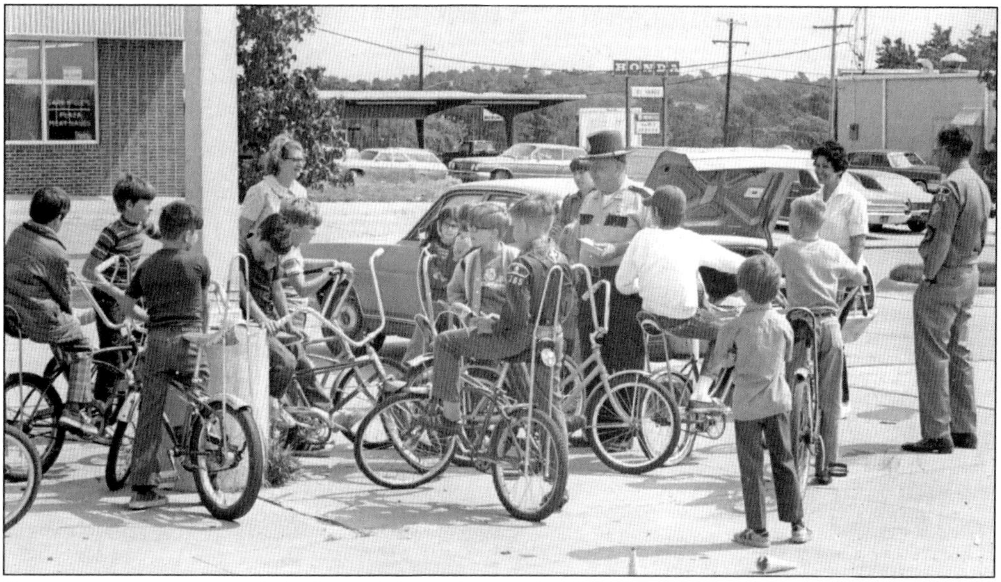

Scouts congregate at a Cub Scout bike rodeo at the Holiday Plaza in the late 1960s or early 1970s. The Scouts brought their bikes to be inspected and then completed an obstacle course on them. (Courtesy of the Lansing Historical Museum.)

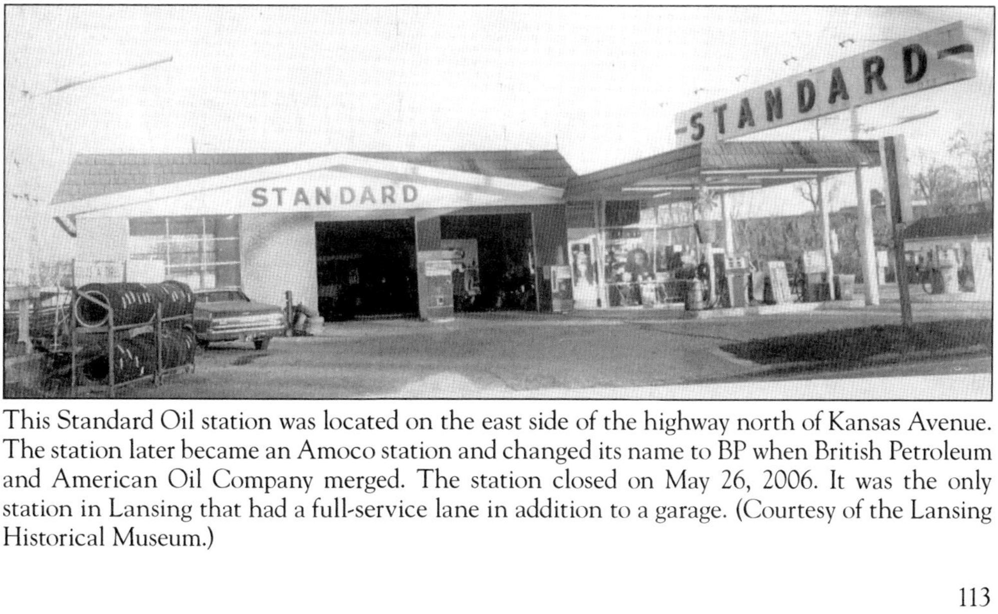

This Standard Oil station was located on the east side of the highway north of Kansas Avenue. The station later became an Amoco station and changed its name to BP when British Petroleum and American Oil Company merged. The station closed on May 26, 2006. It was the only station in Lansing that had a full-service lane in addition to a garage. (Courtesy of the Lansing Historical Museum.)

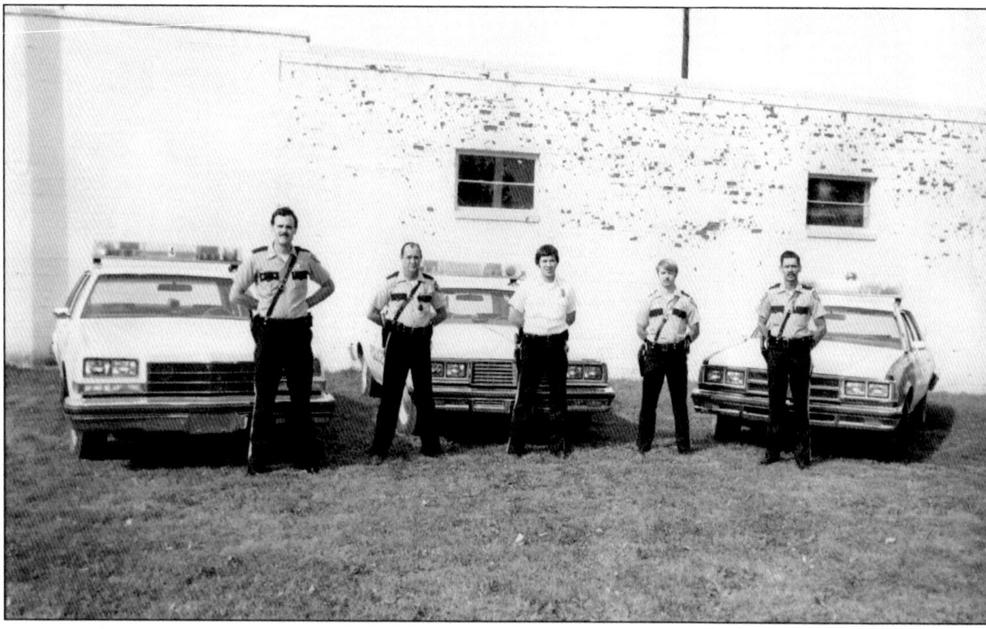

In 1979, the Lansing Police Department had five officers on patrol. This picture was taken by the old fire department on the corner of Kansas Avenue. From left to right are officer Wayne Buford, Sgt. Bob Thomas, Lt. Tommy Powell, officer Michael Smith, and officer Jim Hill. In four years, Smith became Lansing's chief of police and served in that capacity for 16 years. Since 1999, he has served as Lansing's city administrator. (Courtesy of Michael Smith.)

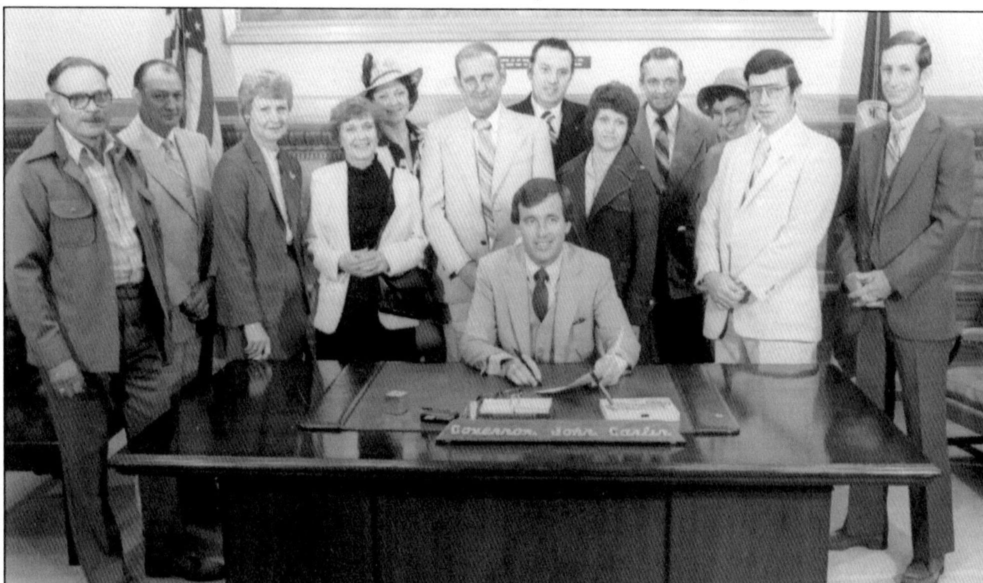

When Lansing's population surpassed 5,000, it became eligible to become a city of the second class. To celebrate the milestone, many witnessed Gov. John Carlin signing a proclamation making Lansing a city of the second class on June 2, 1982. Pictured from left to right are Joe Black, Bob Thomas, Vi Dooley, Ruth Elliot, Virginia Mann, Charles Mann, Lee Koeler, Mrs. Koeler, Kenneth Bernard, Marliese Bernard, Mike Wilcott, and Fred Massey. (Courtesy of Michael Smith.)

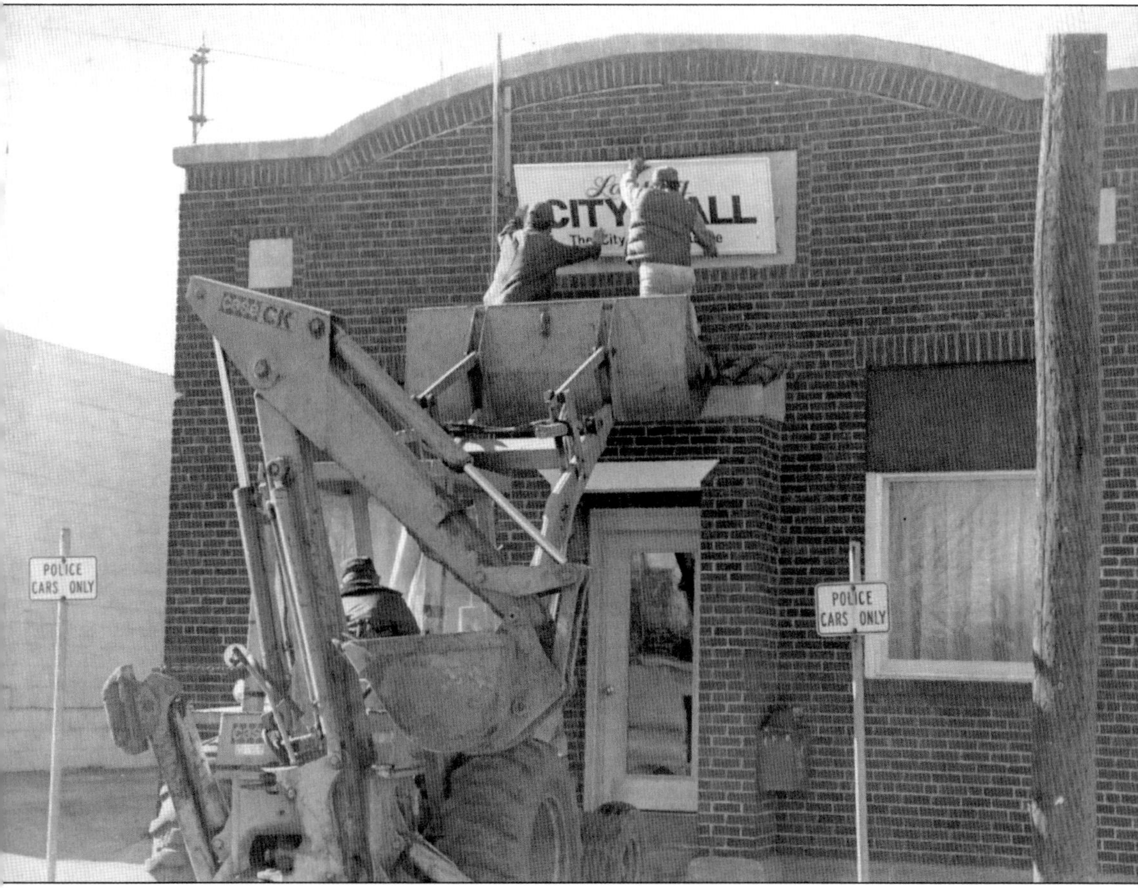

From 1959 to 1990, the building at 108 South Main Street served as Lansing's city hall. Lansing's growing population needed a new city hall, and in 1990, the doors at the new Lansing City Hall at 800 First Terrace opened. The new city hall houses the city's administration, police department, city council, and municipal court chamber. It also houses the Lansing Community Center. (Courtesy of Michael Smith.)

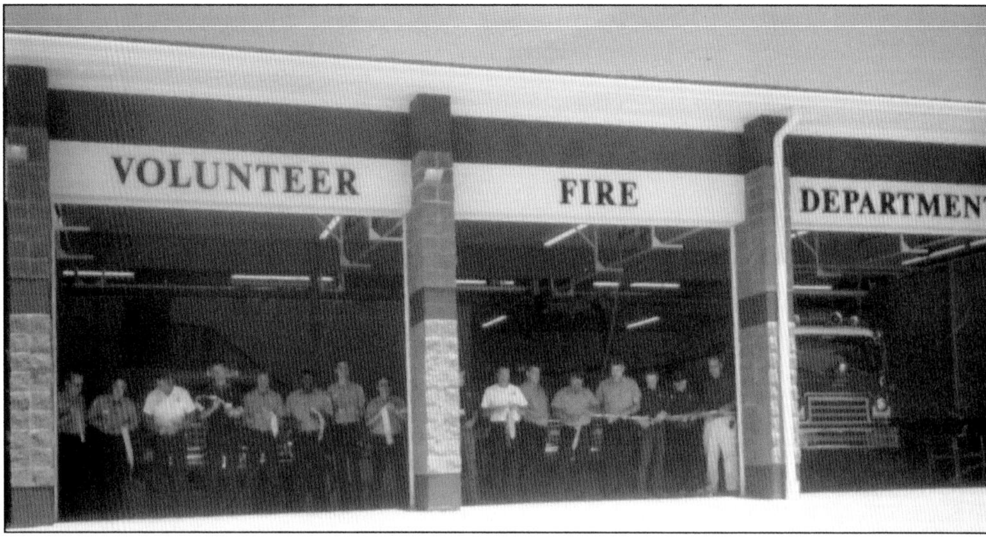

In 1951, the Delaware Township Fire Department building was constructed on the corner of Highway 73 and East Kansas Avenue. As the city of Lansing grew, the fire department had to expand to meet the needs of the community. Three additions were added on to the building in 1961, 1980, and 1985. Finally, a new station had to be built. Members of the fire department and inmates from the Lansing Correctional Facility constructed the new building behind the old one. Upon completion of the new building, a crew demolished the old fire station. On June 24, 2001, the fire department held an open house to celebrate the completion of the new building. In addition to the truck bays, the building has offices and a conference room. Today Leavenworth County Fire District No. 1 has five paid firefighters and 26 volunteers. (Courtesy of Rick Huhn.)

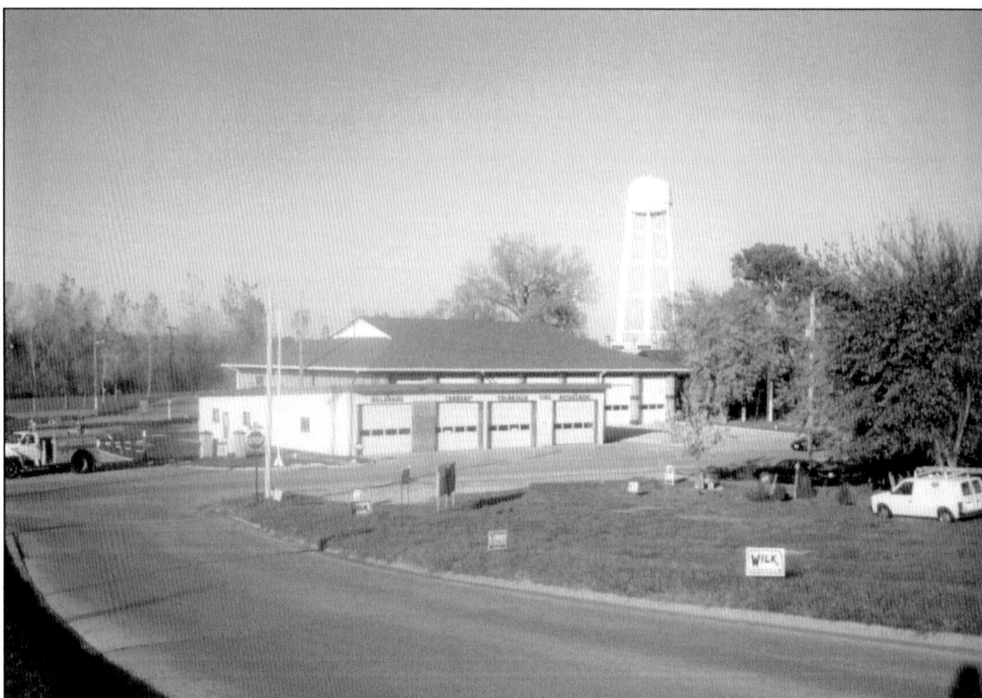

Nine

THE CITY WITH A FUTURE

In recent years, Lansing has lived up to its motto, "the City with a Future." In 2007, the city of Lansing and the Kansas Department of Transportation completed a $17 million Main Street System Enhancement project. The project added enhanced turn lanes, lighting, and other safety features to one of the busiest north–south highways in Kansas. This infrastructure improvement has made Lansing an attractive location for businesses. In the past few years, Carriage Hills Crossing, the Lansing Depot Shops, and Eisenhower Crossing have all been built with businesses moving in. As of the spring of 2008, preparations are underway for the 34-acre Lansing Towne Center Project, which will have 200,000 square feet of retail space.

Lansing's two industrial parks, Lansing Business Center and Larkin Industrial Park, are located on Gilman Road in south Lansing. New tenants moved in this past year and offer a variety of options for potential development.

In the fall of 2008, the new Lansing Elementary School opened its doors to students and teachers. The school is one of the largest in the state and has a capacity for more than 900 students. The new facility features computer labs, a gymnasium with bleacher seating for 600 spectators, and other amenities that provide a 21st-century learning environment.

In addition to the elementary school, Lansing High School has a new auditorium that seats 900 people. The stage is large enough for a 150-piece band to perform. The backstage area has makeup rooms, storage space, and restroom facilities. A large commons area with amenities connects the auditorium to the gymnasium.

The Kansas Regional Prisons Museum is a planned project, which will be located behind the current Lansing Historical Museum. Leavenworth County is the only county in the United States that has a military, state, federal, and private prison. The museum will feature the unique history of the area prisons and educate the public about the corrections industry. The museum's educational program will be an asset to educators' curriculums. Lansing has a bright future ahead as a growing community with excellent schools, neighborhoods, and businesses for the citizens to enjoy.

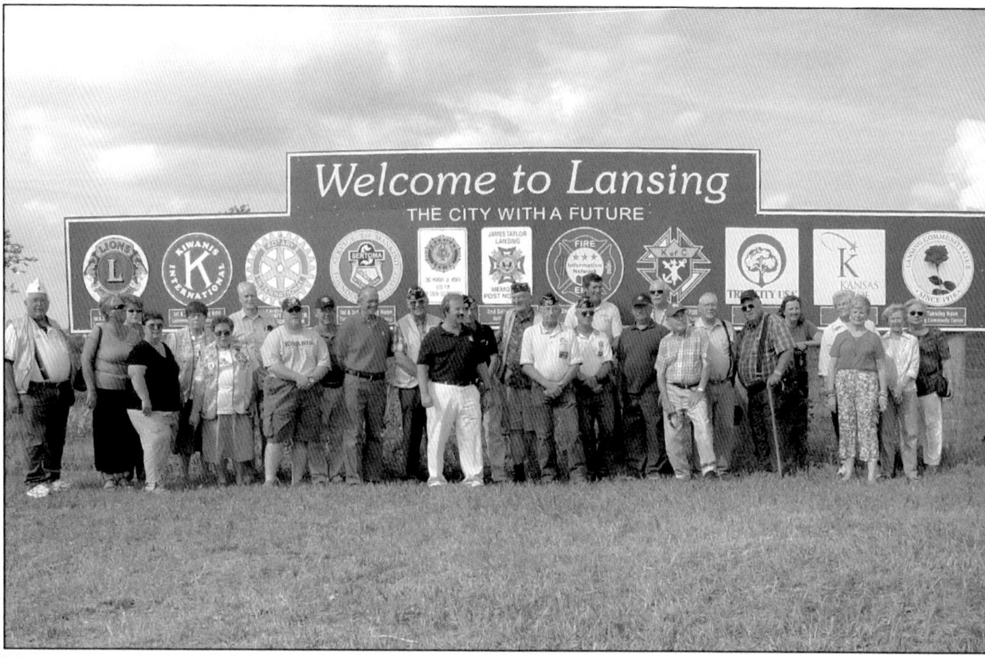

Visitors traveling north on Highway 73 will be welcomed by a new "Welcome to Lansing" sign. Eleven service organizations whose members have volunteered countless hours of community service are featured on the sign along with the city of Lansing's motto, "the City with a Future." (Courtesy of the City of Lansing.)

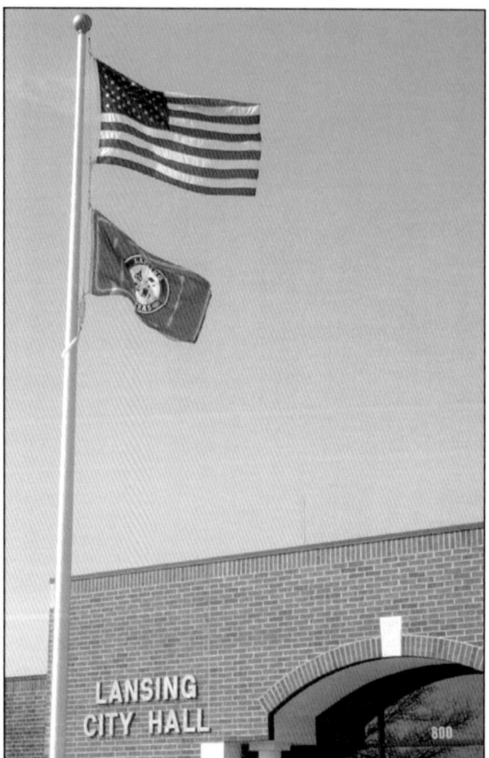

The City of Lansing staff consists of over 70 employees who are proud to serve the community. From snow removal in the winter to maintaining the city parks in the summer, Lansing's employees strive to provide excellent services for citizens. The administrative offices and police department are located in city hall. The Lansing City Council meetings and municipal court sessions are also held in the building. (Courtesy of the City of Lansing.)

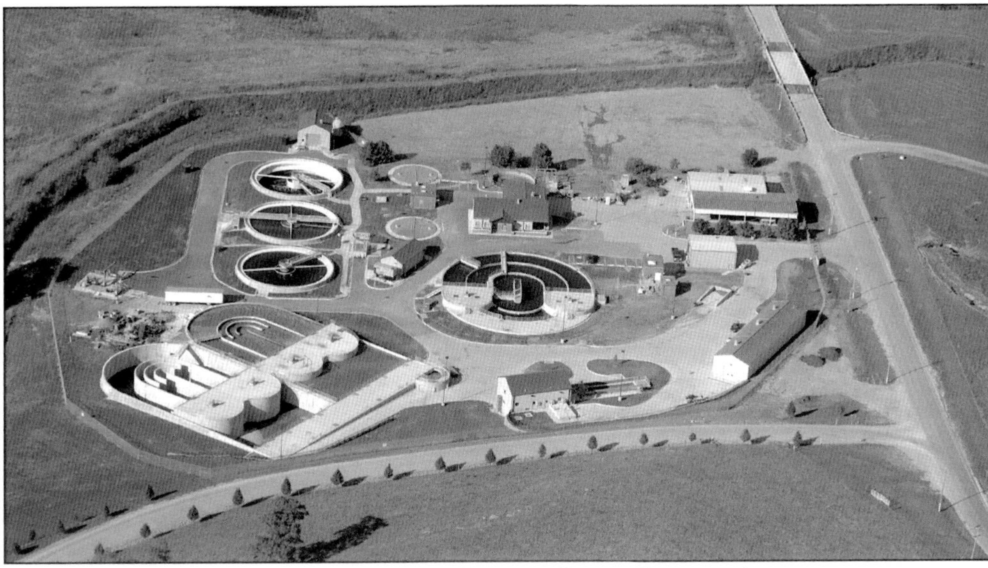

In 1981, the City of Lansing decided to build a 1.4 million-gallons-per-day wastewater treatment plant at the confluence of Nine Mile and Seven Mile Creeks. It proved to be an ideal location, as all the wastewater generated inside the city limits is able to flow by gravity to the facility. In 2006, the city completed a $15.8 million expansion and upgrade to the wastewater facility. This construction project was designed in November 2001, and construction began in September 2003. The project was completed in August 2006. The new facility has the capacity to treat 3.2 million gallons of water each day. (Courtesy of the City of Lansing.)

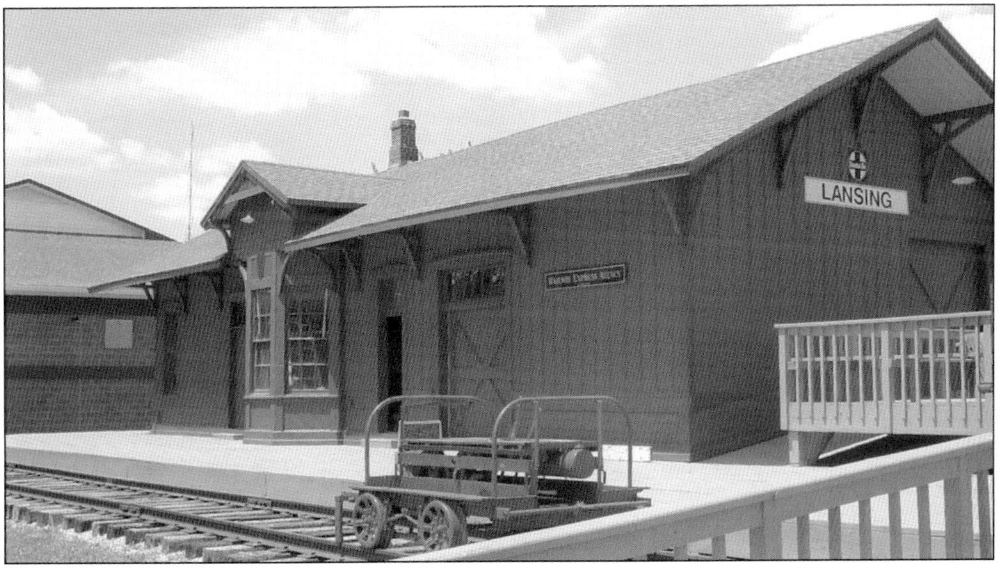

Demolition of Lansing's 1889 Santa Fe Railroad depot appeared evident in 1989. At that time, some enterprising Lansing citizens formed the Lansing Historical Society to save the depot from destruction. The depot was given to the society with the stipulation that it move the building from its original location. The Lansing Correctional Facility offered a location on its grounds, and the depot has resided there since 1992. The society restored the building to house the Lansing Historical Museum. The building is only one of two original public-commercial structures left of the original downtown. (Courtesy of the City of Lansing.)

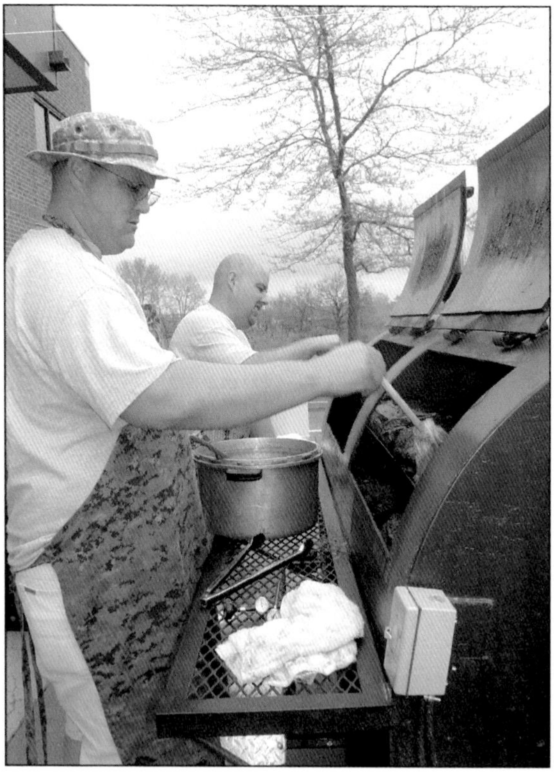

The annual Brew, Blues, and Bar-B-Q festival begins the first weekend of May. The festival hosts barbecue teams from the region to compete in a Kansas City Barbeque Society–sanctioned event. Bands take the stage to play blues music during the festivities. While listening to good music, visitors may participate in the people's choice event to vote for their favorite barbecue. (Courtesy of the City of Lansing.)

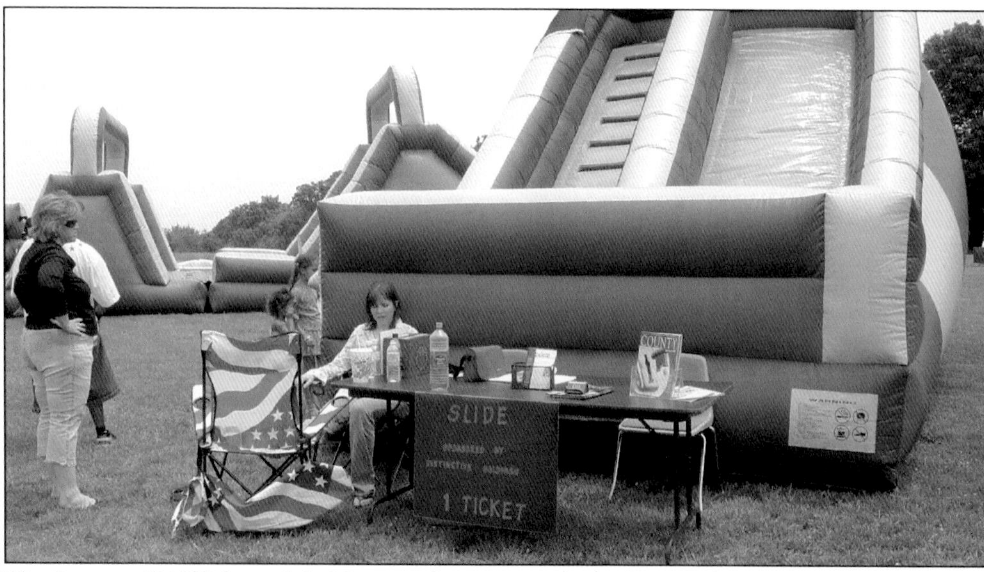

The Lansing DAZE festival, held in combination with the Brew, Blues, and Bar-B-Q, features a fun day of family activities, entertainment, displays, crafts, and great food. A favorite activity for children is the inflatable rides. The event features participation of many community organizations, including a car show, art show, and pancake breakfast. The festival comes to a close on Saturday with a dance and fireworks show. On Sunday, runners compete in the annual On the Run five-kilometer race, and cyclists compete in the Women's Criterium. (Courtesy of the City of Lansing.)

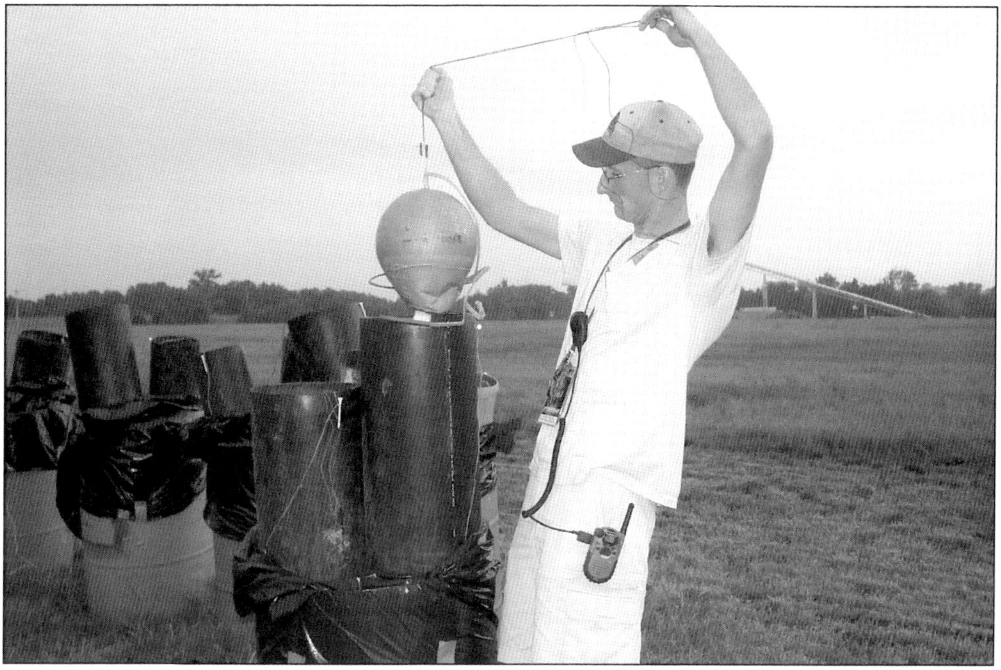

Every year, Lansing residents look forward to the Fourth of July fireworks show. At dusk, the audience is treated to a spectacular fireworks display set to music. Here Jamie Miller is preparing fireworks for a show. (Courtesy of the City of Lansing.)

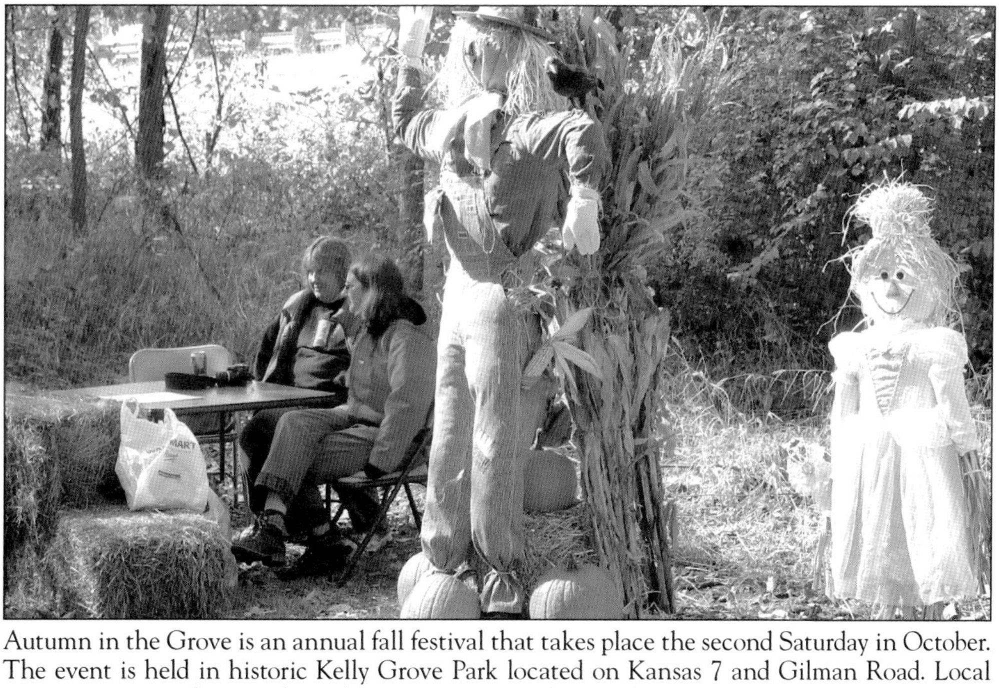

Autumn in the Grove is an annual fall festival that takes place the second Saturday in October. The event is held in historic Kelly Grove Park located on Kansas 7 and Gilman Road. Local organizations, crafters, and vendors participate in the fall-themed event. Festival participants can paint pumpkins, eat caramel apples, and buy produce from the farmers' market. (Courtesy of the City of Lansing.)

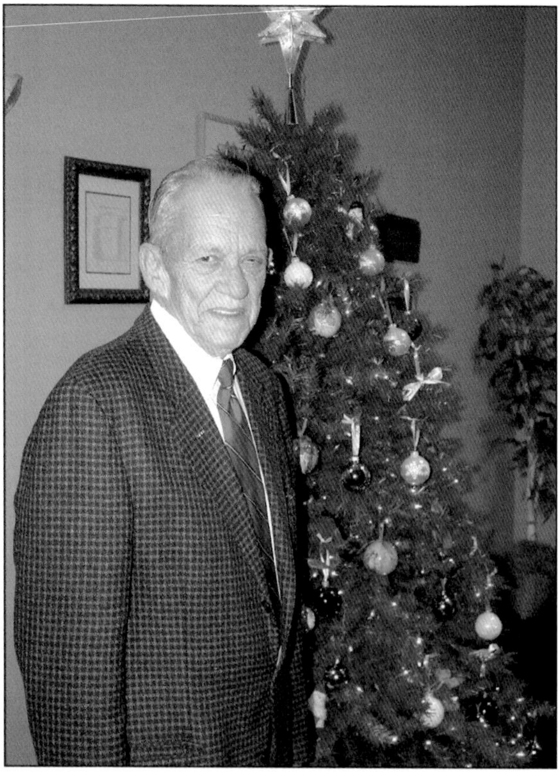

The annual Mayor's Christmas Tree Fund is a way for area residents, businesses, and community organizations to provide some Christmas cheer to the less fortunate. From area civic organizations, such as the Lions Club and the Kiwanis Club, to the Boy Scouts and Girl Scouts, the event continues to grow and collect toys, clothes, and food and raise funds for needy area families. (Courtesy of the City of Lansing.)

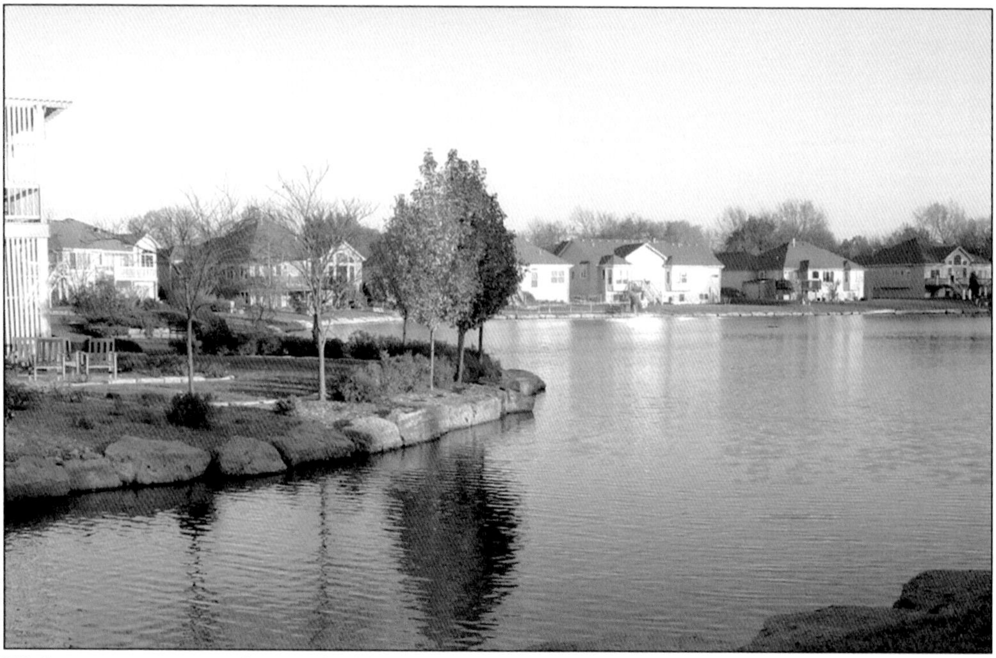

With a growing population, builders have constructed many beautiful homes in Lansing. These homes are located in Fairway Estates, a subdivision located off Eisenhower Road near the Leavenworth Country Club. Lansing's population is quickly approaching 11,000 residents. (Courtesy of the City of Lansing.)

Quality health-care providers are essential to Lansing residents. Lansing's medical community continues to grow, providing excellent care and services to area residents. The Eisenhower Medical Plaza is a recent addition to Lansing's business community. In addition, Associates in Family Healthcare, Rock Creek Imaging, Preferred Physical Therapy, and Leavenworth-Lansing Family Health Center are located in Lansing. (Courtesy of the City of Lansing.)

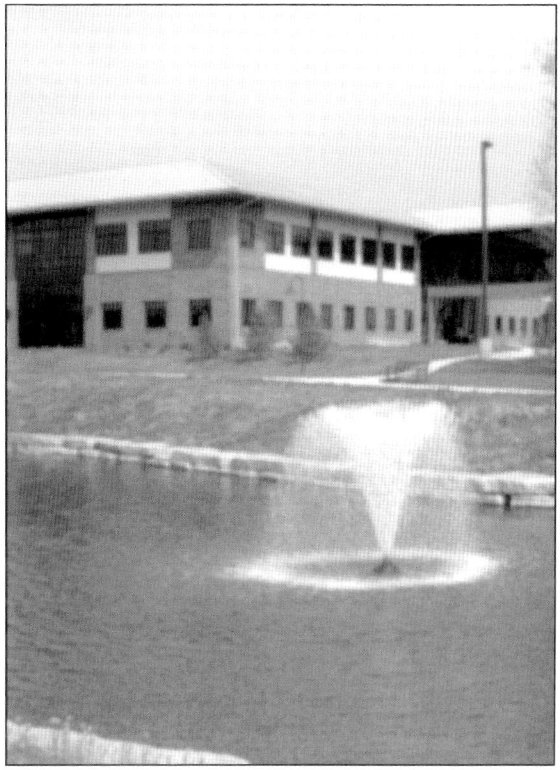

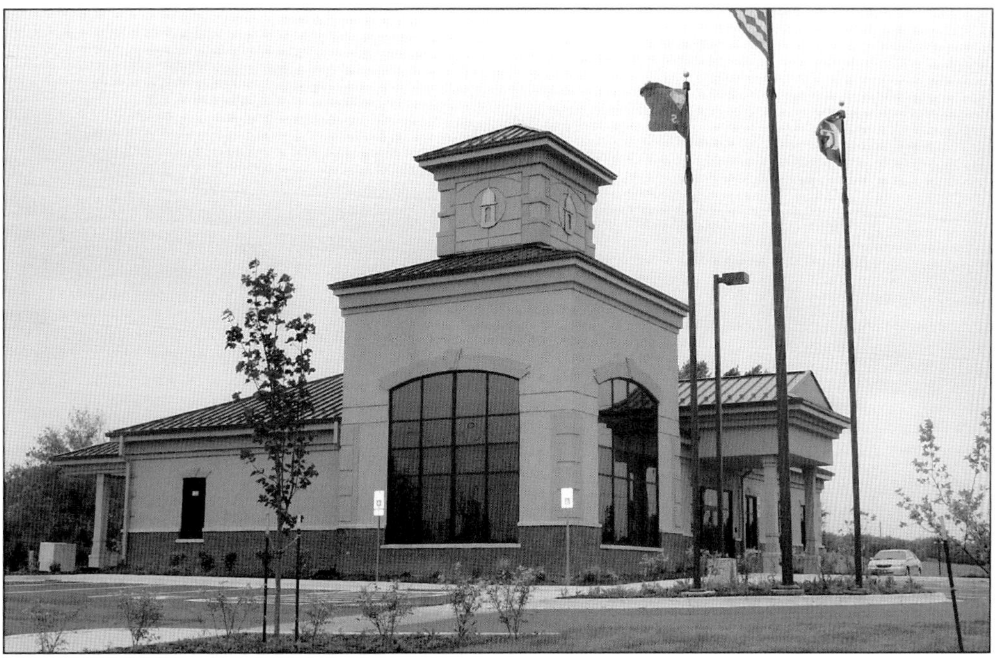

As Lansing continues to grow, new businesses are calling it home. In the past few years, Mid-American Bank (pictured) and First National Bank have opened in the Towne Center development. In addition, several businesses have opened in the new Carriage Hills Plaza located off Main Street. (Courtesy of the City of Lansing.)

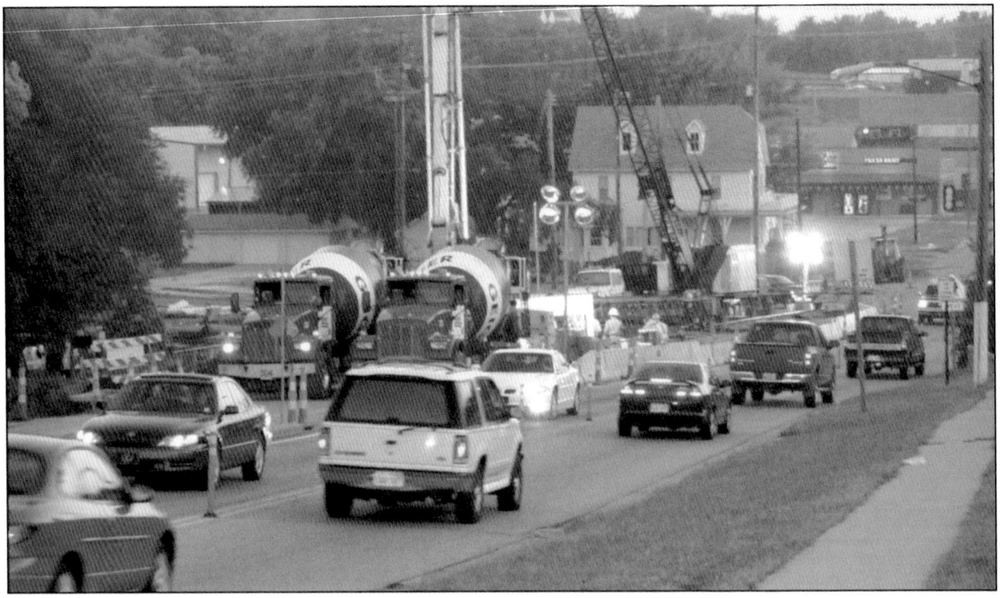

In 2006, the City of Lansing and the Kansas Department of Transportation embarked on the two-year Main Street System Enhancement project. Main Street/Kansas 7 is one of the busiest north–south highways in Kansas. To improve highway safety, construction workers added enhanced turn lanes and new lighting. The project cost $17 million and has led to many businesses locating along Main Street with the prospect of more to follow. (Courtesy of the City of Lansing.)

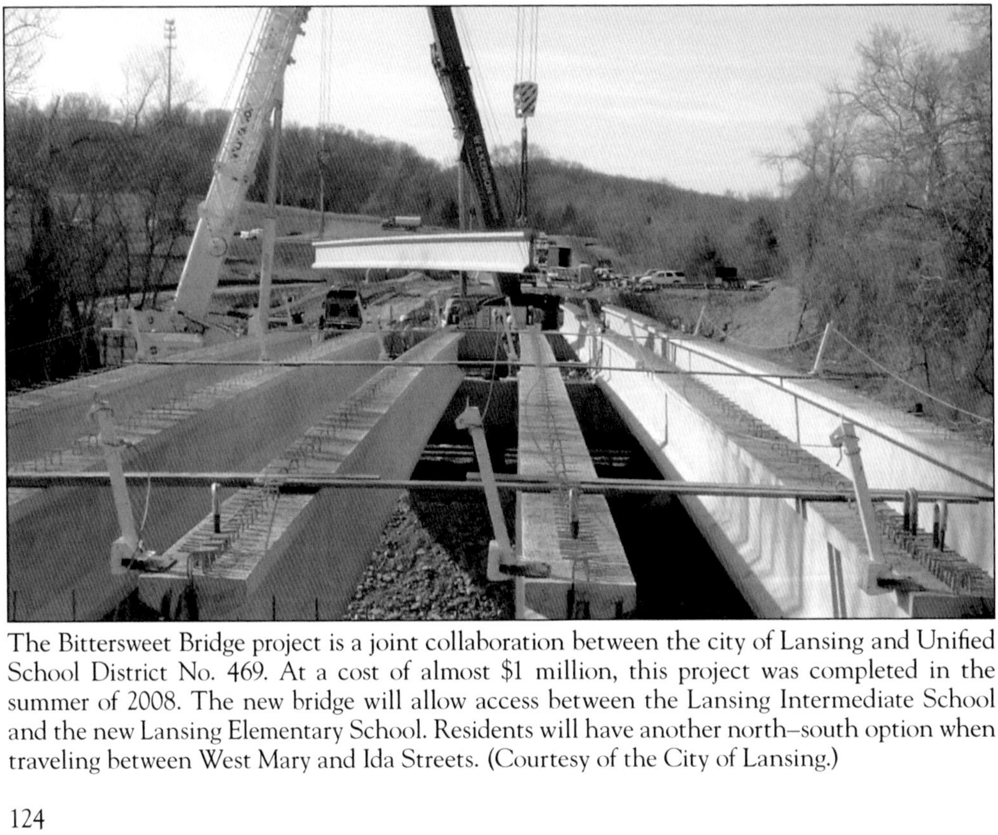

The Bittersweet Bridge project is a joint collaboration between the city of Lansing and Unified School District No. 469. At a cost of almost $1 million, this project was completed in the summer of 2008. The new bridge will allow access between the Lansing Intermediate School and the new Lansing Elementary School. Residents will have another north–south option when traveling between West Mary and Ida Streets. (Courtesy of the City of Lansing.)

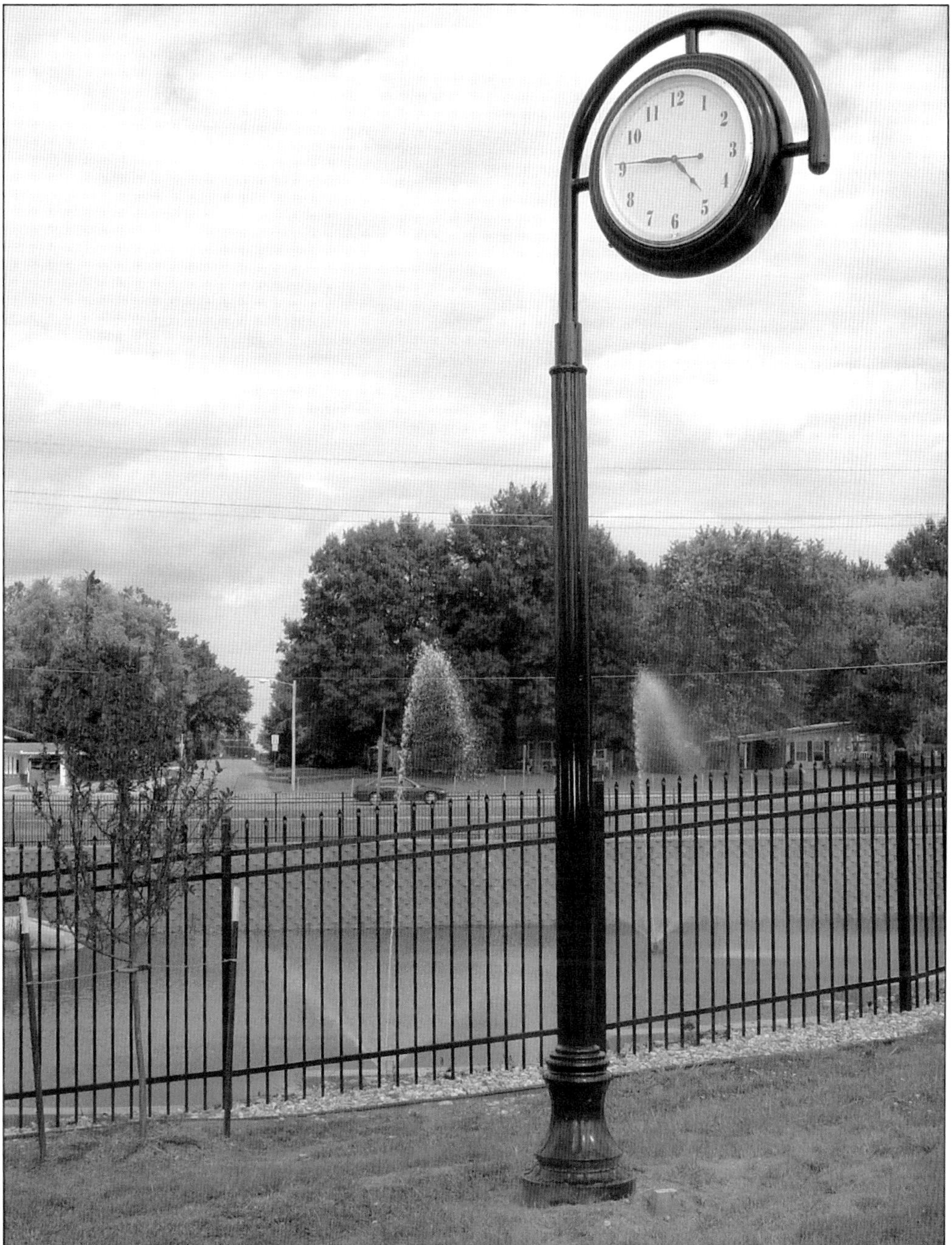

The city's growth and recent infrastructure improvements have led to the development of Lansing Towne Center. This future development is a 34-acre commercially zoned area in the heart of Lansing and within the Main Street Overlay District. The project will be completed in three phases. Two of the first tenants in the Lansing Towne Center area are First National Bank and Trust Company and Mid-American Bank and Trust Company. The development plans include over 200,000 square feet of retail space, with a hotel, restaurants, and general retail shopping. (Courtesy of the City of Lansing.)

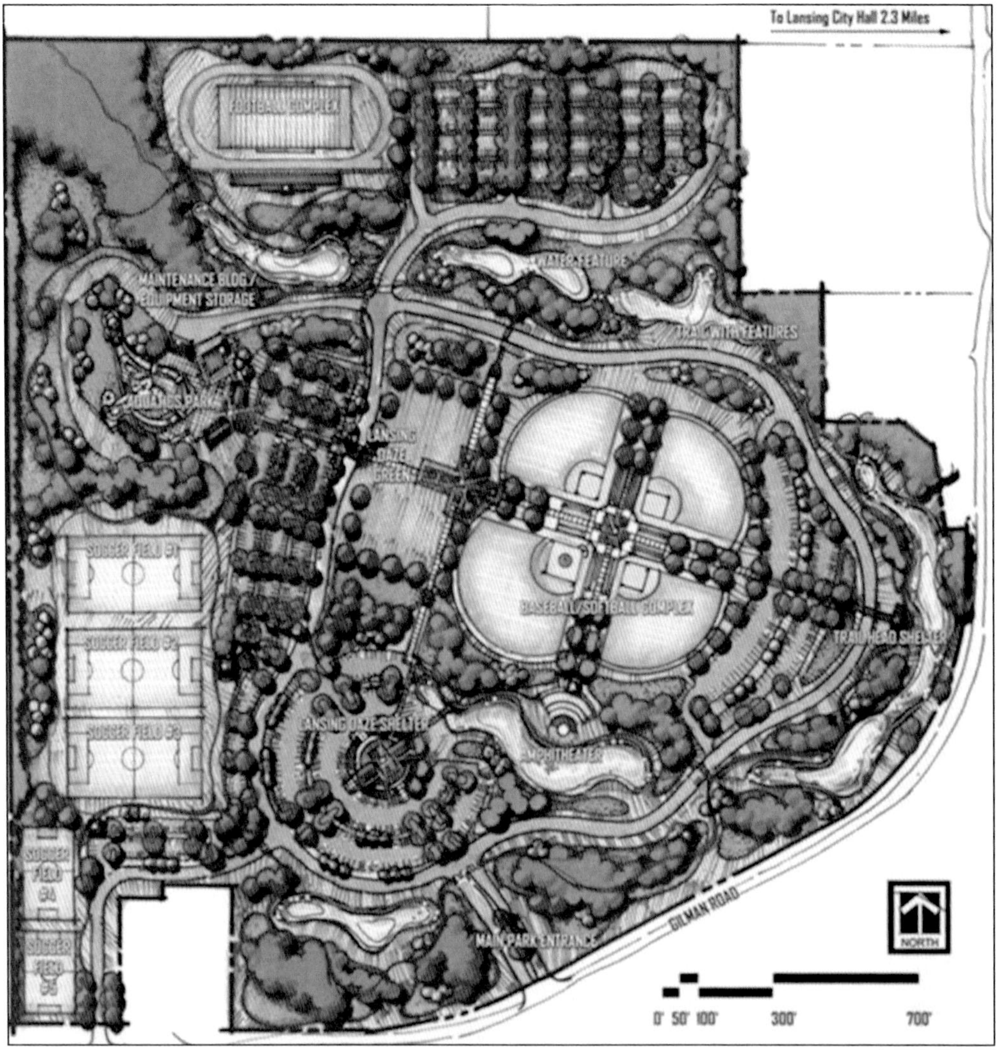

As Lansing grows, more park space is needed for the community's youth to play. Development for a new city park is underway on 4-H Road. This conceptual rendering of the finished park reveals many options residents will have for their recreation activities. The proposal for this 127-acre park will eventually include soccer, football, and baseball/softball fields, a large community park shelter, an amphitheater, and an aquatics park. Phase one includes the entry, a parking lot, and a grading for the site at a cost of almost $2 million. (Courtesy of the City of Lansing.)

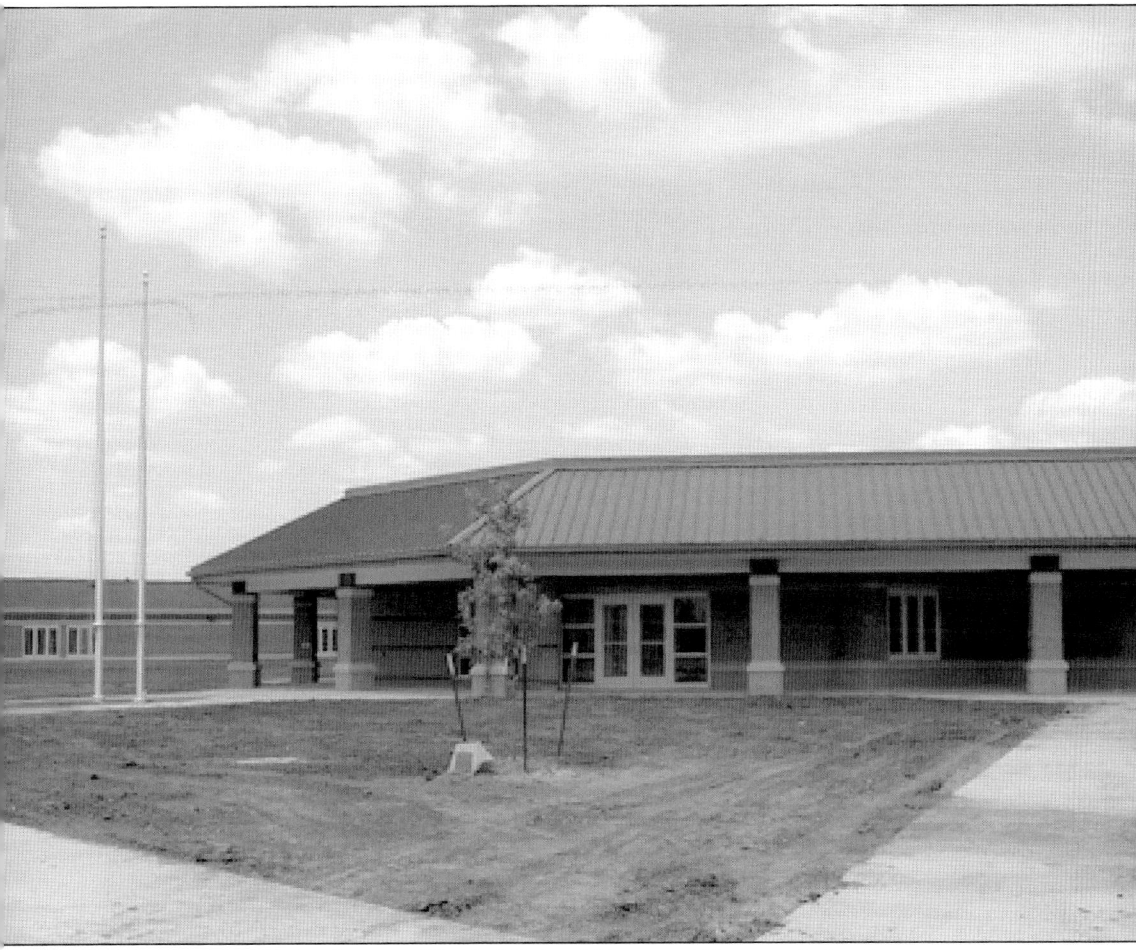

In the fall of 2008, the Lansing Unified School District 469 opened the doors to one of the largest elementary schools in the state of Kansas. The building is home to Lansing students from kindergarten through the fifth grade. (Photograph by Laura Phillippi.)

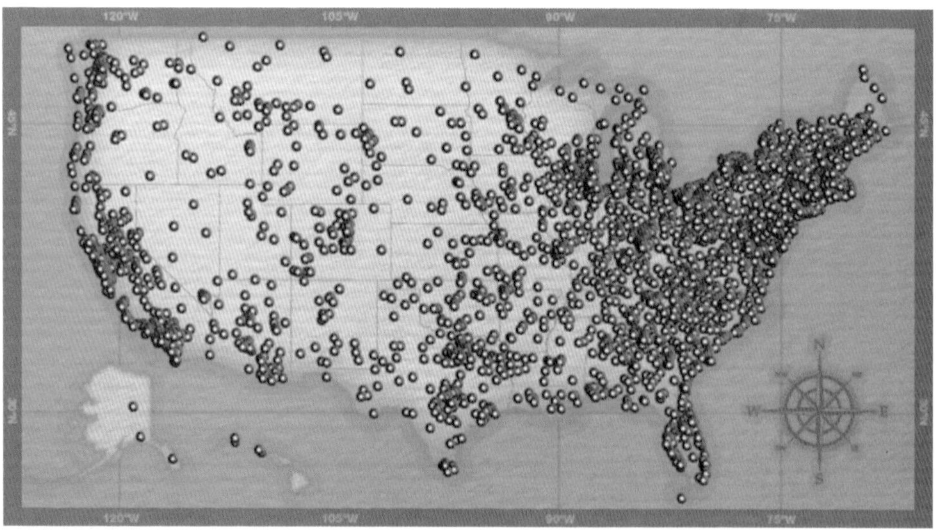